T0093170

Software Durability
Concepts and Practices

Rajeev Kumar

Centre for Innovation and Technology
Administrative Staff College of India
Hyderabad, Telangana, India

Suhel Ahmad Khan

Department of Computer Science
Indira Gandhi National Tribal University (A Central University)
Amarkantak, India

Raees Ahmad Khan

Department of Information Technology
Babasaheb Bhimrao Ambedkar University (A Central University)
Lucknow, India

CRC Press
Taylor & Francis Group
Boca Raton London New York

CRC Press is an imprint of the
Taylor & Francis Group, an **informa** business

A SCIENCE PUBLISHERS BOOK

First edition published 2023
by CRC Press
6000 Broken Sound Parkway NW, Suite 300, Boca Raton, FL 33487-2742

and by CRC Press
4 Park Square, Milton Park, Abingdon, Oxon, OX14 4RN

© 2023 Rajeev Kumar, Suhel Ahmad Khan and Raees Ahmad Khan

CRC Press is an imprint of Taylor & Francis Group, LLC

Library of Congress Cataloging-in-Publication Data (applied for)

ISBN: 978-1-032-34478-2 (hbk)
ISBN: 978-1-032-34480-5 (pbk)
ISBN: 978-1-003-32235-1 (ebk)

DOI: 10.1201/9781003322351

Typeset in Palatino
by Radiant Productions

To My Mother

Late (Smt.) Indu Srivastava

Preface

The millennial lifestyle is marked by digital technologies that are driven by software applications. The software developers are confronting several challenges in designing and delivering high quality software that can cater to the varying needs of the present day end users. Moreover, the ubiquitous use of software places the users' personal data at high risk.

Hence, the emerging need for the developers is not only to make a commercially viable and durable end product that would substantially reduce the expenses and resources spent on maintaining the software, but also to safeguard the data of the users who avail of those systems. Given the alarming increase in the instances of data poaching and data breaches, informed users are more judicious in their options while investing in software applications. The demand for software that offers security intertwined with optimum efficacy as well as durability so that the user is not taxed with undue expenses in maintaining the software, is gaining traction. This, in particular, is the pattern of requirement amongst the users of software applications in healthcare, financial institutions, and those domains that work with highly classified data. While efforts are constantly underway in the context of achieving the desired level of security of the software systems in use, the "Durability" quotient still needs intensive study.

The present endeavour undertaken by the authors of this Book is to centre stage a one of its kind "Durability Concepts, Practices, and Applications" that would serve to be instrumental in assisting the developers working in this domain. The practitioners are always in search of better ways to manage software services for a long duration. However, there is no straightforward solution available for the problem of improving the life span of software. Furthermore, practitioners are trying to achieve durable software, but unfortunately, they are ignoring the basic concept of durability. Without in-depth research about the attributes that contribute to durability, there is no way of ensuring durable software performance. If durable software does not have good quality, then a user will lose his/her trust in the software. That is why the durability of software is as important as software quality.

The critical examination of literature surveys and best practices in this league led the authors to establish that durability is defined as the time during which the software performs strongly. Hence, it can be emphatically stated that without paying attention to durability, the software may start failing after deployment. Further, ignoring durability may adversely affect the service life of software. In addition, less durable software is likely to fail in the market. In this row, the envisioned treatise, "Software Durability: Concepts and Practices", authored by Rajeev Kumar, Suhel Ahmad Khan, and Raees Ahmad Khan merits to be a significant contribution. This Book seeks to investigate the key tenets of Durability and, thereafter, establish a standard operating procedure that could be put to use by the developers for designing software with enhanced longevity.

The persistence of this book is to define concepts related to software service life. In the context given, the book clarifies the traits, varieties, and myths of software and explores the qualities and connections associated with durability in order to maintain software services for a predetermined period of time. This book comprises real-time case studies of durability issues and their mitigation plans to present an observable view on loopholes and how to fix them for more durable software. Literature on software durability tells us that the first step is to know about the problem. The book provides knowledge about durability, risk, estimation, knowledge, and governance based on five main characteristics, i.e., dependability, trustworthiness, usability, security, and human trust. The book serves as a complete package to get acquainted with assurance and risk management from a software durability perspective. It helps us learn more about the idea of durability, its multidimensional approach, threats and the different kinds of threats, risk, techniques for reducing risk, and suggested measures.

This book presents a set of criteria for evaluating software durability and develops a framework to simplify the process of evaluation in order to increase the useful life of software and assist developers. This unique concept is further developed throughout the book. According to the authors, it will be useful for both risk management and durability assessment. The most important parts of the book look at the relationship between software durability and software quality; the durability assessment and risk management frameworks that contribute to software durability; the risks that come with adding software durability; and a review of the five main characteristics of durability.

The book explores the benefits of combining software dependability and durability to lengthen the software's service life. The book examines the connection between dependability and durability as well as the durability's life cycle and fault criteria. It also looks at the ways, frameworks, and management tools that can be used to combine the concepts of dependability and durability. Further, it discusses how to categorise and explain easy-to-use security and durability aspects. The need for software to last a long time is highlighted and established as a design trait in this book, which should cause developers to reconsider how they create software.

The goal of the book is to define the evolving trends in the software development process in the context of durability concepts such as automated code reviews, coding standards, software durability standards, cost management solutions, low-code or no-code solutions, and durability assurance. The book examines the requirements and significance of durability in software engineering. It is challenging to validate the findings in the absence of any standard index values or information for durability assessment. The goal of the book is to fill in this research gap. The authors have created a novel paradigm that, if used, will assist developers in evaluating durability in actual software design scenarios in order to present workable solutions. The book also points out key areas that need to be improved if there are to be big changes in how long-lasting and secure software is made.

This book is done in the area of software durability or software life span, which is one of the biggest concerns in today's era. Software organisations need to focus on this area to get long-term performance from software with low maintenance costs. Therefore, the developers need to focus on durable software. The book will help practitioners improve the life span of software.

Acknowledgments

The tedious journey of life comes as a blessing with the objective of learning by following the fruitful path bestowed with many enigmas and also with many results. All should be laid to rest with the Almighty, because we are not alone and will not remain alone because it is He who created this path full of hopes and learning and who transforms an ordinary human into a human of reason and rationality. This book is a very insignificant contribution to the vast ocean of knowledge, whose caretaker is the Almighty.

The authors would like to offer their heartfelt gratitude to everyone who helped them develop and evaluate the work in this book. The authors of the book are very thankful to the publishing house and the people who work for them for overseeing and monitoring the book's development process, as well as taking so much care and skill in completing the project. We are indeed indebted to Dr. Alka Agrawal for all her help during the drafting of the book. Positively, we do not hesitate to state that without her help, it would not have been possible for us to complete the book.

We are also thankful to Ms. Nimisha Pande for her continuous support in reviewing the entire contents during the drafting of the book. We couldn't have finished the book without her assistance. Furthermore, we are also thankful to Dr. Kavita Sahu for her continuous encouragement, moral support, and consultations during the drafting of the book. We are thankful to Mr. Tauheed Qidwai (Director, SAQ Infosys) for granting us the permission for assistance for experiments. We express our sincere thanks to all the experts from India and abroad for honouring us with their valuable observations during the Expert Opinions.

Thank you also to everyone who contributed to the book's chapter reviews. The authors also express gratitude to the editors who collaborated with them, corrected errors, and thoroughly reviewed numerous sources while the book was being written. In this book, Mr. Vijay Primlani did a great job of reviewing and managing the content. He also kept in touch with us during the process of finalising the topics in the book.

Contents

Key Features of the Book

Software quality is an important component that tends to increase durability. Durability is a crucial consideration when assessing the quality of software. Software design development is based on the reuse of market-available requirements rather than being a one-time built-in procedure. The term "software durability" refers to the effectiveness and lifespan of software under ideal maintenance. This book, focusing on software durability and its assurance in practice, has been planned to suit the needs of its audience. Ten key features that distinguish it from other books include the following:

- Addressing the concept of a new paradigm in software engineering: durability.
- Identifying the main parameters and sub-parameters of software durability.
- Proposing the conceptual framework of software durability assurance.
- Addressing the risk management activities in the early development of durable software design.
- Integrating durability engineering into software dependability, trustworthiness, usability, security, and human trust.
- Recommending a fuzzy-based decision-making technique for durability assessment.
- Using a real-world example to demonstrate the evaluation technique.
- Addressing the concept of software durability testing in detail.
- Proposing the theoretical framework of source code analysis for building durable software.
- Addressing the future prospects of durability in software engineering.

This book is aimed primarily at software durability and will be beneficial to graduates, postgraduates, researchers, and other practitioners who are working in the areas of Software Engineering and Information Technology Management.

Envisions: This book, focusing on software durability and its assurance in practice, has been planned to suit the needs of its audience. The authors intend to meet the following Envisions:

- Broad Audience: The Book takes up a hitherto unexplored entity in the world of Software Engineering, the Durability factor, and intends to address the queries of a larger audience, including academicians and practitioners.

- Durability Assurance Embedding: Concepts of software durability assurance have been modelled as a phase-embedded activity rather than treating them as separate and post-development activities.

- Learning by Objectives: Each chapter of the book starts with a set of objectives, to which a prospective should be targeting to achieve rather than leaving the student directionless.

- Review Questions: Each chapter ends with three types of review questions, including objective type, short answer type, and descriptive through-provoking questions.

- Key Terms: Each chapter ends with a list of key terms. As these terms generally refer to certain abstract concepts, they may be used for better and more precise communication.

- Bibliography: Each chapter ends with a list of key references for the concepts in the chapter to enable the users to find in-depth information related to the contents of the chapter.

- Useful Links: Lists of useful website addresses have been appended to each chapter for quick references on needed topics.

CHAPTER 1

Software Durability Concepts

1.1 Objectives

The digital age has necessitated the use of high-quality software in all the spheres of present-day interactions, be it in education, financial institutions, healthcare, or other commercial purposes. However, the phenomenal growth in the use of software is accompanied by a consequent increase in the complexity of the system. More complex features inbuilt into the system compromise the durability as well as the security of the system in use. Despite the best efforts of the developers, achieving the desired level and extent of durability in high-quality software is still a challenging task.

Software's lifespan is determined by several factors, including its development life cycle. Businesses are striving hard to upgrade the software to extend the life of applications. The intent is to provide user-friendly software that meets the diverse needs of a given domain and, at the same time, save on the money and time invested in ensuring the durability of the software. The developers must follow a set of procedures at the very beginning of the Software Development Life Cycle (SDLC). After a software release, identifying and fixing bugs may be a time-consuming and costly process.

It is significantly easier to create a durable software design than to fix one that is vulnerable. Though software durability is critical for providing high-quality services, it isn't easy to achieve throughout the process of development. Developers can extend the life of software during its working life, thus reducing the likelihood of software failure. The goal of this chapter is to define the concepts of the durability of software.

When creating a roadmap for software durability, keep the following goals in mind:

- To create a plan for the introduction of software durability that considers the other essential variables.
- It is highly desirable to identify the attributes and their relationships concerning durability in order to sustain software services for a specified duration.
- To determine and research software durability goals for future design.
- To review the literature available on software durability and its characteristics.
- An arrangement is used as a quality benchmark to discover and evaluate the long-term software needs for serviceability.

Given the software-related goals, trying to build long-lasting software is highly desirable. Integrating software durability into the development life cycle is the best method for this. Moreover, should the features that affect and enhance the durability be worked upon in the initial stages of the software development, it would save on the expenses and rework required later in the long-term development of the software.

1.2 Durability: The Need for a New Paradigm

The value of the software's services is comparable to the value of the software itself. Software and its operationality are valued above extended runtime services. These services must also ensure that the data handled by software is accurate. Software developers are beginning to recognise the value of long-term services. As a result, it is quickly becoming one of the essential needs in software development. Company procedures are nearly uniform and confident in many areas of business, such as finance and accounting. They don't differ significantly amongst businesses, and they are consistent in terms of timing. As a result, the software development companies must focus on long-term services while their products are being used to remain competitive in a global environment. Furthermore, with the growing demand for software that lasts longer and is more serviceable, developers are being driven to work on long-lasting software (long life-span).

Durability is an essential premise as it is the basis of software service over an extended length of time. This study will help identify the existing difficulties that should be fixed to ensure software durability and a path forward in the service period. The service supplied by software has an impact on the quality of the software. Durability is a novel concept that requires more profound attention to be addressed through a variety of dimensions. As a result, many different fields are attempting to address it, including psychology, civil engineering, and sociology. For development companies, achieving comprehensive services is becoming increasingly important. There are various reasons to be concerned about software's extended service life, and some of the most important ones are as follows:

- We need to build and follow the appropriate policies and documentation targeting the software development organisational structure.
- It is highly necessary to explicitly specify the software durability evaluation policies during the software development life cycle.
- To improve the working life of software, guidelines, processes, and proposals must be provided for sustaining the services.
- For confident design, durability development teams must collaborate with software development teams to include durability concepts into the various development methods in use.
- An appropriate tool is highly demanded for service assurance of durable software.
- Policies, guidelines, processes, checklists, and infrastructure should be updated regularly to accommodate the user's needs and technological developments.

The discussion above stated that enhancing software's working life will be a new challenge for the software business. Furthermore, software durability assessment is a valuable technique to predict the long-lasting durability of software products or software services and help in further improvements.

1.2.1 Emergence of Software Durability

Because software is regularly released with little to no security, weaknesses are both encouraged and mitigated. There is no patch, culminating in further vulnerabilities in the future. It is reasonable to hypothesize that the design will remain functional across the program's entire life cycle and that services and quality will emerge and disappear.

As a result, the designers and users may emphasize the relationship between durability and the rest of the software architecture. Software durability refers to the usefulness of a piece of software's service life, such as design and construction with optimal maintenance. The term can be used to describe the complete software development life cycle by contrasting the design's service life with its functional undesirability. Except for the operational components of the software, all of the other aspects require varying levels of service maintenance, repair, and replacement throughout the software development life cycle, according to a study of international

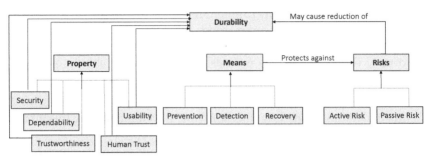

Figure 1: General Activities for Durability of Software.

studies. The extent and strength of these service demands are highly dependent on how well software and systems are synchronized and how readily they can be regularly maintained, fixed, and replaced.

Software durability may be regarded as a function of service quality and service life during the development cycle. There are three critical requirements to consider when it comes to service quality:

(i) The software developer's minimum codes or quantifiable quality.

(ii) The item's minimum acceptable quality, indicating that it must be replaced; and

(iii) Failure.

As indicated in Fig. 1, risk should be avoided in order to achieve software durability. There are two types of risk in the software development stage (active and passive). When risks are properly managed through detection, prevention, and recovery, the durability of software improves.

1.2.2 Pertinent Gaps

The lack of inherent durability measures causes the software's durability issue. It's all about common sense when it comes to determining software durability. Researchers and industry professionals have put in a lot of work to ensure software resilience. It may, however, be harmed by delayed evaluations, which are vital to both durability and quality assurance. For worthwhile software development, an effort must be made for early and exact software durability estimation. It appears that having a potentially successful approach for evaluating software durability early in the software development life cycle, on schedule, and precisely, is unavoidable. It is critical to establish what to measure earlier in the development life cycle, organise the variables to make them manageable and functional, and produce durable software that functions well for extended periods. It is commonly accepted that software durability must be incorporated from the beginning of the software development life cycle, as soon as the design phase begins.

Some known durability problems in the software may not be addressed during development due to time restrictions or other factors. These problems are being evaluated, prioritized, and corrected. Furthermore, maintenance is an ongoing process that continues until the software is no longer used or replaced by new software. Thus, the long life of life software, is decidedly more profitable an investment for any organisation. Integrating software durability in the early stages of development significantly reduces the cost, time, and effort incurred in software maintenance.

Some recognised software durability issues may go unaddressed during the development due to time constraints or other considerations. These problems are being evaluated, prioritized, and corrected. Furthermore, maintenance is a continuous process that continues until the software is no longer used or replaced by new software. There is a need to optimise maintenance costs and time and increase the durability life duration of software services due to high maintenance costs and time. It has become more durable and profitable for organisations with the help of long-life software. Integrating software durability throughout the early stages of development leads to cost, time, and effort savings in software maintenance.

1.2.3 Formulation of the Issue

Because the expenses on maintenance have inevitably increased, the practitioners are now attempting to develop software that will last longer in use. The concern now is optimising the available resources for saving on the expenditure on maintenance and improving durability to meet the future difficulties posed by new software issues. Because design is known as the skeleton or blueprint of software, the developer should focus on the design phase rather than maintenance to control and manage service within the life duration of working software. At this stage, including durability is relatively simple. Simultaneously, if durability requirements are ignored at this phase, the future design may be less reliable. A single design flaw will manifest itself over the successive stages of the software life cycle, making it more difficult to identify hazards as the process advances. Reducing design errors, on the other hand, reduces rework and consequential costs.

Software durability is in high demand these days. Furthermore, software that is dependable and usable for an extended period of time is deemed durable. This chapter introduces software durability by leveraging its needs and importance in the present-day context. This challenge necessitates a definition of "longer software durability". Furthermore, through the qualities, a relationship between software and durability is required. In order to get a quantifiable assessment of software products and improve product durability, software durability attributes must be prioritized. Software designers focus on durable software services during the development process, supporting prioritised software durability attributes and decision-making processes.

Early quantitative analysis allows for the evaluation and assessment of software durability. It serves as the foundation for determining the software's long-term viability. Program durability evaluations will aid in resolving trade-offs between software goals and maintenance costs or rework. Software durability evaluation helps improve, guide, and regulate software durability integration early in the development process. According to a preliminary literature review, the software produced is no longer durable, even though many durability challenges have indeed been addressed. The following are some of the problems in this regard:

- There is a requirement for a software durability mechanism.
- A technique to optimize the software maintenance process is a prerequisite.
- Throughout the stage of development, a way to extend the period of software design service is required.
- It is necessary to bridge the gap between software quality and durability properties.
- A software durability development framework is required, which is a complex undertaking that requires in-depth examination.
- There is a requirement for a software evaluation system.
- A technique to understand the user's expectations of software is required.
- It is necessary to bridge the gap between software durability considerations and actual implementation.
- A system that may aid in the better monitoring and administration of software under development throughout its life cycle is in great demand.
- A technique to reduce the amount of work necessary to produce long-lasting software is required.

The elimination of unnecessary expenses, time, and effort spent on maintenance by focusing on durability, from the beginning of software development with an increased operational life span, is a context of concern both from the industry as well as the end users' perspective. However, their T isn't a single foolproof mechanism for dealing with software durability. A viable assessment approach is required to overcome design software durability concerns. As indicated by the ideas in the preceding references, the early availability and implementation of quantitative assessments of durability is an essential factor in the efficient delivery of software.

1.3 Software Perspective

1.3.1 Software Components

The early twenty-first century's software development environment presents new problems for everyone, including durability. Previous practices have demonstrated that software's durability isn't as efficacious as it should be. Although the development organisations spend a significant amount of money and effort in resolving durability challenges, they are unconcerned about the software's long-term viability. The "software development life cycle" refers to the process of incorporating durability into software during its development. Developers encounter new hurdles in meeting customers' criteria while designing software as the demand for long-lasting software grows. Software development encompasses durability attributes, durability strategy, durability design, durability testing, and durability management from a durability standpoint. Unfortunately, durability is frequently only considered in isolation and at a late stage in the development process. Cost, time-to-market needs, productivity effects, customer satisfaction concerns, and other factors force organisations to impose development limits. As a result, there is a mismatch between the creation of long-lasting software and the development of short-lasting software.

Hence, one of the software challenges that has gained a lot of attention in recent years is durability. The desire for durability determines whether a company succeeds or fails in the market. While industry and researchers have reached an agreement, software durability is still far from being assessed. Furthermore, software durability is defined as the software's ability to remain operational for a specific amount of time. The durability problem is classified as follows: After a particular interval of time, the software begins to deteriorate. The durability of software can influence its expiration time. In a highly competitive market, software with inadequate endurance is likely to fail. As a result, the software development companies are focusing more on assuring software's long-term viability. It is necessary to explore the relationship between software durability, its properties, and cost to produce cost-effective software durability. Software specialists must analyse the software development concerns, durability design, and user happiness to reset the evaluation. Figure 2 depicts the link between software issues, user needs, and evaluation.

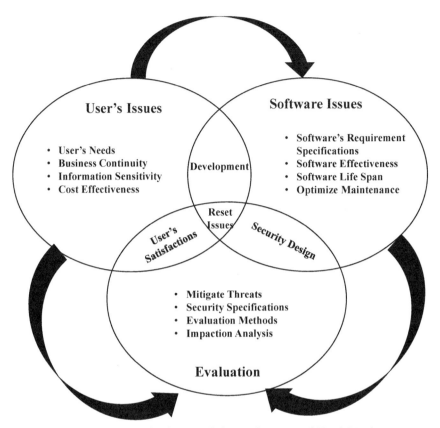

Figure 2: Relationship between Software, Security, and User's Needs.

Three steps are shown in Fig. 2 for resolving the concerns cited in the discussion above. User issues and software issues are essential for development, but user issues and evaluation are crucial for user satisfaction. Security design is also based on software issues and evaluation. In addition, NASA released a report on software maintenance costs. This article discusses how the cost of software maintenance has risen unavoidably. It is necessary to design flexible, long-lasting software to lower these costs. According to a survey published in 2016, software maintenance consumes 60% of time and money. This collection of software maintenance reports focuses on a specific problem: non-durable software.

According to another study, the service life of working software impacts software durability in the early stages of development. This paper highlighted the issues of software durability that depend on its dependability and trustworthiness and the variations between software durability, consistency, and survival. Our contribution cites durability as a software element to help solve this problem, focusing on software durability to extend its life and efficacy. It has also been discovered that if the functional life of the software can be predicted, the cost and time spent on maintenance may be minimized.

Software development is a complex process, and qualities such as effectiveness must be examined. Identifying qualities during the development life cycle can help to optimize maintenance issues and reduce the time and money spent on them. Users and businesses rely on technology, and technology is meaningless without software. The inclusion of potential parameters that lead to the improvement of software quality is considered essential. The discovery of new factors aids in the advancement of software quality.

1.3.2 Software Characteristics

Software is a collection of computer programs, operations, rules, and data. How good software is treated is influenced by a variety of things. What distinguishes an excellent software product is what it offers and how well it can be used. Software attributes are influenced by three sorts of factors: operational, transitional, and maintenance. The accompanying Fig. 3 explains and illustrates these concepts.

Figure 3: Characters of Software.

Operational: Operational parameters are those that govern how well software performs in real-world situations. The following criteria can be used to assess it:

- Budget: The amount of money spent on the software development life cycle should be carefully planned.
- Usability: The ability or suitability of anything to be used.
- Efficiency: Efficiency refers to achieving the highest performance by employing the fewest number of inputs to produce the greatest output.
- Correctness: A computer's or other electronic system's ability to accomplish a set of functions.

- Dependability: The quality of being trustworthy and reliable.
- Security: Things you do to protect somebody or something from attack, danger, robbery, etc.
- Safety: The state of being safe means not being dangerous or in danger.

Transitional: The following elements impact the software quality when it is migrated from one platform to another:

- Software Portability: Software portability refers to the ability to move software from one machine or system to another.
- Interoperability: A computer system's or software's ability to share and utilize information.
- Reusability: The ability to be used again or repeatedly.
- Adaptability: The capacity to be modified for a new use or purpose.

Maintenance: All factors that describe how well software can maintain itself in an ever-changing environment are included in these categories:

- Modularity: The use of individually distinct functional units, as in assembling an electronic or mechanical system.
- Maintainability: The ability of an item to be retained in or restored to a specified condition.
- Flexibility: The ability of a joint or series of joints to move through an unrestricted, pain-free range of motion.
- Scalability: The ability of a computing process to be used or produced in a range of capabilities.

1.3.3 Software Types

Software is a collection of information that tells a computer or other electronic device how to operate, function, and carry out specific tasks. Hardware, on the other hand, refers to the actual system and parts that do the actual work. Software is simply another name for a computer programme, and a programme is a set of instructions that tells the equipment how to operate. The language used to write such instructions is one that computers can understand. All software is based on the input > process > output principle and logic. For the programme to run, it needs the input, or data. Think about pressing a phone button. Then, a series of inquiries based on a set of rules are made. For instance, should the button cancel a purchase or issue an invoice? The outcome is what takes place as a result. When your printer first turns on, the invoice emerges from the tray.

Software can range in complexity from the simplest single line of code to the most complicated operating system, Windows, from Microsoft.

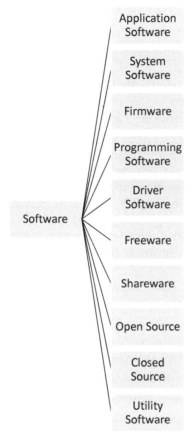

Figure 4: Various Software Types.

The software works along with other programmes to create a cohesive system (Fig. 4). The dozens of software parts that make up a smartphone are designed to work together. Code languages and styles range in size and scope. The software that drives a modern microwave is very different from the programming that powers an Apple Mac. Numerous types of software are described in the section after this one, including:

a. Application Software

Application software is a programme or group of programmes created with end users in mind. There are many different types and sizes of application software.

➢ *Examples*

- Word Processing Software: Google Docs, Microsoft Word, WordPad, and Notepad

- MySQL, Microsoft SQL Server, Microsoft Access, Oracle, IBM DB2, and FoxPro
- Spreadsheet Software: Google Sheets, Apple Numbers, and Microsoft Excel
- Multimedia Software: Media Player, Winamp, QuickTime, and VLC Media Player
- Presentation Software: Google Slides, Microsoft Powerpoint, Keynotes, Prezzy
- Customer relationship management (CRM) software (HubSpot, Microsoft Dynamic 365), project management tools (Jira, Monday), marketing automation tools (Marketo, HubSpot), enterprise resource planning (ERP) software (SAGE, Oracle, Microsoft Dynamics), treasury management system (TMS) software (SAP S/4HANA Finance, Oracle Treasury), business intelligence (BI) software (SAP Business Intelligence, MicroStrategy, Microsoft Power BI)
- Information Worker Software: documentation tools, resource management tools
- Communication Software: Zoom, Google Meet, Skype
- Encarta and Britannica dictionaries; MATLAB for math; Google Earth and NASA World Wind
- Simulators for flight and science
- Using media players or web browsers to access content
- Apache OpenOffice, Microsoft Office365, Apple's iWork, LibreOffice, G-Suite, Oracle E-Business Suite
- Software for Engineering and Product Development: IDEs, or Integrated Development Environments
- Email Software: Microsoft Outlook, Gmail, Apple Mail.

➤ *Benefits*

Applications are the lifeblood of our digital devices. Mobile app developers create solutions that enable companies to advertise and sell online. The stock market is operated by financial software. The banking system uses software to transmit money and record transactions. If your business needs a digital solution, it will probably take the form of an app.

b. System Software

Programs that control the computer itself are referred to as system software; examples include the operating system, file management tools, and disc operating systems. It acts as a foundation for other software (or DOS). Function libraries, system services, printers, additional device drivers, system preferences, and other configuration files are all included in the designs. Examples of system software applications include assemblers, compilers, file management software, system utilities, and debuggers. The system software is necessary and gives programmes a platform to run on, whereas application software is optional and won't shut down your device if it is uninstalled.

➢ *Examples*

System software runs things in the background, and operating systems are an example of system software.

For desktop computers, laptops, and tablets:

- Microsoft Windows
- MacOS (for Apple devices)
- GNU/Linux
- For smartphones:
- Apple's IOS
- Google's Android
- Windows Phone OS

Game engines, computational science software, industrial automation software, and service applications are some further examples. Some people categorize programming software and driver software as forms of system software and operating systems. However, in the following two sections, we will go through each of them separately.

➢ *Benefits*

Open-source operating systems let businesses create their OS.

c. *Programming Software*

What is the process of creating software? Using programming software is the answer. The majority of code is written in English and follows a strict format or syntax. Machine code is then generated from high-level programming languages. This is accomplished via a compiler, which is a sort of software. Programming software, often known as a programming tool or a software development tool, is a program that helps software developers and programmers create, debug, and manage other programs and applications. Although there is some controversy about this, programming software is considered to be a subset of system software.

➢ *Examples*

Plain-text editor programmes can be used to develop computer languages like Java or PHP, but more robust, industry-standard tools are also available. Compilers, assemblers, debuggers, interpreters, and other programming software are examples. All of this software is combined in integrated development environments (IDEs). The majority of software developers make use of programming software apps such as:

- GitHub
- GitLab
- Android Studio
- Visual Studio Code
- Eclipse
- XCode
- Notepad++
- Atom

They're termed IDEs, or integrated development environments, and programmers use them for a reason.

➢ *Benefits*

IDEs have functions like code error highlighting. Additionally, they include built-in compilers that let you test an app on a computer before running it through its paces on a phone. Finding a bug spanning hundreds of lines of code in a simple text editor is practically impossible. On the other hand, an IDE makes this process easier, which speeds up software development and makes it more reliable.

d. Driver Software

The driver software enables a computer to communicate with its hardware, including peripherals and control and input devices. By obtaining information from the operating system and giving the hardware instructions to carry out particular actions or tasks, it achieves this. The hard drive and processor, for example, each have their own drivers. If the wrong software is installed, the device won't work properly. In prior iterations of Windows, device drivers were the misery of the workplace. The proper driver must be installed before using new peripherals, like a printer. It took a very long time to get the right driver software online after the CD was lost. Fortunately, Windows and other operating systems manage and install drivers invisibly. A machine that is optimised and useful is the end product.

➢ *Examples*

All hardware devices require drivers. For example:

- Graphic cards
- Network cards
- Mouse and keyboard

The OS detects a USB flash drive as a new device when you insert it into your computer. The driver is then immediately installed to make it function.

➢ *Benefits*

Drivers are under the category of system software. Nothing would function without them. Hardware companies frequently create driver software. Linux and Chromebooks, on the other hand, are sometimes disregarded due to their modest market penetration. The coding community, thankfully, comes to the rescue. Someone creates the code that allows the device to function correctly on their system. They then make the driver available for others to download and use on the internet.

e. Freeware

There's a difference between freeware and free software or open-source software. The source code of freeware software is not exposed or shared. The software's owner, on the other hand, does not charge anyone to use it. Freeware licenses differ in terms of what can be done with the software and who can share it. Some developers only allow their software to be used for personal or private purposes. Businesses require a paid license or written approval. GPT-3 is an example of this; only approved developers and marketers can access the program. Always read the fine print and be aware of freeware licenses that grant copyright.

➢ *Examples*

Freeware software examples cover a broad base of valuable applications from audio to virtual machines.

➢ *Benefits*

You don't have to spend anything to get fully developed software. If you don't like the features, you can uninstall them. There are no businesses that will 'force' you to upgrade. Freeware also facilitates the sharing and growth of the online community. Developers can show off their skills, while businesses can benefit from some fantastic apps.

f. Shareware

Shareware, like freeware, is free to use and share with others for a limited time. It serves as a form of assessment. Before making a purchase, you can test out some or all of the features.

➢ *Examples*

WinZip is one of the most well-known shareware programs. It began in 1991 when Windows didn't contain compressing software. Even thirty years on since then, It still receives a lot of downloads. Although the free trial is limited in duration, all versions include encryption.

➢ *Benefits*

Trial of the software can be availed for free before purchasing an exclusive license with shareware. Some are time-limited or have a limited feature set. "Try before you buy" is an excellent way to see if the program is suitable for your company's requirements.

g. Open Source Software

If the software is open source, you can examine the exact code in which it was developed. Overly restrictive software licences restrict what another developer can do with the source. On the other hand, the philosophy behind open source is to promote development. Open source refers to software that is continuously improved for all users.

➢ *Examples*

The Linux operating system exemplifies open-source software. Developers can get the source code and make any changes they want. As a result, new Linux variants can help meet a specific demand.

➢ *Benefits*

Github.com is the most popular place for programmers to save and exchange code. Developers can quickly locate the proper solution to their problems because repositories are frequently open-source. They can get free elements or clone entire projects.

h. Closed Source Software

The majority of applications are closed source, meaning that the original code is not accessible. The requirements for obtaining a license are rigorous. It is forbidden to copy or crack the software without permission. The app can be public or private, but it must be paid to use.

➢ *Examples*

Closed-source software is any program that hides or encrypts its source code. Video conferencing, for instance, is possible with Skype. Although it is free to use, Microsoft charges a fee to high-volume users.

➢ *Benefits*

Closed source software is designed for commercial usage. Programmers frequently write code. This is a financial investment. As a result, businesses do not want their funds disbursed without a comparable return.

i. Consider the Case of Utility Software

Utility software is used to analyze and enhance the functioning of a device. The majority of these software applications work in conjunction with the operating system. They monitor performance and notify the system if an issue, such as overheating arises.

➢ *Examples*

The Task Manager displays all open processes in Windows. It demonstrates how well each performs over time as well as how much memory they require. Utilities also include anti-virus and software applications.

➢ *Benefits*

Overheating must be closely monitored, and viruses must be screened. Utility software assists in the preservation of a stable condition of affairs. It's designed to keep your system working smoothly and protect it from damage caused by heavy use.

1.3.4 Software Myths

Since the dawn of time, man has been surrounded by myths, superstitions, and misconceptions. Software engineering, a relatively new and advanced sector, is no exception. Unlike classic legends with underlying life lessons, myths in software engineering only confound business people, end-users, software durability managers, and engineers themselves. As an outsourcing software durability development firm, we deal with the effects of software myths all the time. False assumptions and beliefs stymie communication and product development. Some clients have unrealistic or stereotypical expectations. Others are wary of making critical judgments and are hesitant to do so. We'd like to dispel some common misunderstandings concerning software durability engineering. Eight common software myths about software durability are:

Myth I: Software durability development is a linear process that can be predicted

Most people feel that creating software with long-term durability is analogous to manufacturing or building a house from blueprints. All that the squad needs to do now is keep to the plan as visualised. This isn't true, for better or worse. Software durability development can be predictable and straightforward for simple, short-term initiatives, like a landing page. Fixed-price contracts are built on this foundation. Software durability development gets ahead without a hitch as long as the product requirements are explicit and well-documented, the correct technology stack is chosen, human resources are sufficient, and communication is frequent and fluid. With the typical waterfall SDLC model, it appears to be very simple. The sequential manufacturing flow, on the other hand, is currently deemed stiff. Agile approaches are preferred by development teams worldwide because they are more flexible but less predictable. In most cases, it is impossible to provide a project with an exact time estimate. It's a good idea to think about each function as thoroughly as possible as soon as possible. Project requirements, on the other hand, rarely remain constant throughout the development process. Both internal and external

Factors that can stretch a project's timeline

	Internal Factors	External Factors
Slow Down	Adding more persons to project at a late stage	Replacement of key people in project
		Internal politics
Delay the Software Project	Technology Transfer	Change in consumer taste
		Competitor launching similar product

Figure 5: Development of Software is Linear Process.

changes can have an impact on software products (Fig. 5). Furthermore, developers may encounter writer's block or receive new ideas and insights daily.

When developing software for long-term use, you must factor in the possibility of failure. Although extensive project planning and documentation are necessary, plans should be viewed as early hypotheses that are constantly changing.

Myth II: Adding/changing features is simple

This myth is the polar opposite of the one before it. Some clients assume that a simple set of generic criteria is sufficient for development; further specifics can be added later. Some people misunderstand Agile to mean "no more planning and documentation". Others believe that changing things is as simple as changing a few lines of code. Starting development without a clear set of requirements will result in the loss of time and money at the very least, and, project failure in the worst-case scenario. Software durability engineering processes are expedited, and product quality is improved with proper documentation. "Scope creep" wreaks havoc on timelines and budgets. "Feature creep" does the same thing and harms the usability of a product.

Furthermore, if the requirements keep changing, the team will be unable to test the product fully. In reality, you must strike a balance between time, cost, and features. At the very least, if you overestimated the flexibility of software durability early in the development phase, strive to include most modification requests as soon as possible. They may require re-design, additional resources, or the entire development process to be repeated at a later point.

Myth III: There is a one-size-fits-all technology or methodology

Because it appears to assure success, the most recent or most popular technology or SDLC approach is appealing. Unfortunately, teams must examine more elements to that aim, focusing mainly on the client's needs and essential software duties. There's no need to go overboard if something more straightforward and less expensive will suffice. Another variant of this myth asserts that one programming language is superior to others. Software engineers enjoy praising their work while criticizing others. Remember that each language has a specific function, and the benefits of each can only be assessed within the context of a particular outcome or project. 'Suitable' does not imply 'trendy.' 'Maturity' does not mean 'depreciation'. It's fine to change strategies and technologies in response to changing company needs (proven, for example, by advanced web applications).

Myth IV: Testing is unnecessary (or testers)

People who believe in this myth do so for a variety of reasons. People outside the IT field, for example, assume that anyone can assess software durability. On the other hand, only QA professionals comprehend the general workings of software durability, dependencies, and the effects of one module on another. Clients sometimes refuse to test because it takes too long. Using QA techniques such as code review, the quality of software durability may be efficiently measured at any stage of the development process.

Furthermore, test automation cuts down on testing time. A related myth is the high cost of quality assurance. Automated unit testing, while reducing the number of problems by up to 90%, raises development costs by 30 to 50%. However, you will spend less money on testing at the development stage than on maintenance or correction later.

Myth V: It is possible to create bug-free software

A bug-free product is a great goal to strive for, but it's unlikely to happen unless your software is fundamental, well-written, and thoroughly tested. Even the most skilled testers can't guarantee that the software is bug-free in the vast majority of circumstances. It is conceivable to try all paths, but complete testing is never achievable. Some eventualities are impractical for the team or the client to implement during development and can only be accomplished after the project has been launched.

It's not a calamity when bugs appear as long as they aren't catastrophic. They are something that can be worked out over time. Furthermore, this procedure is linked to product enhancement. Simply test the functions of your software as soon as possible and keep an eye out for bugs.

Myth VI: The product must be flawless on the first try

It's a fundamentally erroneous belief. Nobody knows what "perfect" looks like until the thing is used. It's preferable to create a Minimum Viable Product (MVP) with only the most essential features rather than expect (and wait for) the developers to complete the entire project. Place the MVP on the market, start making money, gather feedback, and make improvements. If you're creating an online business, focus on the essential buying capability first, then add features to the foundation, such as making the experience more personalised and engaging. Kudos to the product development team, if they succeed the first time. However, there is another risk: the unit may become complacent and stop coming up with new ideas. Regular updates are required for successful goods, and tests are a vital part of the innovation process.

Myth VII: When a product is released, the project is finished

The concept is appealing, but software products are more like live organisms in that they have life cycles and are vulnerable to change. Markets, businesses, and technologies are all changing at breakneck speed. End-users are increasingly demanding new features and enhancements. Users feel irritated when an application is incompatible with their device or operating system. For the company, this represents lost income and more untapped potential. The best software durability necessitates ongoing maintenance. Its seamless operation can only be ensured through security updates, bug fixes, and routine maintenance. It's ideal to have post-release support, a long-term product development strategy, and the flexibility to adapt to changes quickly.

Myth VIII: A successful development project translates into a successful product

The right specialists or outsourcing partners can help you organise a suitable project development process and ensure that the end product is high quality. They'll complete it on time and within budget. They cannot, however, guarantee the product's market success. For a mobile application, for example, the correct monetization strategy and promotion are only a few of the elements to consider.

1.4 Software Durability

Quality is an essential aspect of software that contributes to its long-term durability. Durability is a vital factor to consider when assessing software quality. Software design is not a one-time built-in process; instead, it is based on the reuse of current market standards. The focus of this chapter is on the software's service life and how it relates to quality. Typically, the software is given with little to no durability, resulting in short service life. Patching is done to mitigate them, which leads to further vulnerabilities. It's common to assume that the design will be used throughout the software's life cycle and that services and quality will come and go. In fact, most designers and users do not reckon with durability's relationship with the rest of the software architecture. The functionality of the software takes precedence over durability. This is indeed a fallacy. Software durability is used to define the usefulness of a piece of software's service life when properly maintained.

As Nathan Ensmenger discusses in his paper "When excellent software goes bad: the surprising durability of an ephemeral technology", there has been a lot of work done in the field of software maintenance in terms of durability. According to this study, there is a need to concentrate more on issues associated with maintenance achievement. It has been argued that software durability is related to software serviceability and that achieving durability may improve the software's serviceability. Software durability is described as "a software product's service is durable if it performs efficiently and effectively for the user's satisfaction over the duration expected by the user."

1.4.1 Definition

Software's role in our lives is expanding by the day. The existence of highly durable software can substantially enhance people's personal and professional lives, while poor quality software can significantly impair them. The durability of secure software is crucial in the most complicated software systems, such as airline flight control or nuclear power plants. In today's environment, businesses are preoccupied with identifying and addressing difficulties during the software development life cycle. Some crucial qualities can be focused on to help directly or indirectly address these difficulties. Durability is one of these traits. It's also known as software's "working life" or "longevity". The long-term durability of software is critical in sensitive domains such as banking and finance. The software is also affected by durability, either directly or indirectly. Based on a review of past work and best practices, the authors have characterised software durability as follows:

"Software durability means the solution ability of serviceability of software to meet users' needs for a relatively long time."

Durability refers to how long a software solution will continue to perform appropriately and fulfil the industry standards. Organizations include durability throughout software development for a variety of reasons, including:

* To deliver more extended services in a given service environment, hence reducing problems.
* To cut down on maintenance time by lowering the work required to patch defects by delivering long-lasting and safe software.

Addressing, measuring, and improving software durability, are the key reasons for looking at durability and services simultaneously.

Numerous durability attributes are linked to feature attributes. These characteristics help determine the software's long-term viability.

1.4.2 Durability Factors

Durability is a significant factor of software quality that affects its characteristics such as usability, maintainability, etc. In the early years, durability needs were identified and categorised in the form of durability attributes. These attributes are used to enhance the service life of software through identification, classification, and measurements. These attributes depend on the durability or how long-lasting software will be.

Furthermore, it is difficult to assess whether the software will be durable enough to handle unpredictable future needs. The durability concept is multi-dimensional and multi-criteria in nature. The majority of the time is spent on creating highly durable software that meets the desired software quality standards. To assess software durability, its attributes should be identified in a quantified manner. The features are the same as the need for quality software that meets durability requirements as well. The researchers found the most crucial durability attributes, including software dependability, human trust, software trustworthiness, software security, and software usability, discussed in Table 1.

Software and durability attributes that affect the life span of software are defined in Table 1. Among these software durability attributes, the researchers have recognised three attributes that also affect software durability, i.e., dependability, trustworthiness, and human trust. The description and relationships of software and durability attributes are specified in the next chapter.

Table 1: Software Durability Attributes.

S. No.	Durability Attributes	Definition
1.	Software Dependability	Dependability refers to a company's ability to provide service that can be relied on.
2.	Software Trustworthiness	The certainty that the software will work as planned is referred to as trustworthiness.
3.	Human Trust	Human trust is defined as the readiness to put one's faith in software.
4.	Software Usability	Usability refers to a user's ability to utilise software to get quantifiable objectives with efficiency and satisfaction.
5.	Software Security	Software security refers to the durability of the software's confidentiality, integrity, and availability in a way that ensures its long-term viability.

1.4.3 Durability Planning

The primary goal of innovation development is to benefit humanity in terms of social advancement and protect clients from malicious attacks. Paying attention to the software at each stage of the development life cycle can lead to higher reliability and customer satisfaction. The software significantly improves quality to suit corporate needs. According to experts, the process of factor identification occurs during the evaluation process. Practitioners must focus during the early stages of software development. However, this is not always possible. Developers are finding it increasingly challenging to achieve durability throughout software development. Durability must also be considered, which includes durability features, classifications, and measurements. Durability aspects must be considered at every stage of software development. In the field of durability engineering, durability qualities are regarded as extremely important. The identification of durability attributes during software development aids in the improvement of durability. These characteristics are essential in the realm of software engineering. Furthermore, durability characteristics are incorporated to create solid cryptographic arrangements and find a way to assign durability requirements to improve durability during the software development life cycle.

The duration of a software's service life is affected by its durability. This statement bolsters the notion that there must be a durability-related feature. Durability should be seen as one of the supporting properties of durability in this regard. In terms of software, durability refers to the length of time that software provides services. As a result, it appears that the emphasis on durability has shifted to the software's durability. The administrative life of the product is directly or indirectly connected with durability. The durability of software is also affected by durability, either directly or indirectly. This study aims to conclude the theoretical and empirical realities of durability through assessment. Commercial software programmes usually have certain apparent features that provide them with a competitive advantage. The main objective of this contribution is to reduce the effort required to manage and control durability. Assessment of durability may be helpful in improving durability and achieving optimal maintenance for a period.

1.5 Durability Evaluation

Durability as a feature of high-quality software assumes a significant role in profiting from the market and meeting the software's needs. The importance of maintenance in maximising software durability cannot be overstated. The goal is to figure out "what works now in terms of optimal software maintenance and improving the life span of software services" from both a practical and theoretical standpoint. It can be seen that maintenance is 60–80% of the total cost, and development is at most 20% of the software life. Like most companies today don't seem to acknowledge, they primarily focus on faster development and set due dates without proper estimation of durability. This forces the developers to *dump and go*, which subsequently makes maintenance harder.

It is a challenge to identify the changes in design for improving the durability and turn them into optimal maintenance of software products. The following are the leading causes of software durability failure: insufficient involvement of durability designers during the software development process; insufficiently defined durability needs; and experts constantly focusing on the maintenance process rather than design to optimise maintenance and improve durability for a longer life span of software. To enhance software's working life or service life to better understand maintenance issues, practitioners must focus on the software design and its durability.

Practitioners may not optimise the maintenance difficulties of a profitable and successful software product without it. Software durability is essential for optimising maintenance difficulties. Furthermore, software durability and its qualities are ambiguous and have various interpretations; their descriptions are frequently linguistic and confusing. Moreover, it is widely acknowledged that expert judgement is usually skewed. It is suggested that fuzzy logic be used to model the uncertainties in expert preferences. There is no framework/method available for software durability assessment and improvement during the software development process to enhance the durability for a life span.

1.6 Models of Durable Software

There is little work available in the field of software durability. Some researchers have defined durability in terms of trustworthiness, while others have defined it in terms of dependability and human trust as follows:

Celia Chen, 2017 [1]
The author described why it is essential to measure maintainability and the best ways to accomplish the same. According to the author, high maintenance can cost approximately 75% of the total cost of software development. Furthermore, the author defines software maintainability as the simplicity with which a software system may be repaired or modified to fix bugs, increase performance or other features, or adapt to a changing environment. It explains how minimising the cost and time spent on

software maintenance improves its durability. According to the author, some measures can help the software developers objectively monitor and examine a project's maintainability. The study discussed the necessity of understanding software maintainability and a framework and some of the best approaches for measuring it.

Kelty C., Erickson S., 2015 [2]
The study talks about how to create long-lasting software that is easy to maintain. According to the authors, software durability is determined by its various applications in the social, economic, and cultural fields. Robustness and maintainability are two factors that contribute to durability. Maintainability is described as a never-ending process in the article, which reduces durability. The experimental results they presented could be valuable in a variety of situations. The article clarifies that poor design is a primary cause of software's lack of durability. They advise the developers to look for ways to ensure the software's durability by design because it still has to be improved for a better user experience.

Nathan Ensmenger, 2014 [3]
 The author asserts that software durability and software serviceability are two sides of the same coin. Long-term services are a key issue, as is the high cost of software maintenance. The author also analyses the working life of durability, which reduces over time. As a result, for long-term software, durability is crucial. The study also links durability with maintenance, as time spent on maintenance can be reduced when the aspect of durability in software is considered. The author concludes that if durable software is not produced, maintenance will become a central issue in software, computing, and technology history.

J. J., Cusick, 2013 [4]
Using a virtual toolbox, the author defined long-lasting ideas in software engineering in terms of concepts, methods, and approaches. During the software development process, he stressed upon the significance of keeping a balance between durability and quality.

E. V. Bartlett, 2013 [5]
The author defined the process of maintenance as invariably increasing these days, but the longer working life of software may decrease the cost of the maintenance process. The author has also suggested ways to reduce the time spent on the maintenance process. According to it, the durability of software plays an essential role in maintaining quality. The study underlines that poorly planned maintenance techniques can raise life cycle costs and impair software dependability and service life. Reliability and durability are both important for longer service life and the user's satisfaction. After high-profile design breaches, the practitioners are now

trying to improve design because it is not enough. The author concludes by differentiating the terms of reliability and durability, as most of the time, they are considered the same. According to the author, there is a minimal and negotiable difference between them.

Ernie Hayden et al., 2014 [6]
The authors described patch management as a solution for regular maintenance to increase the service life of the software. The study notes that Patch and vulnerability management is still one of the essential prerequisites for a successful program. With the framework presented in the article, patch management is introduced within the design phase of the software development process. It also includes the defect management process. Its internal structure had ten unique steps to be taken to search for and patch defects and vulnerability flaws.

Van Der Linden, 2010 [7]
In his research, the author has provided principles for improving the quality of software's non-functional qualities. According to this study, software development strives to generate software systems that meet two categories of requirements: functionality and quality. Non-functional attributes (NFAs), such as performance, durability, and availability, are one component of software quality. This study looks at how software developers might meet NFA criteria by following appropriate principles throughout software development. The various effects of multiple rules on NFA quality and the interactions among the guidelines themselves are a challenge that complicates developing procedures. This study has produced a step-by-step technique that provides software engineers with a valuable set of guidelines for improving the working life of software and obtaining high-quality software. The study tabulates the effects that the different approaches would have after applying the guidelines provided by the author for improving the lifespan of the software.

Malik Hneif, 2011 [8]
The author has proposed a method for durability analysis of development systems in computing. To analyse the software's high failure rate, this report focused on a systemic view of software engineering. In this work, durability is proposed as a critical property of software development and a quantifiable sign of a system's ability to prevent bugs and failure. This study presented an approach to software system development in computer science and defined a method for maintainable development to assess the durability of development systems.

Basil Vandegriend, 2006 [9]
This study discusses some guidelines on how to create software that is maintainable with minimum risk and impact. This paper discusses the

specific challenges faced by the developers while maintaining software. The author discusses that some organizations have separate software maintenance groups from the software development group. The maintenance team may need to make emergency bug fixes or release defect fixes quickly, while the development team keeps on working on new features.

Robert C. Feenstra et al., 2009 [10]
The authors described the need and importance of durability in software engineering for different environments by reducing the maintenance costs during the early stages of the development life cycle. They defined "durable software" as software that doesn't change with time. In addition, this study suggests a new reason to explain why the conventional hedonic methods may overstate the price decline of personal computers.

Ruth Thomas, 1994 [11]
The author described the importance of durable and low-cost educational software. He also signified that there is a need for stable and cheap software in educational software. He has given a concept and an issue to optimise the software development life cycle for cost-effectiveness. According to his research, developers should focus on the details of the design to achieve durability in s/w.

Lack of funds for maintenance and time affects software durability, and many contributors have addressed this problem. Further, some of the contributors have focused on trustworthiness, dependability, human trust, and usability separately, but no one, as yet, has discussed it all together. In addition, there are only a few studies that focus on software design to assure the durability of the software. Still, the practitioners are trying to find a way to enhance the durability of the software.

1.7 Experts' View

Experts who haven't worked on the software (to avoid myopia) but are familiar with software development (including architecture and code analysis issues) have access to the source code and documentation. They can perform static analysis and understand the software's requirements and operating conditions are ideal. If test coverage is good, tests are executed methodically, and at least some of the testing is done under actual operating conditions. Software testing, including unit, integration, and system testing, gives a wealth of information regarding software durability.

If high-quality operational data is available for a sufficiently long period, operational data (failure reports, etc.) provides a solid foundation for stochastic durability analysis. Software durability estimation is not a one-day process. It is also hard to implement because no effective standard methodology is available yet for practical durability estimation. This issue makes software durability maintenance vaguer and more complex. To make it more understandable and straightforward, this book aims to numerically identify the durability estimation process and propose a guideline for it.

Users' needs are changing these days with regard to durability because new threats are generating the challenges in the maintenance process. Further, users do not want an interruption in their business for a long time through the maintenance process of software services. That's why the practitioners are continuously trying to solve this problem. In this regard, many practitioners have focused and put forward their comments related to these issues. DeMarco and Lister quoted, "Quality is free, but only to those who are willing to pay heavily for it" [12]. Quality product standards and definitions evolve over time. At first, it fulfilled the user's basic needs. Now durability needs are added to the essential requirements in software.

For a very long time, the software development community has recognised the need to incorporate a human dimension into its work. Surprisingly, however, understanding user needs for durability is increasingly common these days. The importance of durability has been recognised in recent years, maybe due to several increased cases of attacks reported by the media [13]. Lehman's first law of maintainability states that "a programme that is used undergoes continual change or becomes progressively less useful" [14]. Strengthening Lehman's fact, Nathan Ensmenger says, "Maintenance is a Misnomer" and also a "Dull and Dirty Work of Maintenance" [3]. In this row, Mr. Tekinaslan states that the first 90 percent of the code accounts for the first 90 percent of the development time and the remaining 10 percent of the code accounts for the other 90 percent of the development time [15].

Regarding rapid development, Steve McConnell did an interesting experiment by giving the same software to five different development teams. Each development team had a diverse list of objectives that included memory use, output readability, programme readability, minimum statements, and minimum programming time [16]. As a result, only four out of five developers were able to achieve at least two objectives. This shows that achieving all the objectives in one development is not possible.

In Clean Code: A Handbook of Agile Software Craftsmanship, Robert C. Martin states that "It is not enough for code to work" [17]). Durable software development aims to develop software whose durability can be quantified. Kevin Mitnick says that "companies spend millions of dollars on firewalls, encryption, and secure access devices, and it's money wasted because none of these measures address the weakest link in the security chain" [18]. The weakest link in durability can be identified by finding vulnerable holes in software design. According to Bruce Schneier, "If you think technology can solve your durable service problems, then you don't understand the problems, and you don't understand the technology" [19]. Technology doesn't mean that it will make itself durable. Durability is not built in a day, and it is developed in steps: durability by design, development, etc. Gary McGraw states that software durability is about integrating durability practises into how you build software, not integrating durability features into your code [23]. Hence, designing durability through the steps increases the durability of the whole software life span. Although Thomas C. Gale observes that "good design adds value faster than it adds cost" [20].

Further, Gabriel Morgan of Microsoft Corporation said, "Build high-quality software, leverage industry practices, and plan to build quality into your solution; but be sure to prioritise carefully" [21]. In 1995, Sutherland described the cost of maintenance during the use of software services in the United States as more than $70 billion annually for more than ten billion lines of existing code [22–23]. According to these statements by the practitioners, it is clear that there are so many loopholes in software design, and to improve the life span of software services, durability is the key point [24]. Durability must be perceived as one of the foremost concerns to address for improving the life span of software services.

1.8 Conclusion

Despite the requirement of establishing software and durability simultaneously during development, especially during the design phase, the researchers discovered a gap. More so, between the quality attributes as identified by the existing research done in this domain and the best practices that needed to be adhered to by the developers. Building the relationship between software and durability is highly demandable to minimize the gap, and advanced research is required to strengthen the concept. The available literature can be divided into three patterns: in the first category, the approaches try to improve durability during the development life cycle. The second category of techniques is identifying methodologies that will enhance software durability, either after development or during later stages of development. The identified approaches in the third category are essential and can be used to estimate and enhance the software durability of software service life span.

Points to Remember

- Software durability management is not a one-day process.
- There are no standard rules available as of now to manage the software durability.
- Adding the feature and updates after the software development is not a commercially viable option.
- Patching creates loopholes for the software attackers.
- To create effective software durability, we need to incorporate attributes of software and durability on the same platform.

Review Questions

Objective Type Questions

1. Which one of these is a software characteristic?
   a. Operational
   b. Dependable
   c. Complexity
   d. Trustworthiness
2. Which one is not a software type?
   a. Application
   b. Firmware
   c. Utility
   d. Graphics
3. What is application software?
   a. Google Docs
   b. Firmware
   c. MacOS
   d. Windows
4. Which one is system software?
   a. MacOS
   b. Google Docs
   c. Microsoft Word
   d. VLC Media Player

5. Which one is programming software?

   a. Google Docs
   b. VLC Media Player
   c. Android
   d. Android Studio

Short Answer Type Questions

1. What is durability?
2. What type of software is available in the industry?
3. Enlist some of the software myths.
4. What is application software?
5. What do you understand about software myths?
6. Give a brief overview of software durability.
7. What are durability factors?
8. What do you understand by software security durability?

Descriptive Questions

1. Give an introduction and discuss software durability and its factors.
2. Discuss the types of software types and myths.

References

1. Chen, C., Alfayez, R., Srisopha, K., Boehm, B. and Shi, L. 2017. Why is it important to measure maintainability and what are the best ways to do it? In Proceedings of the 39th International Conference on Software Engineering Companion. IEEE Press, pp. 377–378.
2. Kelty, C. and Erickson, S. 2015. The Durability of Software, Meson Press, Germany, 1(5): 1–13.
3. Ensmenger, N. 2014. When good software goes bad: the surprising durability of an ephemeral technology. In MICE (Mistakes, Ignorance, Contingency, and Error) Conference. Munich, pp. 1–16.
4. Cusick, J.J. 2013. Durable Ideas in Software Engineering: Concepts, Methods and Approaches from My Virtual Toolbox, Bentham Science Publishers.
5. Bartlett, E.V. and Simpson, S. 2013. Durability and Reliability, Alternative Approaches to Assessment of Component Performance over Time, Available at: https://www.irbnet.de/daten/iconda/CIB8616.pdf, Last Visit Sep 20 2018.
6. Hayden, E., Assante, M., and Conway, T. 2014. An Abbreviated History of Automation & Industrial Controls Systems and Cyber Security, A SANS Analyst Whitepaper.

7. Van Der Linden, D. and Wupper H. 2010. A method for durability analysis of development systems in computing. Research Number, 117 IK, pp. 1–17.
8. Hneif, M., Lee, S.P. 2011. Using guidelines to improve quality in software non-functional attributes. IEEE Software, 28(6): 72–77.
9. Vandegriend, B. 2006. How to Create Maintainable Software, Available at: http://www. basilv.com/psd/blog/2006/the-importance-of-maintainable-software. Last Visit Sep 25 2018.
10. Feenstra, R.C. and Knittel, C.R. 2009. Re-assessing the US quality adjustment to computer prices: the role of durability and changing software. In Price Index Concepts and Measurement, University of Chicago Press, pp. 129–160.
11. Thomas, R. 1994. Durable, Low Cost Educational Software, In Computer Assisted Learning: Selected Contributions from the CAL'93 Symposium, pp. 65–72.
12. Develop Zone. 2016. Available at: https://dzone.com/articles/the-ultimate-list-of-100-software-testing-quotes-2, Last Visit Jan 24 2018.
13. Continuous Delivery: How to Have the Reliable Software Releases to Production at Any Time. 2018. Available at: http://www.softwaretestinghelp.com/what-is-continuous-delivery/, Last Visit March 31 2018.
14. Jansson, A.S. 2007. Software Maintenance and Process Improvement, CMMI, UPTEC STS07037.
15. Tekinaslan, H. 2018. Available at: https://twitter.com/htkaslan last Visit Jan 24 2018.
16. Professional Software Development. 2006. Available at: http://www.basilv.com/psd/blog/2006/how-to-create-maintainable-software last Visit Jan 30 2018.
17. Martin, R.C. 2009. Clean Code: A Handbook of Agile Software Craftsmanship, Pearson Education Press.
18. Mitnick, K. 2000. Available at: https://www.theregister.co.uk/2000/03/02/kevin_mitnick_was_no_hacker/ last Visit Jan 24 2018.
19. Schneier, B. 2009. Schneier on Security, John Wiley & Sons, pp. 1–2.
20. Coders Trust. 2018. Available at: https://coderstrust.tumblr.com/post/116455270040/top-20-coding-quotes last Visit Jan 24 2018.
21. Implementing System Quality Attributes. 2007. Available at: https://msdn.microsoft.com/en-us/library/bb402962.aspx last Visit Jan 30 2018.
22. Sutherland, J. 1995. Business objects in corporate information systems. ACM Computing Surveys, 27(2): 274–276.
23. McGraw, G. 2006. Software Security: Building Security In, Volume 1, Addison-Wesley Professional.
24. Kumar, R. 2018. Fuzzy Multi Criteria Decision Analysis for Security Durability Assessment, PhD Thesis [Online]. Available at: https://shodhganga.inflibnet.ac.in/handle/10603/262367.

Useful Links

https://www.squareboat.com/blog/different-types-of-software-with-examples
https://www.geeksforgeeks.org/types-of-software/
https://www.leadwithprimitive.com/blog/the-4-main-types-of-software
https://en.wikipedia.org/wiki/Software_durability
https://onix-systems.com/blog/10-common-software-myths-dispelled

CHAPTER 2
Assuring Software Durability

2.1 Objectives

Software design is a progressive activity that involves constructing a proxy to create specific descriptions of objects and designing software to accept goals using well-established processes and constraints. The research begins to classify conditions, tactics, or actions that lead to software degradation and financial loss. Energy risk evaluations, secure rights records, rumours about events going in the opposite direction, and previous approval or certifying exams are all part of gathering evidence and building a foundation.

The demand for software maintenance has risen as a result of the increasing use of software services. It encourages the developers to minimise the cost and time spent on software maintenance to reduce risks for the users while using the software's protected services. Developers should strive to create secure and long-lasting software as a solution to these issues. The inventors have presented a system for assessing software durability to improve the functional life span of secure software and assist developers.

The inventors have also introduced a new concept of software durability and certain necessary actions for incorporating software durability into software architecture. In addition, the inventors have produced some key recommendations and a basic approach for establishing guidelines to aid in the development of software with a longer life cycle. When creating a plan for software durability, keep the following goals in mind:

- To create a software durability assessment framework that takes into account a variety of other essential variables.

- To determine and assess the respective factors of software durability.

- To determine and explore the risks associated with the software durability inclusion into the software quality.
- To establish the relationship of software durability with software quality.

2.2 Five Touch Points for Software Durability

The expected service life duration of software is known as software durability. Because new security dangers emerge every day, the use of software and the need to update security grows over time. If these risks become active, services will fail, and the software will crash as a result. As illustrated in Fig. 1, there are a variety of software durability features that can be employed to improve software life span, including reliability, usability, security, trustworthiness, and human trust. A brief description of these attributes is as follows:

2.2.1 Software Dependability

For many computer-based systems, system dependability is the most critical system attribute. The user's level of trust in a system is reflected in its dependability. It indicates how confident the user is that the system in use will work as intended and will not "fail" in normal use. Dependability encompasses system attributes such as reliability, availability, and security. All of these factors are linked.

System failures can have far-reaching ramifications that affect a large number of people. Because they are not dependable, users may reject systems that are unreliable, harmful, or insecure. The implications of a system failure that results in economic losses or physical damage can be highly costly. Data loss can occur as a result of unreliable systems, with a significant recovery cost.

When a user can rely on a computer and its software to perform as intended, it is said to be "safe". This concept is debatable since it assumes that users' computer and software behaviour expectations include care. However, it is useful in emphasizing the significance of dependability. Dependability and its co-attributes have an impact on software endurance. Dependability refers to a company's ability to provide services that can

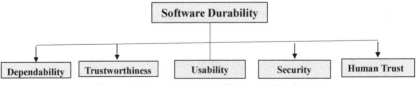

Figure 1: Main Attributes of Software Durability.

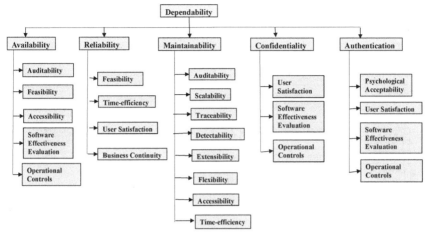

Figure 2: Attributes of Dependability affecting Durability.

be relied upon. The user's expectation of software service life duration, according to the dependability criteria, is vital. As a result, in these terms, trustworthy software aids in the strengthening of durability. As illustrated in Fig. 2, there are numerous aspects of dependability, but only a few are affected by durability.

Figure 2 depicts the reliability characteristics that influence the life span of software services. The definition emphasizes the importance of trust justification. As a result, it is linked to qualities like confidentiality, authentication, and dependability. An alternative, quantitative definition that offers the criteria for assessing if the service is dependable is the capacity to avoid service failures that are more frequent and severe than what is acceptable to the user(s).

2.2.2 Software Trustworthiness

Every day, confidence and faith in a system's ability to work as intended are put to the test, whether due to planned or unexpected operational problems, environmental consequences and system dangers, or hostile unauthorised individuals. Systematic attention to a system's fundamental traits and gathering adequate proof that the necessary characteristics are being met are required for confidence and trust. To supply resilient and lucrative industrial solutions, trustworthy software is required.

Analysis and proactive measures in software architecture, design, implementation, testing, and operation are necessary to develop a dependable, robust, safe, privacy-preserving, and secure system. The safeguards must address potential faults in analysis, design, and code quality that could expose the software to security risks, threats, or theft. When software functions as intended for a given purpose when needed,

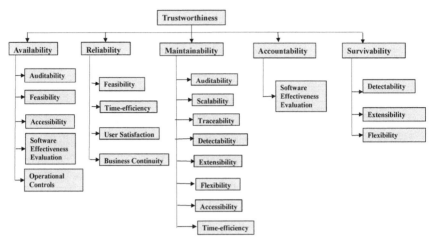

Figure 3:   Attributes of Trustworthiness affecting Software Durability.

with current changes, and without undesirable side-effects, behaviours, or exploitable vulnerabilities, it is considered trustworthy. The certainty that the software will work as planned is referred to as trustworthiness. There are many aspects of trustworthiness, but only a handful have an impact on longevity, as shown in Fig. 3.

The factors of trustworthiness that determine the lifetime of software services are depicted in Fig. 3. As a result, availability, reliability, maintainability, accountability, and survival are all factors that influence trustworthiness. Furthermore, durability necessitates that the programme works for a set period by enhancing the maintainability of software services and therefore increasing trustworthiness. Operational resilience is a set of approaches that allow people, processes, and information systems to adapt to changing patterns, which enhances trustworthiness. This word expresses the fact that software maintainability has an impact on its long-term security. The quantitative concept of trustworthiness suggests that availability, reliability, accountability, and survivability are all related to trustworthiness.

2.2.3 Software Usability

Usability is described as a system's capacity to allow users to perform tasks in a safe, productive, and efficient manner while still having fun. Usability, as defined by software engineering, is the degree to which individual consumers can use software to achieve measured goals with efficacy, efficiency, and satisfaction in a quantified context of usage.

The object of usage can be a software application, website, book, tool, machine, process, vehicle, or anything else with which a human interacts. A usability study can be carried out by a usability analyst as a primary job

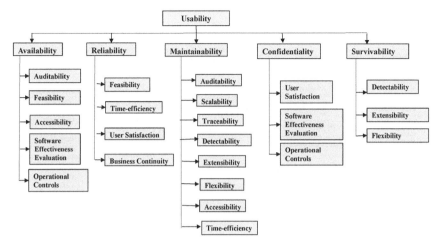

Figure 4: Attributes of Usability affecting Software Durability.

function or as a subsidiary job function by designers, technical writers, marketers, and others. It's used in consumer electronics, communication, and knowledge transfer objects (such as a cookbook, a document, or online help), as well as mechanical objects like a door handle or a hammer.

A software interface's simplicity or ease of use does not always imply that it is usable. Making everything simple is not the same as usability. The five key enhancements that make for usable software, according to the end user's experience, are availability, reliability, maintainability, secrecy, and survivability. Software durability and usability are also features that complement one another. There are various usability qualities, but only a handful of them are affected by software durability, as shown in Fig. 4.

Figure 4 shows the attributes of usability that are affecting the life span of software services. Hence, according to its definition, usability depends on availability, reliability, maintainability, confidentiality, and survivability.

2.2.4 Software Security

If integrity, authentication, or availability of software is jeopardised, it is considered insecure. Data can be stolen, content can be monitored, vulnerabilities can be introduced, and programme behaviour can be changed when software systems are infiltrated. Malware can cause a system crash or a Denial of Service (DoS). Software security is a mechanism that protects software against malicious assaults and other hacker risks so that it can continue to function normally even when under attack. Security is required for integrity, authentication, and availability. Some of

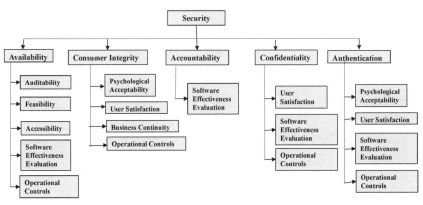

Figure 5: Attributes of Security affecting Software Durability.

the security's properties, such as availability, consumer integrity, and so on, have an impact on durability. Figure 5 depicts the impact relationship.

Figure 5 shows the attributes of security that are affecting the life span of software services. Hence, security depends on availability, consumer integrity, accountability, confidentiality, and authentication.

2.2.5 *Human Trust*

Human trust is frequently characterised as a difficult issue in which the trustworthy party owes a moral commitment to the trusting party. "Human trust in software" refers to the customers' faith in web developers. Consumers' trust in the internet is based on the software design and the web's ability to perform for the expected amount of time while preserving their personal information.

Human trust is typically regarded as a delicate issue involving human-human contact in which the trusted party owes a moral obligation to the trusting party. Consumers' faith in developers is referred to as "human trust" in software. Consumers' trust in software is based on the product's design, which ensures that it will work for the expected amount of time. The qualities of software durability and human trust strengthen one another. There are many aspects of human trust, but just a handful have an impact which is shown in Fig. 6.

Figure 6 depicts the characteristics of human trust that influence the longevity of software services. Durable software will increase human trust and, as a result, consumer confidence in an organization's software services. Human trust is the readiness to put one's faith in software. Reliability, consumer integrity, accountability, confidentiality, and authenticity are five criteria that may affect human trust, according to its definition. These factors are inextricably linked to human trust. As a result, the effectiveness of these five factors is critical in fostering more vital human trust.

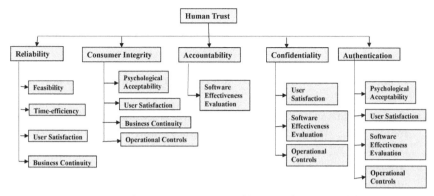

Figure 6: Attributes of Human Trust affecting Software Durability.

There has been a lot of research done to try to understand and characterise the strategies that can be used to upgrade software. While there has always been a gap between hypotheses and practises that is difficult to bridge, the problem could be alleviated by adopting a uniform nomenclature and making research results more accessible. It has been attempted to construct a quantitative assessment of durability attributes for determining the importance using the durability analysis.

Identifying durability characteristics early in the software development process is crucial for evaluating the impact of these features on the product's life span. Decision-makers may be able to make suitable decisions and actions based on the assessment of durability attributes. However, decision-makers must not only understand durability traits but also their mapping in order to take suitable action.

Figures 2 to 6 depict several aspects of software service endurance. For example, confidentiality affects software effectiveness, user satisfaction, and operational controls; availability affects auditability, feasibility, accessibility, software effectiveness evaluation, and operational controls; reliability affects feasibility, time-efficiency, user satisfaction, and business continuity; maintainability affects auditability, scalability, traceability, detectability, accessibility, time-efficiency, extensibility, effectiveness, and flexibility; and maintainability affects auditability, scalability, traceability, detectability, accessibility, time-efficiency. Full descriptions of the aforementioned hierarchy or mapping are followed at each level.

Figures 2 to 6 depict the software durability hierarchy, which is divided into three layers. An attribute at one level influences one or more attributes at a higher level, although the effects are not identical. The values may be different. Reliability, for example, has an impact on dependability, human trust, and trustworthiness, but the impact values are not equal. The hierarchies of attributes aid in distinguishing the effects of similar attributes on higher-level attributes. Practitioners must understand and assess software durability during the software development process in order to provide extended software services.

There are eight attributes at level 2 which affect software durability and are defined as:

- *Confidentiality*: Confidentiality refers to allowing authorized access to sensitive and secure data.

- *Consumer Integrity*: Consumer integrity is defined as the attribute maintaining the consistency, accuracy, and trustworthiness of consumers all over the life cycle of a software product.

- *Authentication*: Authentication is the factor that is responsible for the identity of the user profile. It is the process of determining whether a user is, in fact, the one who the user claims to be.

- *Reliability:* Reliability is the ability to consistently perform according to its specifications. It is considered to be a very important aspect while designing software.

- *Maintainability:* It is the probability that a system can be repaired in the said environment or situation.

- *Accountability:* Accountability means that every individual user who works with the software should have specific responsibilities for durability assurance. These tasks include individual responsibilities as part of the overall durability plan because software may become vulnerable to a responsible person such as a developer.

- *Survivability:* Survivability is the ability of a system to fulfill its mission, in a timely manner, in the presence of attacks, failures, or accidents.

- *Availability:* Availability means the information is accessible by only authorized users. Availability, in the context of a computer system, refers to the ability of a user to access information or resources for a specified duration.

There are fourteen attributes at level 3 that are defined as follows:

- *Auditability:* The capability of supporting a systematic and independent security process for obtaining audit evidence and evaluating it accurately to determine the extent to which audit criteria are fulfilled.

- *Scalability:* Scalability is the measure of how well security can grow to meet increasing performance demands.

- *Feasibility:* A feasibility study is an analysis of how a project can be completed successfully, accounting for factors that affect it such as economic, technological, legal, and scheduling factors.

- *Detectability:* Detectability is responsible for the detection of security failures or crashes in software for a particular duration of time.

- *Accessibility:* Accessibility is the degree to which a software security service or environment is available to as many people as possible.

- *Time-efficiency:* The capability to provide the appropriate performance of security, relative to the number of resources used under the stated conditions within the specified time duration.

- *Extensibility:* The ease with which security can be enhanced in the future to meet the ever-changing security requirements or goals.

- *Psychological Acceptability:* Acceptance in human psychology is a person's acceptance of the reality of a situation; recognizing a process or condition without attempting to change it or protest against it.

- *User Satisfaction:* User satisfaction is a degree of how secure the service that has been provided by an organization is to meet the customer's expectations.

- *Business Continuity:* Business continuity encompasses a loosely defined set of planning, preparation, and related activities for software security which are intended to ensure that an organization's critical business functions will either continue to operate within a period or not.

- *Software Effectiveness Evaluation:* Effectiveness is the degree to which something is successful in producing the desired result and realising the envisioned target.

- *Flexibility:* The capability of secure software to respond to potential internal or external changes affecting its value in a timely and cost-effective manner.

- *Operational Controls:* The most difficult task of management includes monitoring the behavior of individuals, comparing security performance to some standard, and providing rewards as specified.

The first-level, second-level, and third-level qualities that depend on the durability, either directly or indirectly, were divided by the researchers into three primary tiers based on the discussion that came before them. The researchers can evaluate the software's durability thanks to these characteristics. Software can last longer if a process is well-planned, well-organized, and simple to manage during the software development life cycle.

2.3 Quality Assurance: Durability Perspective

Software Quality-Durability Assurance (SQ-DA) is a technique for ensuring the quality and durability of software. It's a set of steps taken to guarantee that the project's processes, procedures, and standards are acceptable and correctly implemented over time. Software Quality-

Durability Assurance is a process that happens at the same time as software development. Its goal is to improve the software development process so that the problems can be identified and resolved before they become major issues, as well as to make the product more long-lasting. SQ-DA stands for Software Quality and Durability Assurance, and it can be added as a form of umbrella activity that is employed throughout the software development lifecycle.

2.3.1 Software Quality-Durability Assurance

- A quality-durability management approach.
- A multi-testing strategy is used to ensure durability.
- Engineering technology for software durability that works.
- Measurement and reporting mechanisms

2.3.2 Major Assurance Activities

- *SQ-DA Management Plan:* Make a plan for how you will carry out the SQ-DA throughout the project. Think about which set of software durability engineering activities is best for the project. Check the level of SQ-DA team skills.
- *Set The Check Points:* The SQ-DA team should set checkpoints. Evaluate the performance of the project based on the collected data on different checkpoints.
- *Multi-Testing Strategy:* Do not depend on a single testing approach. When you have a lot of testing approaches available, use them.
- *Measure Change Impact:* The changes made to correct an error sometimes reintroduce more errors when attempting to measure the impact of change on the project. Reset the new change to check the compatibility of this fix with the whole project.
- *Manage Good Relations:* In the working environment, managing good relations with other teams involved in the project and development is mandatory. The lousy association of the SQ-DA team with the programmer's group will impact directly and badly on the project. Don't play politics.

2.3.3 Benefits

- Software Quality-Durability Assurance (SQ-DA) produces high-quality software.
- The high-quality and durable application saves time and money.
- SQ-DA is beneficial for better reliability.

- SQ-DA is valuable in the condition of no maintenance for a long time.
- High-quality commercial software increases the market share of a company.
- Improving the process of creating software.
- It improves the durability, and hence, the quality of the software.

2.3.4 Disadvantage

There are several disadvantages to quality-durability assurance. Some of them include adding more resources and employing more workers to help maintain durability and quality, among several others.

2.4 Durability Assurance Framework

Durability must be incorporated and examined from the inception of software development to extend the life span of software services while minimising the maintenance costs and time involved. Before the application is supplied to the user, durability features must be tested and certified. Development costs can be more precisely defined and controlled if the software is developed using an appropriate approach that integrates durability. It also saves money and time on maintenance, which can improve durability. The goal of this research project is to investigate the potential for developing a metric to evaluate durability at the early stages in the life cycle of software development so as to maximise the total life span. The basic idea is to examine software durability during the design process and minimise the maintenance time and cost as soon as possible. Hence, in the initial stages of the development process itself, a system for durability should be devised, which may help with knowledge of durability during the design phase. Since the design phase creates the software's structure, making modifications and fixes is easier than doing them later. As a result, at this stage, an adequate methodology for durability assessment is required. The framework could aid in the development and verification of durability.

Every industry, including finance, education, and communication, is dependent on various software platforms. The increased use of software services invariably increases the maintenance process. This puts the developers under even more pressure to reduce maintenance costs and time so that users cannot receive continual software services. As a response to this challenge, programmers are attempting to create secure and long-lasting software. In this league, the authors have outlined a paradigm for assessing durability to extend the operational life of secure software. The envisioned methodology offers a roadmap for determining durability with a focus on software quality improvement. This framework also includes some critical actions for simplifying and incorporating durability into software architecture. In addition, the authors have enlisted and cited an elementary approach that, if prescribed, would help the developers in producing software with a longer operational life span. This study also encapsulates several key recommendations in the same row which will facilitate the developers' task.

2.4.1 The Framework

Organizations constantly focus on new concepts to acquire user trust to create more adaptable, usable, and durable software. To improve user satisfaction, businesses want to provide more durable software that delivers more comprehensive services. Unfortunately, a faster development pace and a lack of software documentation prevent them from achieving the long-term goal. During their literature review, the authors discovered that existing techniques for developing durable software are theoretical or just naive practices. Most firms that are attempting to accomplish software safety fail to consider its long-term viability. However, focusing on software durability at the same time will meet the user's needs and protect the user's investment in durable software. As a result, developing durable and long-lasting software remains an arduous undertaking.

It is a proven fact that including durability during development phases lowers costs and reduces rework. Most specialists have concentrated on the deployment phase of software development to improve service life and reduce maintenance time and expense. However, durability is still an issue of concern. Researchers and practitioners have advocated incorporating durability during development phases, but no one has presented a step-by-step strategy to improve the software's life span. Furthermore, no research has been found that discusses incorporating durability into software development processes. As a result, there is a need to establish a method that provides step-by-step instructions on including durability in the development process. The authors created the Software Durability Framework (SD^F), which offers comprehensive guidance for incorporating durability into development in response to this need.

2.4.2 Premise

The framework, as visualised by the authors, is a diagram that depicts a complicated procedure. It provides a step-by-step approach for completing the intended research work. This framework is a living document that can be updated and amended as needed to meet the user's demands. This framework can be a widely used method for incorporating software durability into the software development process. The framework makes the following assumptions to achieve durability:

- The framework extends the life of the software during its service life, focusing on lowering maintenance costs (time and money).
- During the framework installation process, the list of durability attributes can be changed. A subset of the provided set of durability attributes can be specified, or extra durability attributes can be added.
- The durability hierarchy's tiers are not final. It is modifiable due to variations in the number of attributes.

The use of this Software Durability Framework (SDF) is the next step in improving the software's life span, extending its life span by lowering the cost of maintenance and time structured in the entire process.

2.4.3 Generic Guidelines

The proposed durability assessment framework comprises five phases or steps (as shown in Fig. 7). These are:

- Factor Identification
- Classification
- Assessment
- Validation
- Packaging

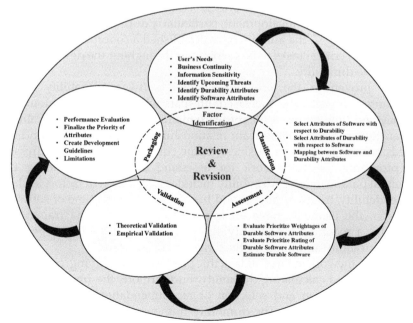

Figure 7: A Framework for Integrating Software Durability Activities at Design Phase.

The appropriate principles, relevant durability factors, and levels of attributes are identified in the first phase, the Factor Identification phase. The next phase, the classification phase, determines whether the construct adheres to the recognised principles for each of the indicated durability qualities to improve durability. Prioritization of durability qualities is done during the evaluation process to measure durability confinement through that construct. A durability algorithm has been developed. The fourth phase entails the verification of the obtained outcomes or assessments. The packaging phase, the fifth phase, examines performance based on validation. Following that, a developer guideline for the software development life cycle is presented. In each of these stages, there is a lot of review and revision. This step revisits the entire strategy for prospective improvements and returns it to its previous phase from the present one.

2.4.4 Framework Development

Over the last decade, software development companies have experienced remarkable growth, increasing in tandem with rapid technological advancements. The rising use of software in practically every human profession, including defence, business, media, and sports, is a significant reason for this expansion. There is a need to design durable and safe software that can be used for a long time, based on user demand and investment in the software. Though there is a lot of study on integrating durability during development, there is none on integrating durability throughout software development, particularly during the design process. As shown in Fig. 7, the authors have established a conceptual framework that outlines critical tasks to be carried out throughout the design process to improve durability.

As proven in the previous chapter, software durability has a substantial impact. The increased lifespan will reduce the amount of money and time required for software maintenance. Mapping durability parameters can find a significant relationship between durability and the needs and importance of business. Some concepts have been addressed in providing the framework for assessing durability, including the essential parameters, i.e., durability includes a collection of factors such as dependability, trustworthiness, and human-trust. At the time of software creation, the elements have an impact on durability. The framework provides a roadmap for identifying and mapping durability aspects to assess durability and improve the longevity of software.

The framework in Fig. 7 aids in this process by identifying, classifying, evaluating, and calculating durability. Furthermore, the framework aids in the identification and selection of recommendations for integrating all development efforts. The durability framework contains five phases: factor identification, classification, evaluation, validation, and ultimately, the packaging phase, which results in the formulation of instructions. The review and revision procedure will be carried out as needed. The following sections go through all of the durability activities that must be completed during each phase.

2.4.4.1 Attribute Recognition

The primary stage in most problem-solving tasks is to identify factors or attributes. The concept of crucial solutions, as well as relevant data, is the emphasis of this stage. The primary goal of this phase is to identify aspects of durability based on the needs of the users, the sensitivity of the information, and potential threats. The requirement or expectation in terms of software is referred to as the user's need. The variables highlighted here are recognised as crucial considerations and aid in developing a roadmap for durable and long-lasting design. A pragmatic approach should be taken when identifying factors that have a significant impact on both durability and reliability. If irrelevant aspects are taken into account, a durable design can become convoluted, worthless, and ineffectual. As a result, only those durability factors that affect software design should be examined and finalized.

2.4.4.2 Attribute-to-Attribute Mapping

Initially, software attributes concerning durability will be classified in this phase, and vice versa. The mapping or relationship between the durability factors should be established after that. The embedded relation of one characteristic with the other and vice versa is referred to as mapping. This attribute mapping creates a hierarchy of relationships between the attributes, which will aid in the quantification of durability. The link between durability aspects is then created by using best practises and a unified set of regulations. At this stage, all of the identified elements that may impact the design must be cross-verified. To control design, these durability factors must be addressed. All the detected durability factors are mapped, and a durability factor hierarchy is built. Durability can be broken down into three quantitative characteristics: trustworthiness, dependability, and human trust.

2.4.4.3 Evaluation

Durability is inextricably linked, and enhancing one while simultaneously strengthening the other improves the overall life span of software. The software will have a long durable service life if durability is improved. The durability evaluation will assist in achieving objectives at a lower cost. The examination will also help discover which elements have a negative or positive impact on software durability. Multiple methods can be employed for this, with soft computing-based methods such as AHP (Analytic Hierarchy Process), Fuzzy Analytic Hierarchy Process (Fuzzy AHP), and Delphi Analytic Hierarchy Process (Delphi AHP) being prominent.

The assessment of durability aids in the enhancement of software's service life. Longevity and durability appear to be inextricably linked. Improving one leads to the improvement of the other. It means that assessing durability improves service life span and considering serviceability increases durability. Durability evaluation will also aid in achieving the objectives while reducing the amount of money spent on them. A more safe and long-lasting system may be developed, as well as one that is less vulnerable over time. If suitable evaluation findings are not obtained, the fifth phase, "Review & Revision", can be carried out using various procedures and instruments, such as expert opinions.

2.4.4.4 *Validation*

The validation procedure guarantees that the produced model does the job it was designed to achieve. After assessing the long-term software, it's crucial to evaluate performance. It can be done in either a quantitative or qualitative manner. Though numerical or quantitative assessment is preferable in this situation, sensitivity analysis might be used.

The validation process peruses the actions that go into checking the building process and ensuring that the final product is what it should be. The values employed in the models are valid measurements for the design constructs, and it's helpful to look at them in an empirical setting. The first step, "theoretical validation", involves ensuring a theoretical foundation through literature review and analysis. The second phase, "empirical validation", consists of testing the constructed models with real-world data to provide accurate measures of the required properties. The third phase, "Review & Revision", can be completed using various methods and techniques, including expert opinions and the contextual interpretation and inference of the data collected. Informal reviews and adjustments might take place at any point during the development process. The final section, referred to as "finalization", refers to the acceptance of legitimate models and their quantitative values for software.

After assessing durability, it's crucial to evaluate performance. After considering durability as a raw aspect, performance evaluation is used to measure the improvement. There are two methods for assessing performance: quantitative and qualitative. Although no numerical or quantitative assessment is possible in this circumstance, sensitivity analysis can be used to examine the situation. If the outcomes are unsatisfactory, the procedure can proceed to the review and revision phase.

2.4.4.5 *Suggestions*

Durability guidelines are prudent advice to reduce the time and expenses incurred in maintenance while the software is in use. These guidelines will assist in calculating the values of durability to improve serviceability while reducing software maintenance time and expense. Prioritized criteria are mapped to select or identify development recommendations based on the assessment. The guidelines have been based on the previous methodologies proposed by various practitioners. The input to this procedure is software factors, and the output is a collection of guidelines.

The guidelines that are created have an impact on the factors that are related to them. These effects can be beneficial, adverse, or have no effect at all. It is necessary to map the links between guidelines and factors to understand the consequences. This relationship map aids in identifying conflicts between the chosen criteria and higher-priority factors. Guidelines should ensure two attributes: The guidelines must, first and foremost, have a beneficial impact on the high-priority factors. Second, the development guidelines adopted should have only homogeneous relationships with one another. To achieve a set of non-overlapping development guidelines, the relationships between all chosen development standards must be determined. Development guidelines are defined based on prioritised variables. Figure 8 depicts a step-by-step approach for generating durability guidelines.

2.4.4.6 *Review and Revision*

The step of review and revision is common to all the processes because it can occur during the development process. This process is both informal and crucial, as reviewing and revising a framework makes it more manageable. All phases of the process are reviewed and revised as needed to produce more refined recommendations.

2.5 Risk Management Activities in the Early Development of Durable Software Design

Until recently, software engineering had shifted the responsibility of ensuring a product's long-term durability to an additional design phase. Due to the increasing exposure of design defects and the expanding influence of malicious code, dealing with design life span is becoming increasingly vital when it comes to development. It is an effective strategy for reducing the risk of software failure. It depends on how the duties of classifying, investigating, and monitoring risk are handled in the design process.

Basic Steps to Select\ Identify a Set of Guidelines

```
Input       :   Software Durability Factors
Output      :   Set of Guidelines for Improving Security

Step 1: Collect the development guidelines related to given factors.

Step 2: For each required factor
Select\Identify the development guidelines related to given factor
Step 2.1:
    if
      guideline procedures are not conflicting to another factor's
      guideline procedures
    then
      continue
    otherwise
      form the experts comment and literature of best practices, some
      steps of development guidelines are rejected, according to the
      choice of the designers and create\select new steps
      without conflicting
Step 2.2:
    if
      same factor has two different guidelines
    then
      identify some steps that supports single development guideline for
      given factor, according to the choice of the designers
    otherwise
      continue

Step 3: For overlapping guidelines of two factors
Step 3.1:
    if
       priority value of factor 1 = priority value of factor 2
    then
       select guidelines steps that are supporting the priorities
       values of both factors
    else
        continue
Step 3.2:
    if
      priority value of factor 1 ≠ priority value factor 2
    then
      select one of the factor is next rank and select guidelines
      steps, according to the choice of the security designers
```

```
Repeat these steps for each required factor.
```

Figure 8: A Procedure for Creating the Guidelines and Perceptions.

A robust design is vital during software development since it can serve as a safety net in the event of a failure. Since the software needs to be protected from hazards and managed throughout the development process, a design is required to ensure that this is possible and that the software becomes durable. The framework depicted in Fig. 9, is used to construct a long-term software strategy that incorporates risk and its management as inputs for software durability and verification and validation at every level of software design.

The development of software that is long-lasting is a natural progression. As part of this method, risk documentation and control are essential. The main challenge of risk management in software is not to eliminate all risk but rather to reduce risk to a reasonable level while maintaining the product's ability to function. Early risk management efforts should be made to assure the durability of various software modules. Every known threat in system software is examined for risk in both standard and accountability settings.

The designer needs to determine whether or not a risk decrease is intended in a risk estimation problem. Throughout the design verification process, risk controls are estimated and implemented as part of the design output. The value of risk control measures is established during the design validation phase of the software development life cycle. The top design advancements can eliminate minor risk problems in unrestrained design output.

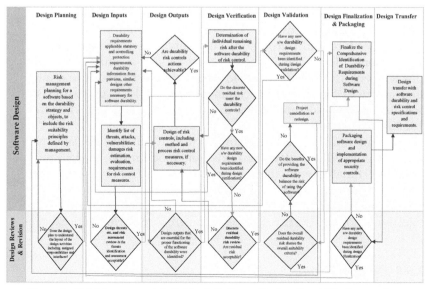

Figure 9: Risk Management Activities in Software Design: Durability Perspective.

After the announcement of the software to the marketplace, the risk management activities of the software should be connected to durability management developments. Software design activities directed at managing risks should be maintained by software durability documents. Fig. 9 shows the risk management activities concerning durability that overlap with the universal design development as distinct.

2.5.1 Design Planning

Software design is the progressive activity that constructs a proxy to produce explicit descriptions of attributes and designs of durable software to accept goals using well-established methodologies and restrictions. The development begins to classify conditions, strategies, or performs that could risk software impairment and monetary wastage. Collection and foundation of evidence contain energetic risk valuations; secure rights records, contrary event rumours, past approval, or certifying examinations.

Software design planning should specify the wanted properties; authorization of this, including suitable ability, is vital to confirm the necessary analysis of thinkable durability distresses. The review part of this planning is to determine whether the design plan can apprehend the design layout and its activities. If the response is inevitable, it will drive to the next drift stage; otherwise, it will go back to the undetected plan.

2.5.2 Design Inputs

Design inputs for software are taken in one or the extra leaflets to create continuous design activities. Design inputs contain the concern of given procedure and purposeful, durability, and control of the design requirements. Risk management processes are a production of risk management activities of the risk, which should be residential into the atmosphere of the design development process. Risk analysis classifies potential harms, susceptibilities due to threats, and damages from a durability perspective.

Any modifications to the identified design features, disclaimers, risk control methods, and related hazards from modern risk analysis must be sensibly estimated with constant maintenance. The review shows that the design inputs are essential before they are improved into the design conditions. According to the flow of data information in Fig. 9, if this objective is not achieved, design development is reviewed until executions are finalized.

2.5.3 Design Outputs

Design outputs are usually of three types. Its first type contains the requirements for the appearance of the software design and those essential for its risk-free and appropriate procedure. The second type of design output communicates the necessities for obtaining, behavior, assembly, delivery, and analytical. The third group includes principles of software risk identification. The design outputs of software durability will consist of the specific risk control procedures and where there will be the requirement for those risk control connections.

These risk control actions should relate to the development process of software. It appears that the risk control measures of software are obligatory and the features for risk control movements are capable of being adept or not. Whether the review and revision parts of design output would test the achievement of design outputs that are essential for the proper working of software durability were emphasised or not. If the answer is positive, the flow goes to the next part of the chart, otherwise, it drives back to the design input for adding new inputs for appropriate operations.

2.5.4 Design Verification

Verification actions are directed at actual steps and stages of design. The basis of verification is a three-branched methodology relating to examinations, assessments, and analysis. Verification techniques that create conformance with a design input are a satisfactory means of verifying the software's durability with respect to design. Design verification of software should produce objective confirmation that acknowledges whether risks were substantiated or not. Durable design verification of software verifies if control measures were affected, and risk control measures were defined to be functioning so that the distinct acceptability ethics happens. It resolves the specific residual risks after the software durability of risk control in software design development. It additionally studies if any unmarked durable design has been acknowledged or not.

2.5.5 Design Validation

The challenges and beginnings of invalidation are exemplified by drawing correspondence to design research. Specific validation follows revisions, such as scientific studies and procedures of models of security viruses are discussed, including infected methods to adapt them to the design of software security engineering.

The empirical validation area involves three major segments. First is pre-tryout: a small fragment of the software design document is being occupied to identify and mitigate the design imperfection with the support of both tools, and then, after assessing the trustworthiness, discretely compare it. The second is tryout: an enormous security necessity document module for a commercial zone is being occupied with classifying and mitigating the software design imperfection with the improvement of both the framework and tool and then assessing the constancy distinctly. The third is statistical analysis, in which the statistical analysis is implemented using either the framework or tool.

2.5.6 Design Finalization and Packaging

Positive verification and validation process requirements are determined and experienced again and again. Here, the need for the finalisation of software security design originates. Software design would reduce the probabilities of any modifications in software design from the developer's view of all security requirements enhanced for secure software being considered in this process. This flow diagram process finalises the widespread identification of security requirements during software design. It completes the packaging of software design prepared for certification and the implementation of security controls and measures in software design processes.

2.5.7 Design Transfer

Design transfer of software covers the areas designed to transform the validated software or system into a validated method. By estimating software or security design verification and validation behaviours while assessing security risk early in the development design, the transfer of a design to development will be more valuable and robust. In the design transfer, the designer should certify the enactment and efficiency of specific risk control measures. The developer should certify that all obtainable or newly acknowledged risk-related concerns are resolved prior to announcing the design to assembly.

2.5.8 Design Review

Design reviews of software should conclude if any discrete residual risks and any inclusive residual risks are sufficiently transferred to suitable characters with customers. This fragment of the flow diagram indicates in each part of the software design if the following planned ranges or activities are concluded or not. If not, then that portion of the flow diagram is reviewed for every category of vulnerabilities as to whether all threats have been recognised or not, software risks are applicably evaluated, and forthcoming risk control procedures are acknowledged. The conduct of design reviews is necessary for a new era of software security. Frequently changing security requirements produce unknown risks.

2.6 Importance of the Frameworks

The growing number of events involving software failures demands an effective strategy for reducing time and expenditure on the maintenance of software. In addition, as the phase progress, the cost of software maintenance increases. As a result, the developers recommend improving the software's life span through design to reduce the overall maintenance costs. Still, there appears to be a disconnect between durability characteristics. Furthermore, no effort to increase software performance for the design phase has addressed the fundamental issue. During the literature evaluation, it was observed that no framework for durability assessment had been developed [11–12].

As a result, the approach presented in this chapter helps to close the gap between software design and implementation. It has two benefits: it measures the durability of software, which aids in developing cost-effective, long-lasting software. Overall, it allows you to answer questions like "what is the software's durability?" and "which attributes are responsible for less durable software?" Simultaneously, it permits the answer to the question of "how much has durability improved?" The following are the implications of the framework:

- It may aid in identifying and minimizing underlying software maintenance at an early point in the software development life cycle, resulting in a durable end product.
- It could aid in determining the impact of durability during the software development process.
- It could aid in the development of alternate versions of long-term software in development.
- It may be helpful in determining whether the new versions of the two software versions are more durable than the old ones.
- It may aid in determining which version of the software is more durable among the various designs.

2.7 Conclusion

After a thorough analysis of the literature and various industry settings, it was discovered that maintaining overall functionality is more complicated than creating it. In this circumstance, durability appears to be a turning point. It is possible to ensure that software is maintained over its predicted long life by developing and using it. However, ensuring long-term durability is indeed more complex than generating it. Overall, durability software may provide greater protection, and durability software is less vulnerable over time. The authors have created a system for integrating durability, which has been termed the *"durability assessment framework"*. It includes all the activities that are necessary to improve long-term durability. Developers can use this framework to create software that has a more durable working life to meet the users' expectations. Furthermore, this effort lays the groundwork for outlining development principles that will make it easier for the developers to maintain the CIA for a longer time.

Points to Remember

- Software durability management is not a one-day process.
- There is no standard rule yet available to manage the software durability.
- Adding the feature and updates after the software development is not a piece of cake.
- Patching creates loopholes for the software attackers.
- To create effective software durability we need to incorporate attributes of software and durability on the same platform. For which a framework is needed.

Review Questions

Objective Type Questions

1. Which is not one of the software durability attributes?
   a. Maintainability
   b. Dependability
   c. Human-Trust
   d. Trustworthiness
2. Which one is not a step of generic guidelines of framework development?
   a. Classification
   b. Assessment
   c. Validation
   d. Verification

3. CIA triad does not include the attribute:
   a. Confidentiality
   b. Integrity
   c. Availability
   d. Authentication
4. Which one is a type of validation in SD^f?
   a. Theoretical
   b. Verification
   c. Numerical Analysis
   d. Prospective
5. Which one is the touch point of software durability?
   a. Trustworthiness
   b. Authentication
   c. Maintainability
   d. Windows

Short Answer Type Questions

1. What is durability from a software perspective?
2. What are the generic guidelines to develop a software durability framework?
3. Explain trustworthiness in durability.
4. What is Survivability role in durability?
5. What do you understand by maintainability?
6. Give a brief overview of the software durability design framework.
7. What are durability attributes and sub-attributes?
8. Explain the Design relationship between durability attributes and sub-attributes.

Descriptive Questions

1. Discuss the software durability framework and explain its mechanism.
2. Discuss software quality-durability assurance (SQ-DF).

References

1. Boegh, J. 2008. A new standard for quality requirements. IEEE Software, 2: 57–63.
2. McGraw, G. 2006. Software Security: Building Security In, Volume 1, Addison-Wesley Professional.

3. SaaS Industry Market Report: Key Global Trends & Growth Forecasts. 2018. Available at: https://financesonline.com/2018-saas-industry-market-report-key-global-trends-growth-forecasts/ Last Visit on 04 Sep 2018.

4. New Data: Software as a Service Industry Revenue up 23% This Year as Shift to the Cloud Continues. 2017. Available at: https://www.geekwire.com/2017/new-data-software-service-industry-revenue-23-year-shift-cloud-continues/ Last Visit on 05 Sep 2018.

5. CA Veracode Report. 2018. Available at: https://techbeacon.com/sorry-state-software-security-secure-development-key, Last Visit Oct 22 2018.

6. Dehaghani, S.M.H. and Hajrahimi, N. 2013. Which factors affect software projects maintenance cost more? Acta Informatica Medica, 21(1): 63.

7. Dalton, M., Kannan, H. and Kozyrakis, C. 2007. Raksha: a flexible information flow architecture for software security. ACM SIGARCH Computer Architecture News, 35(2): 482–493.

8. Carr, N.G. 2003. IT doesn't matter. Educause Review, 38: 24–38.

9. Kelty, C. and Erickson S. 2015. The durability of software. Meson Press, Germany, 1(5): 1–13.

10. Kumar, R., Khan, S.A., and Khan, R.A. 2015. Revisiting software security: durability perspective. International Journal of Hybrid Information Technology (SERSC), 8(2): 311–322.

11. Khan, R.A., Khan, S.A., Agrawal, A., and Kumar, R. 2018. Security durability assessment framework. Indian Patent, Application Number: 201711032601.

12. Khan, R.A., Khan, S.A., and Kumar, R. 2015. Managing software security risk; design perspective. Indian Patent, Application Number: 1781/DEL/2015.

Useful Links

https://www.squareboat.com/blog/different-types-of-software-with-examples
https://www.geeksforgeeks.org/types-of-software/
https://www.leadwithprimitive.com/blog/the-4-main-types-of-software
https://en.wikipedia.org/wiki/Software_durability
https://onix-systems.com/blog/10-common-software-myths-dispelled

CHAPTER **3**

Integrating Dependability with Software Durability

3.1 Objectives

The terms "dependability" and "durability" are always used to describe the software's ability to offer assistance that can be relied upon for any duration. To understand the two terms in their independent entities, it would be best to state that the dependability of the software is the quality of being trustworthy and the capacity to be relied upon. Whereas durability signifies the software's ability to withstand stress or force for a specified amount of time. Interestingly, though, failures, dangers, errors, quality, and faults are all important from a coordinated perspective of dependability and durability. Moreover, a unified structure that would consist of the elements of both reliability and durability would be an ideal mechanism to strengthen the life span of the software. In addition, the following goals were kept in mind when making a road map for this chapter, which goes against this premise:

- Define the relationship between dependability and durability, including the life cycle and fault parameters for durability, and talk about the techniques, models, and management tools that can be used to combine the ideas of dependability and durability. To summarise the basic concept of dependability.
- Discuss Dependability Analysis into Durability concepts.
- Giving a basic framework for integrating dependability and durability with its characteristics.

3.2 Fundamental Principles

With the technological development of the computing and communication fields, it is becoming increasingly important to ensure that software's durability and dependability are able to withstand the challenges posed by increasingly organised applications of the present day [1]. The security and survival of complex information systems embedded in the infrastructure that supports advanced society have become a top priority in both the national and international circuits. People and businesses are building or buying more and more complicated computer systems that they have to rely heavily on for service or maintenance [2].

This Chapter's goal is to propose the methodology for designing the desired level of software dependability and durability. Another important factor is safety. Although reliability and safety are comparable, there is one key difference: safety can tolerate a certain amount of fault tolerance. For the purposes of this discussion, Fig. 1 shows that software dependability encompasses characteristics such as Attributes, Mean, Impairment. Software dependability is the degree to which a computer system can be trusted to the point where its services can be relied on. Furthermore, the basic concepts of dependability will be discussed in the ensuing sections.

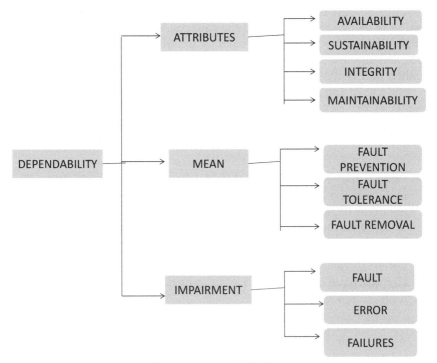

Figure 1: Dependability Tree.

3.2.1 The Evolution of Dependability Concept

The invention of the Babbage Engine in 1830 popularised the idea of dependable computing [3]. Since the early electronic computers had unreliable parts, practical strategies such as error control codes, comparison, triplication, and voting were developed to improve their dependability. Constructing trustworthy logic structures from less trustworthy components, whose defects are made worse by the presence of additional redundant components, was a concept that E.F. Moore and C.E. Shannon, as well as their grandchildren, developed at the same time [4]. The notions of masking redundancy were first referred to by W.H. Pierce in 1965 under the heading "failure tolerance." [5]. The creation of the B. Randell on reliable computing and fault tolerance in 1975 and the J. Bussolini on fault-tolerant computing in 1971 both contributed to the advancement of the development of a coherent vocabulary and a set of concepts [6–7]. In this context, Laprie did more work that went into the book Dependability: Basic Concepts and Terminology, which came out in 1985 [8].

The dependability of the system is, for many computer-based systems, the most crucial system characteristic. A system's dependability reflects the user's level of confidence in it. It demonstrates how confident the user is and that the system will perform as expected, and won't "fail" in case of typical use [9]. Reliability, availability, and security are all linked system characteristics under the heading of dependability. All of these depend on one another. Numerous people may be impacted by system failures that have extensive repercussions. Users may reject systems that lack dependability, are dangerous, or are not secure. Information loss as well as monetary setbacks caused due to unreliable systems may result in costly recovery costs [10]. Due to the two factors, the cost of dependability tends to rise exponentially when dependability levels are increased. The more expensive the hardware and development methods that are needed to reach higher levels of dependability, the more testing and validation procedures would be needed to show the regulators and the clients that the critical levels of dependability have been met.

3.2.2 Dependability Features

A system's attributes are its characteristics. These can be evaluated to establish the overall reliability of the system. The ability of a computing system to provide reliable services is its dependability. One of the most important and delicate skills one can have is consistency [11]. When someone is trustworthy, they hold themselves accountable and, if they are a leader, they also hold their subordinates accountable. People who are part of such a set up are also trustworthy [12]. Durability improves a wide range of software performance categories; having reliable software benefits the business and the organisation, as well as the developer and user, as it aids in his or her professional development and advancement. Trustworthy software not only consistently works on time but also produces predictable work. Dependable and durable software completes duties on schedule. Especially for durable software systems, dependability is extraordinarily valuable. Developers search for dependability in their software. The concept of dependability comprises the following characteristics [1]:

- Availability: The readiness to provide the appropriate service.
- Reliability: Consistently providing the appropriate assistance.
- Safety: Safety is defined as the absence of catastrophic effects on the customer and the environment.
- Confidentiality: The ability to undergo correction and modification.

The degree to which a system exhibits dependability and durability traits should be viewed in a relative, probabilistic meaning rather than an absolute, deterministic sense; systems are never completely available, dependable, and durable due to the inescapable presence or emergence of errors. Security has been added to the list of dependability and durability attributes [13]. This is consistent with the traditional definition of security, which considers it to be a composite concept. The idea of secondary qualities is very important to security because it helps people to tell the difference between different kinds of information. For example:

- Accountability: The identification of the individual who executed the operation's availability and integrity.
- Authenticity: It is important to consider both the veracity of the message's content and the source of other information, such as the time of transmission.
- Variations: Differences in how the various qualities of durability are emphasised directly affect how the tactics (shortcoming aversion, resistance, evacuation, and anticipating) should be balanced to make the following framework reliable.

Other software durability and dependability characteristics are:

- Maintainability: New requirements indicate how much the framework can be altered.
- Survivability: This represents the system's ability to provide services even if it is under assault.
- Error tolerance: Indicate how easily and tolerably user input errors can be prevented.

How to Achieve Durability-Dependability

- Avoid presenting unintentional errors while encouraging a framework.
- Configure procedures that are effective at identifying the errors in the framework.
- Framework that allows for problem leniency so that activity can continue even in the event of a flaw.
- Create a security measure those guards against external attacks.
- Correctly set up the framework for the environment it will operate in.
- This also includes systems for spotting and thwarting online attacks.

3.2.3 Dependability and Durability Characteristics

This section is discussed in Chapter 2.

3.2.4 Systems, Software, Dependability, and Durability

Software engineers defined words like software dependability and software durability in the 1970s by starting with the several specific types of problems (stuck at nothing, stuck at one, etc.) that could occur inside software [14]. We felt the need for a more comprehensive set of concepts and definitions, however, given not only the lack of any useful classification of configuration defects but also the recognition that, most of the time, identifying a specific component of a confusing software development plan as the problem may be very emotionally taxing [15]. Moreover, our perception was that these definitions needed to be sufficiently recursive to let us fully evaluate problems that can happen within or between framework pieces at any level of software.

Figure 2 elaborates on the relationship between durable and dependable software systems. A clear, repeatable software process is essential for ensuring a low number of software flaws. A well-defined repeatable process is one that can be carried out by various people and does not solely depend on one person's abilities. Regulators utilise information about the procedure to determine whether best practises for software engineering have been followed. It is obvious that the process activities should devote a lot of time to verification and validation (V and V) in order to find faults. Figure 2 organises durable software with dependability with very basic functions.

3.3 Dependability Analysis into Durability Concept

In the early stages of the development of durable frameworks, the quick turn of events and assessment of the models for trustworthiness are

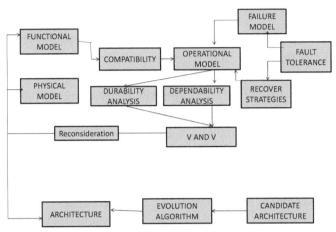

Figure 2: Dependable and Durable Software System.

crucial [16]. The main goals of these models are to find problems with dependability, accessibility, usability, and security.

3.3.1 *Anticipating Faults*

The fundamental principle of dependability states that the one thing the developer must do to meet their dependability requirements is to identify all faults a system is subject to. This goal is easily stated but difficult to achieve, and the goal leads to the notion of anticipated faults [3–5]. An anticipated fault is one that we have identified as being in the set to which a system is subject. It would be done if the techniques for determining the faults to which a system is subjected were perfected, but these techniques are not perfect. The result is that some faults will not be anticipated because they cannot be predicted in advance. In absence of prior information about such faults, a possible pre-emptive mechanism to troubleshoot them can also not be worked upon. Moreover, the effects of such faults on the durability of the system of interest are also unknown. Unanticipated faults are the causes of most, but not all, durability system failures. The two other reasons for durability system's failure are:

- Some system failures result from anticipated faults that were not dealt with in any way. Their effects and probability of occurrence were examined using fault forecasting, and the system designers decided that no treatment was warranted.

- Some system failures result from failures of fault tolerance mechanisms designed to cope with the effects of the anticipated faults.

3.3.2 Generalizing the Notion of Hazard

The notion of hazard arises primarily in the field of safety. Informally, a hazard is a system state that could lead to catastrophic consequences; a system that could lead to a violation of safe operation [6]. A system being in a hazardous state does not necessarily mean an accident will result. Figure 3 shows the hazard identification procedure.

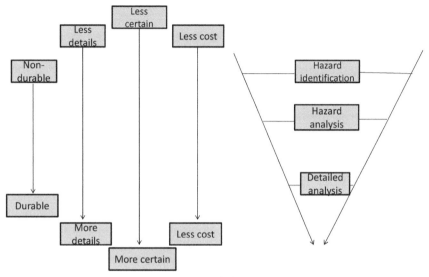

Figure 3: Hazard Identification.

The system should stay in a hazardous state for an arbitrary length of time, and provided there is no change in the environment that leads to loss, there will be no accident. In developing systems for which safety is an important dependability requirement, hazards are the state we have to avoid [7, 12]. By avoiding all the hazards that have been identified, we can be sure that there will be no system operations. In order to arrange for a specific system to avoid hazards, we need to know what hazards are arising. Only then can we seek ways of eliminating them as possible states. Hazard identification is the process of identifying and assessing hazards. A fault is the adjudged cause of an error, and this provides the link between faults and hazards. In order to avoid a hazard, we need to identify the faults that might cause the hazards and make sure that each fault has been suitably treated.

3.3.3 Fault Tree Analysis

Another method for investigating dependability and durability is Fault tree analysis (FTA). The concept was developed in 1962 by Chime

Telephone Laboratories for the US Air Force to use with the Minuteman architecture [9]. The Boeing Company subsequently accepted it and used it widely. One of the illustrative "scientific rationale procedures" that can be found in activities research and framework dependability is the shortcoming tree analysis. Various techniques use block charts of unchanging quality (RBDs). By utilizing the suggested method, Fault Tree Analysis (FTA) can address unusual connections between basic events locally [10–13]. Common avoidance, denial, insinuation, and shifting dependency are all fully supported scenarios. Subordinate occurrences have separate occurrence markers that can be completed as far as the shortcoming tree will allow.

To figure out how much each event or group of events affected that entrance, a few possible probabilities are given in Fig. 4 based on how the events that happened after that entrance were remembered. For example, the occurrence of two completely unrelated events is regarded as a legitimate showing error, and the dependent and dreary events are taken into consideration during the likelihood estimation. Since it combines disproved events, the technique works well for non-sound fault tree analysis (FTA). The legitimacy of the individual components and the engineering logic behind the frameworks leaves the possibility of practical disappointment in the air. The need for a top-to-bottom assessment procedure to identify all probable combinations of disappointment that could result in the loss of the framework's honesty increases with how complex the framework is. Such a method is the FTA.

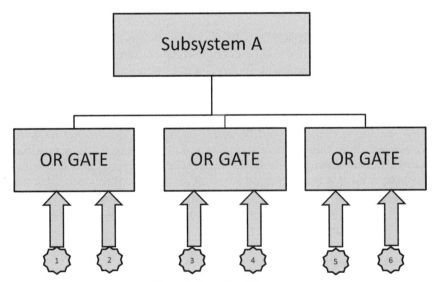

Figure 4: Fault Tree Diagram.

FTA is a hierarchical, logical failure analysis that investigates a framework's troublesome condition by combining a series of lower-level occurrences using Boolean logic. This analysis method is frequently used in security, durability, and dependability design to outline (or obtain a sense of) the event pacing of a health incident or a specific framework level (useful) failure and to identify the most efficient means of risk reduction. FTA is used in high-risk industries such as social assistance, disappointment risk factor, recognisable proof, atomic power, aircraft, substance and cycle, medicine, petrochemical, and other high-risk industries. FTA is also used to fix problems in programming, and it is closely related to the process of finding bugs and figuring out why they happen. Further, a tree of durability and dependability-based fault classes is shown in Fig. 5.

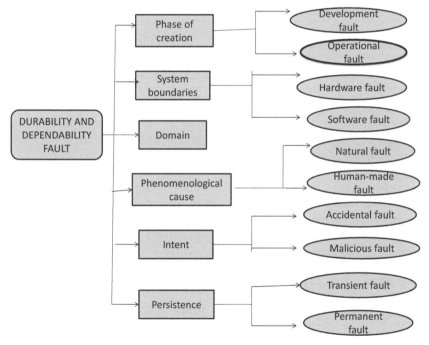

Figure 5: Fault Classes Structure.

3.3.4 *Failure Modes, Effects, and Criticality Analysis*

The methodologies for failure modes, effects, and criticality analysis are used to identify potential failure modes for a product or process (durable software development process), assess the risk associated with those failure modes, rank the issues in terms of importance, and identify and implement corrective actions to address the most serious concerns.

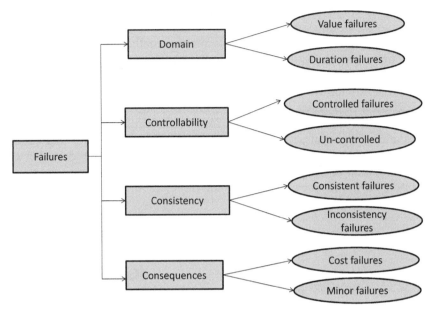

Figure 6: Failure Modes.

Figure 6 shows the different kinds of failure modes that can occur during the durability and dependability analysis of software. The basic steps for doing a Failure Modes, Effects, and Criticality Analysis are as follows:

Assemble the team; establish the rational motive rules; collect and review pertinent subject matter; identify the item or process to be analysed; identify the function, failure, effect, cause, and control; evaluate the risk; prioritise and assign corrective actions; then carry out corrective actions and re-evaluate the risk. The last step is to administer, review, and update the analysis as befitting.

3.3.5 Hazard and Operability Analysis

A Hazard and Operability Study, often known as HAZOP, is a comprehensive methodology to find potential dangers in a work process [14]. This method divides the procedure into parts and examines each step's potential pitfalls by considering any variations in the work parameters. A Hazard and Operability (HAZOP) analysis is a planned or existing process or operation that is structured and methodically examined to find and assess issues that might provide dangers to people or equipment, or obstruct effective operation, which further endangers the durability of software. Although the HAZOP technique was originally created to study chemical process systems, it has since been expanded to analyse other kinds of systems, in addition to software systems and complicated operations for analysing durability [15]. A multi-disciplinary team conducts a HAZOP as a qualitative technique based on guide-words over the course of several meetings. Find out all the ways a software system doesn't behave as planned, what causes them, and what dangers or problems they cause:

- Choose whether measures are necessary to control the software security and dependability risks and/or operability issues and if so, specify how the issues can be resolved.

- Determine what information or activities are necessary for situations where a decision cannot be made right away.

- Ensure that the decisions made are carried out.

- Inform the operator of potential dangers and operational issues.

The HAZOP research should ideally be conducted as early as possible in the software design phase to facilitate the developers' tasks. On the other hand, we require a rather comprehensive software design in order to execute a HAZOP. When the detailed design is finished, the HAZOP is typically performed as the last check as a compromise. An existing facility may also undergo a HAZOP analysis to determine the changes that need to be made in order to lower risk and solve operability issues. HAZOP studies may also be applied more broadly, such as at the following stages:

- At the initial concept stage, when software design drawings are available.

- During the construction and installation of software ensure that recommendations are implemented.

- During commissioning.

- During operations ensure that security and emergency procedures are reviewed regularly and updated as needed.

3.4 The Beginnings of Durability and Dependability Integration

In order to appropriately address the challenges posed by increasingly organised applications and the growing demand for ubiquitous figuring, reliability has developed from trustworthiness and accessibility difficulties, as well as technological advancements in the registering and correspondence areas. Durability [13], as defined ("capacity of a framework to keep on satisfying its main goal notwithstanding assaults, disappointments, or mishaps"), has evolved from pure security concerns; it has acquired a lot of unmistakable quality with the rise in frequency and seriousness of attacks by cunning foes on strategic organised data frameworks [15]. Dependability refers to the ability to withstand in the face of dynamic inadequacies, taking into account all of the mentioned deficiency orders. However, durability and dependability share a lot with everyone. However, in terms of the natives that may be used to carry things out, dependability and durability share a great deal.

3.4.1 Faults and Durable Software Cycle

Different heuristics are presented, and model-based approaches are used for durability examination and detection of the shortcomings [15]. Issue expulsion is a strategy to reduce the number or severity of issues; shortcoming reasoning is a strategy to prevent flaws from occurring or being presented; adaptation to non-critical failure is a strategy to provide legitimate assistance when deficiencies do occur; and shortcoming determining is a strategy to estimate the current number of issues, how frequently they will occur going forward, and what their potential effects will be [16]. Different types of faults with respect to durable software cycles [14] are explained as follows:

3.4.4.1 Fault Prevention

To avoid errors, quality control techniques are applied throughout the planning, assembling, and programming of the software durability development. This process is called "fault prevention". This includes stringent development plan requirements as well as ordered software, data stowing away, modularization, and other programming features. While preparation, strict maintenance procedures, and "secure" bundles prevent connection flaws, protecting, radiation solidifying, and other approaches prevent functional actual faults. Vindictive flaws are controlled by firewalls and other crucial defences.

3.4.4.2 Fault Tolerance

To protect the provision of appropriate assistance in the presence of dynamic inadequacies, adaptation to non-critical failure is expected. It is mostly carried out through error location and ensuing framework recovery. Error identification locates an error message or indicator inside the structure. A mistake that is present but unidentified is called an inactive error. There are two different methods for finding errors: simultaneous mistake location, which takes place while assistance is being provided; and crude mistake identification, which takes place when assistance is not being provided and scans the system for errors that are already present but not being used.

3.4.4.3 Fault Removal

Expulsion of flaws occurs both during the improvement phase and while a process is operational. Three steps make up issue elimination during the development phase of a software life cycle: confirmation, finding, and cure. The process used to determine whether the software durability adheres to specified properties, known as the check criteria, is called confirmation. If not, the next two steps are to determine which error (s) prevented the check requirements from being met and then to make the necessary changes. In most cases, approval is implied by checking the details. Undiscovered design faults may appear at any step of the process, including the detailed stage itself and later stages when evidence is discovered that the software won't function as intended or that the intended action cannot be carried out in a practical way.

3.4.4.4 Fault Forecasting

It is started by acting out an evaluation of the software's behaviour as a deficiency event or enactment. There are two perspectives on assessment: (1) a subjective, or ordinal, assessment that tries to find, describe, and rank the types of failures or event combinations (like broken parts or unavoidable events) that could cause software failures. (2) a quantitative, or probabilistic, assessment that tries to find out how likely it is that different qualities of trustworthiness are met. These credits are then seen as a percentage of the software's durability and dependability.

3.4.4.5 Durable Software Cycle

Whether produced by vendors or in-house development teams, developers need specialisation in planning, building, and supporting large-scale enterprise application software. It's not difficult to create and use one-off and simple interface programmes. Figure 7 shows the general durable software cycle activities. Also, making huge operating systems with millions of lines of code (LOC), like Microsoft XP or big, complicated systems, has its own challenges that this book doesn't cover.

3.4.2 Formal Techniques

"Formal Methods" alludes to numerically exact techniques and tools for planning, confirming, and particularising software [14]. The phrase "numerically thorough" refers to conclusions used in traditional techniques that are thorough derivations of numerical reasoning and formal confirmations that are conclusions in that rationale that are well-framed statements (i.e., each step is observed from a guideline of deduction and thus can be really looked at by a mechanical cycle). The benefits of formal

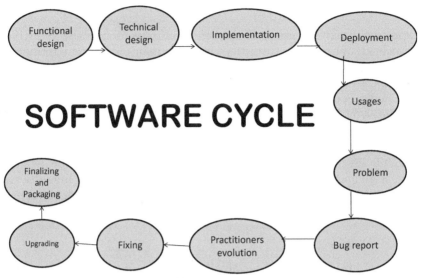

Figure 7: Durable Software Cycle Activities.

approaches are that they enable the developers to examine the entire state space of a computerised plan (equipment or software) and determine whether it is accurate or acceptable for all relevant data. However, this is rarely completed today due to the extreme complexity of true frameworks (save for essential parts of security basics frameworks) [14]. Real-world software uses a number of ways to deal with the astronomically large number of possible states:

- Use formal methods for designing requirements and high-level plans that leave out most of the details.
- Use formal procedures only on the most critical components.
- Analyze software and hardware models with a small number of variables.
- Divide and conquer by analysing system models in a hierarchical fashion.
- Automated verification as far as possible and feasible.

Although mathematical logic is a common thread running through the formal methods discipline, there is no single optimal "formal method". Different modelling methodologies and proof approaches are required for each application domain. Even within the same application area, different tools and methods may work better at different stages of the life cycle.

3.4.3 Durability-Dependability Unified Model

UML-SMs are commonly used to pragmatically represent a system's "correct" behaviour or behaviour in the absence of errors [15]. However, dependability and durability modelling necessitate the specification of system behaviour under various fault assumptions as well as the characterization of system failures. In the case of repairable systems, the repair and reconfiguration actions that eliminate the system's basic or derived failures must also be simulated [16]. In order to construct the system fault assumptions, a software engineer must consider the following: (1) total fault characterization, for example, fault occurrence rate; and (2) total fault characterization, for example, fault occurrence rate. Furthermore, an integrated framework of dependable and durable software is shown in Fig. 8.

The process of determining failure modes and, in particular, system failure states is known as failure characterization. UML does not have the features to model any of the aforementioned reliability concerns completely and rigorously. The DDAM (Durability-Dependability Assessment and Modelling) profile, on the other hand, adds annotations to a UML design that targets the dependability specification. DDAM enables compatibility with UML diagrams by being built as a specialisation of Modelling and Analysis of Real-Time Embedded Systems (MARTE). The MARTE section devoted to quantitative analysis, often known as a general quantitative analysis model (GQAM), is of particular importance to DDAM. Furthermore, DDAM and GQAM, in fact, provide a framework for specifying and analysing dependability with durability.

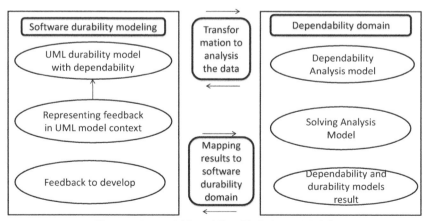

Figure 8: Dependable and Durable Software Model.

3.4.4 Verification by Model Checking

A popular technique for validating intricate interactions, concurrent, and distributed systems is model checking [16]. Model checking uses formal concepts like operations, states, events, and actions to build a behavioural model of the system. The state space explosion problem, which has a large memory consumption and time complexity, is one of the flaws that the model checkers have. A well-known verification method for automatically assessing a distributed system's functional features is model checking. The basic objective of model checking is to use counter examples to identify property violations for durability and restrictions in the system's behaviour.

3.4.5 Correctness by Construction

A revolutionary, practical, and affordable approach for creating software with verifiable integrity for applications that are crucial for security, durability, and safety is known as Correctness by Construction [15]. Correctness by Construction combines the greatest elements of formal techniques and rapid development, two seemingly unrelated concepts. As an illustration, we use progressive development from the latter and exact notations from the former. Correctness by Construction is founded on three straightforward tenets:

- Make it very difficult to make mistakes.
- Despite point 1, make sure that errors are removed as soon as feasible after their introduction.
- Produce fitness for purpose proof as a by-product of development that is inevitable (because showing that the developed system is durable, secure, or safe is often harder than making it so).

These guidelines might seem like rather clear "advice of perfection", but with the correct notations, tools, methods, and mentality, they can be easily attained for achieving dependability in durability construction.

3.4.6 Managing Fault Avoidance and Elimination

Strategies for fault prevention and avoidance locate all possible points where a fault might happen and fill in the gaps [14]. These prevention techniques deal with formal approaches, reusability, software durability design techniques, and system requirements and specifications. They are used to avoid or stop fault occurrences throughout the software development phase. Through the meticulous formulation of the system requirements, programming techniques, and software reusability, they contribute to the system's dependability. However, it is challenging to measure how fault avoidance techniques affect system dependability. So, even though people try to stop problems from happening, they still do. This means that fault removal is necessary.

During verification and validation, reliability-improving procedures called the "fault elimination strategies", are used. They become better by identifying and fixing any flaws that already exist. They are hired to help with the software's validation after the software's development phase. Testing is a common step in fault elimination strategies. Because of this, accurate testing is maximised by reducing component size and interdependence. The challenges that testing programmes face are frequently connected to the high cost of testing and extensive testing. As a result, fault tolerance is required because fault elimination is imperfect.

3.4.7 Misconceptions

A common misconception is that software defects are only introduced during the preparation of the source programme and can only be found by testing, as should be evident from earlier parts of this concept [12]. In many systems, the majority of the software defects are actually introduced in the specification but are usually not found until testing. In some of the software areas that develop systems with high dependability requirements, roughly twothirds of the defects either during testing or in the field were introduced in the specification. The statistics make fault avoidance and elimination a specification of crucial importance.

- Software can be very fragile. A large software system can fail because of a mistake in a single line of the source code.
- The software lifecycle helps identify both the points at which faults can arise and the points at which we might be able to deal with the faults.
- Formal methods provide a variety of analytic results about software artefacts.
- Various techniques can be utilised to achieve software fault avoidance.
- Various techniques can be utilised to effect software fault elimination.
- A combination of techniques should be used to avoid and eliminate as many types of software faults as possible.

3.4.8 Prescriptive Standards

Implementing dependability with durability and security in software is a design decision [4, 7, 11]. However, even in the present context, the delivery of a technical product with an ideal durability mechanism continues to be a challenge for the developers. In this league, maintaining durability attributes such as dependability from the design or development phase of software can produce effective security measures, thereby maintaining data security effectively and minimising the risk of data breaches. To address this research quest, the present study provides an overview of the need for dependability in durability. The key prescriptive standards of this research are:

- The integration of durability with dependability for producing secure software is a domain for intensive research.
- To achieve durability with its important characteristic of dependability, developers need to focus on the prescribed framework.
- The development of software durability lies in the supremacy of its three characteristics. Hence, the following durability-dependability model is of immense importance.

3.5 Conclusion

Software quality includes a big aspect called "programming solidity" and maintainability. The three components of the inquiry into programming consistency are displaying, estimating, and improving. Ensuring that durability has developed to the point where applying fitting models to a problem, might produce useful results. There are several models available, but none of them can capture all of the product's characteristics. Suggestions and reflections should be made to work on the problem. There isn't a general framework that works in all situations. Measuring programming quality and consistency is ludicrous. In terms of estimation, programming, like other specialised fields. How well does the product perform quantitatively? There is no agreeable arrangement, even if the inquiry is direct. Software's unbreakable strength can't be tested directly, so it is roughed out and looked at with other objects using several relevant boundaries.

The connection between improvement and programming, as well as any flaws or disappointments that are discovered, are important considerations. It is challenging to increase software durability. The problem is caused by a lack of understanding of programming unwavering quality and, more broadly, durability characteristics. Up until now, there hasn't been a good solution to the problem of the complexity of the product. It is futile to test every component of a logically modern programming module. It is challenging to guarantee the durability of the end product and certify that it will work for a specific period. We need to make sure that the dependability of the software is ensured for the durability of software. Although it may not be checked enough, durability consistency could become a trustworthiness bottleneck for the software. Durability and dependability are challenging to ensure. Despite of the complexity of the problem, promising progress is still being made in the direction of more durable software. More standardised components and advanced techniques are being used to increase the durability of software.

Points to Remember

- Dependability is the key component for building a more durable and reliable software as it allows a developer to get access to software durability via its service life prediction.
- Dependability is the desire to have someone do something for you when you are unable to do it yourself, whereas durability is the faith you have in someone to accomplish something for a particular period.
- Best Example: We trust our best friends to stand with us in our hour of need; however, we are not always dependent on them for bailing us out of our crisis. On the contrary, a 2-year-old child is solely dependent on the parents for feeding or bathing her/him because the toddlers can't do anything on their own.
- Maintaining software's durability and dependability in the face of errors and failures is crucial, more so in the present era of the ubiquitous use of technology. Software flaws, in contrast to flaws in other components, can have disastrous results if they are not anticipated and addressed properly. This issue has been made worse by the increase in software-based autonomous systems.

Review Questions

Objective Type Questions

1. The seven-position paper was presented in…………..
   a. 1982
   b. 1990
   c. 1981
   d. None of the above
2. ………… is the ability to undergo repair and modification.
   a. Availability
   b. Reliability
   c. Maintainability
   d. None of the above

3. The .... attribute reflects the extent to which the system can deliver services under a hostile attack.
    a. Availability
    b. Survivability
    c. Maintainability
    d. None of the above
4. Fault tree analysis (FTA) is a top-down, deductive failure analysis in which an undesired state of a system is analyzed by using the Boolean logic to combine a series of lower-level events?
    a. True
    b. False
5. Apply formal methods to only the most critical components.
    a. True
    b. False

Short Answer Type Questions

1. What is Fault tolerance?
2. Define Fault removal.
3. What do you mean by formal method?
4. What do you mean by maintainability from a dependability perspective?
5. What is anticipating faults?

Descriptive Questions

1. Describe the Dependable system in detail.
2. What are various Dependability Analysis methods?
3. What is the Fault Tree Analysis? Discuss the dependability model in detail.

References

1. Avizienis, A., Laprie, J.C., Randell, B. and Landwehr, C. 2004. Basic concepts and taxonomy of dependable and secure computing. IEEE Transactions on Dependable and Secure Computing, 1(1): 11–33.
2. Moeinedini, M., Raissi, S. and Khalili-Damghani, K. 2018. A fuzzy fault tree analysis-based risk assessment approach for enterprise resource planning projects: A case study in an Iranian foodservice distributor. International Journal of Quality & Reliability Management.
3. The Engines. 01/01/2022. https://www.computerhistory.org/babbage/engines/.

4. Moore, E.F. and Shannon, C.E. 1956. Reliable circuits using less reliable relays. J. Franklin Institute, 262: 191–208, 281–297. https://cctbio.ece.umn.edu/wiki/images/3/30/Moore_Shannon_Reliable_Circuits_Using_Less_Reliable_Relays.pdf.
5. Pierce, W.H. 1965. Failure-Tolerant Computer Design. Academic Press, London.
6. Randell, B. 1975. System structure for software fault tolerance. IEEE Trans. on Software Engineering, SE 1: 1220–1232.
7. Bussolini, J. 1971. September. High Reliability Design Techniques applied to the Lunar Module, London. Lecture Series Avionics Systems, vol. 47.
8. Laprie, J.C. 1985. Dependable computing and fault tolerance: Concepts and terminology. *In*: Proc. 15th IEEE Int. Symp. on Fault-Tolerant Computing.
9. United States Tri-Service aircraft designation system. 1962. https://en.wikipedia.org/wiki/1962_United_States_Tri-Service_aircraft_designation_system.
10. Avizienis, A., Laprie, J.C. and Randell, B. 2001. Fundamental concepts of dependability. Department of Computing Science Technical Report Series.
11. Bernardi, S., Merseguer, J. and Petriu, D.C. 2012. Dependability modeling and assessment in UML-based software development. The Scientific World Journal.
12. Fault Tree Analysis. 05/08/2019. Available at: https://www.benchmarksixsigma.com/forum/topic/34876-fault-tree-analysis-fta.
13. Kumar, R., Khan, S.A. and Khan, R.A. 2016. Durability challenges in software engineering. Crosstalk-The Journal of Defense Software Engineering: 29–31.
14. Kumar, R., Zarour, M., Alenezi, M., Agrawal, A. and Khan, R.A. 2019. Measuring security durability of software through fuzzy-based decision-making process. International Journal of Computational Intelligence Systems, 12(2): 627.
15. Sahu, K., Alzahrani, F.A., Srivastava, R.K. and Kumar, R. 2020. Hesitant fuzzy sets based symmetrical model of decision-making for estimating the durability of Web application. Symmetry, 12(11): 1770.
16. Kumar, R., Khan, S.A. and Khan, R.A. 2015. Durable security in software development: Needs and importance. CSI Communication, 39(7): 34–36.

Useful Links

https://www.sei.cmu.edu/about/divisions/cert/index.cfm
https://link.springer.com/book/10.1007/978-3-030-40928-9
https://www.coursehero.com/file/72812330/FTA-techdocx/

CHAPTER 4

Integrating Trustworthiness with Software Durability

4.1 Objectives

In the context of software usability and durability, trustworthiness is always a key factor. However, integrating trustworthiness with many other factors and managing the same in a systematic manner is not an easy task. This chapter aims to provide an effective description of software trustworthiness so as to reduce the complexity in this context. The Chapter provides an informative introduction to the software trustworthiness factor in managing software durability perspective for designing software with long-service life. The following objectives have inspired the roadmap for this chapter:

- To define the fundamental principles of trustworthiness with respect to durability.
- To propose the concept of trustworthy design of software durability.
- To propose the extended trustworthy computing initiative.
- To discuss the tools and techniques of durable design for making durable software.
- To suggest the financial benefits of integration of durability, quality, and cost with a unified tactic.

4.2 Fundamental Principles

The trustworthiness of any software system depends on designing software that comprises the different facets needed to ensure the criticality and the efficacious use of the software [1]. All business sectors require trustworthy software, which has a direct impact on the durability of software. Trustworthiness is the key component in software's service life and it is totally and directly connected with the feedback of the end users. Untrustworthy software can be a severe threat to the software user and even be life-threatening in some conditions, such as the like medical operational software [2]. Hence, maintaining trustworthiness for managing durability in software assumes utmost importance in software engineering.

4.2.1 The Evolution of Trustworthiness Concepts

The concept of trustworthiness evolves with the concept of software development [3]. The basic fundamental development concept of software comes under the process of software development life cycle. Trustworthiness relies on the process of software evolution [2]. Evolution is the process that associates situational updates and changes in any type of mechanism and framework with respect to time. Some researchers believe that evolution is a process that allows continuous changes in the software. In order to maintain trustworthiness in software, there is a software trustworthiness growth mechanism (STGM) that provides a conceptual mechanism (as shown in Fig. 1) to maintain trustworthiness for a specific life-span.

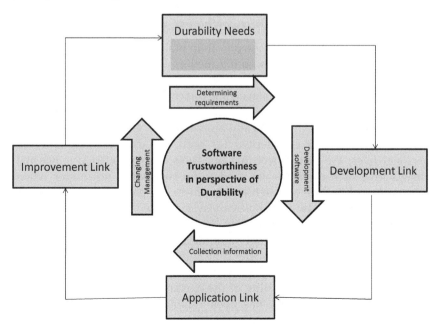

Figure 1: Software Trustworthiness Growth Mechanism Model.

This model includes a conceptual process framework that allows the user to maintain trustworthiness in software development [4–7]. This model consists of a conceptual link, an application link, a development link, and an improvement link. As a working process, there are four phases to this model.

It executes the conceptual phase as the first initial step. During this phase, the developer associates each trustworthiness factor or attribute with the software specification. The development link is the next step of the model, in which the developers employ software reengineering and other design approaches to create effective, durable software based on the needs indicated in the preceding phase. Following this phase, the application link begins to function. The major goal of this phase is to identify and assess various changes that are required in the development of trustworthiness, as well as to identify possible areas for software trustworthiness improvement. However, after applying all three phases of this model, researchers use the fourth and final cyclic process of STGM, which is the improvement link phase, in which we identify and update any untrustworthy software factors. This is the STGM model's entire working process, which is a cyclic process.

4.2.2 Trustworthiness and Durability Characteristics

The section is discussed in Chapter 2.

4.2.3 Systems, Software, Trustworthiness, and Durability

Software is the unseen framework that makes it possible for people to interact, conduct business, and function. Software is at the core of an astounding and perplexing proliferation of capabilities, including everything from operating a washing machine to pumping the water, flying aeroplanes, diagnosing cancer, or just enabling the users to connect wirelessly from practically anywhere [8]. Clearly, having highly trustworthy software is essential for both our digital workplace and personal lives. We just expect that our tools and application suites will always give us the results we need to be successful, no matter where we use them [9]. Both research and business are paying more and more attention to how trustworthy software systems are.

Software application domains are continuously expanding, for example, under the aegis of ubiquitous, pervasive, and ambient intelligence, to name just a few trending subjects [10]. But people will only agree to use these software systems if they are sure that these systems are durable. The long-term viability of the existing practise of not certifying software in a manner that has been established for more traditional technical systems, which are designed in other engineering disciplines and, to a considerable degree, relieve vendors from obligations. Instead, software companies will have a huge advantage in the market if they can prove that their products are high-quality and have long durability.

Every day, a trustworthy system's ability to perform as intended is put to the test, whether due to operational issues (anticipated or unexpected), environmental effects, system risks, or hostile unauthorised parties [13]. It's crucial to pay organised attention to a system's key characteristics and to compile enough evidence to show that the necessary traits are being obtained in order to promote confidence and trustworthiness. Durable software is necessary to build strong and efficient solutions for the industrial sector. Making thoughtful judgments regarding the architecture, design, implementation, testing, and operation is essential for a system to be durable, resilient, safe, private, and secure.

4.3 Designing for Trustworthy Software: Durability Perspective

Many initiatives have been undertaken in recent years to address the problem of insecure and untrustworthy software [14]. Secure, safe, durable, and trusted are some of the phrases that have been used to describe how "solid" a piece of software should be. Recently, the "socio-technical systems" terminology was introduced in the literature on (durable) software development. This idea distinguishes between the real confidence that the users of software place in the software's working or delivery, on one hand, and the software's trustworthiness, i.e., attributes that justify the faith that users place "into" the software, on the other. Unlike trustworthiness, which should largely be the subject of "maintenance" of the relationship between the user and the software in use ("in operations"), trustworthiness is mostly earned during the software development process and can be "lost" later.

4.3.1 Trustworthy Software

Except for strictly theoretical techniques or on a functional level, the software production process has not been fully addressed both in theory and practise until lately, addressing concerns like trust, trustworthiness, or similar [15]. As a result, there has never been a study of existing software development practises and processes with a focus on trustworthiness. Hence, it is important to define the terms "trust" and "trustworthiness" so that it can be examined how trustworthiness is addressed across various software development disciplines. In general, trust refers to a trustor's anticipation that the software will produce the intended outcome, whereas trustworthiness refers to the chance that the same software would meet all requirements of the trustor. In software development, the balance between trust and trustworthiness is critical since any imbalance (such as over-cautiousness or misguided trust) can have significant consequences, such as making it more difficult for people to use the software.

(a) Notation "Trust"

Trust can be defined in software as a feature of every individual trustor, expressed in probabilities and reflecting how certain they are that using the software to achieve a specific goal would result in a good outcome [16]. As a result, trust denotes a situation in which the outcome is still undetermined based on the subjective views and requirements of each trustor. If a stakeholder's trust criteria were effectively met, that is, if their perceptions exceeded or surpassed the standards, the stakeholder would elect to invest trust in the software [17]. By looking at what has transpired in the past, a person who has used software for multiple transactions can (or will) upgrade their level of trust in that software.

Because trust decisions are influenced by subjective considerations, two different trustors may have different levels of confidence in the same software to produce the same outcome in the future, even though they have both observed the same system outcomes in the past. Trustor attributes, which include social elements such as age, gender, cultural background, level of knowledge with Internet-based programmes, and legal perspectives, might impact subjective assessments [15].

(b) Notation "Trustworthiness"

Software's trustworthiness is considered to be an objective property based on the presence (or absence) of relevant qualities and countermeasures that lower the chance of undesirable consequences [14]. Based on trustworthiness criteria, a stakeholder must decide to what extent a software is trustworthy. These standards are logical expressions of quality characteristics in terms of software attributes. The qualities and/or behaviours of software or their component pieces will be examined to determine these quality attributes.

When measuring trustworthiness for a certain attribute, objectivity is determined by meeting certain predetermined metrics for that attribute or by the design process for that attribute adhering to our predefined software standards [10]. As a result, the software's trustworthiness can be measured against the desired performance level or against its ability to prevent a threat from becoming active. Such difficulties are defined by traits of trustworthiness that have two meanings. Until recently, trustworthiness was usually looked at from the point of view of security or loyalty. People thought that single aspects of services, like certification or specific technologies or processes, made them more trustworthy and even made the users trust them more.

Software programmes could offer to cover a set of diverse qualities based on their domain and target consumers to verify their trustworthiness [10]. Trustworthiness should be defined in terms of durability, security, performance, and how the user feels about it. However, trustworthiness is a relative property that depends on the domain and application. This means that software may be trustworthy for some QoS, like performance, but not for security [13]. As a result, trustworthiness and trust should not be thought of as a single construct with a single effect; rather, they are promoted in the context of the standards and metrics for analysis. The purpose and the trustworthiness of a software application are related to specific scenario characteristics such as the application and user groups.

4.3.2 Extended Trustworthy Computing Initiative

Bill Gates' famous "Trustworthy Computing" memo was delivered to all the employees of *Microsoft* in January 2002 [17]. As a result, all Windows Server 2003 development was suspended for two months while the programme managers, engineers, and programmers were taken through exercises aimed at improving their view of security as it related to their product [17]. Everyone working on the operating software had to take a step back and consider the security implications of their work. As a result, *Microsoft's* customers gained a new perspective on the value of safe computing. The "out-of-the-box" behaviour of Windows Server 2003 is perhaps the clearest example of this [13, 17].

Microsoft added the Durable capability to the already established code framework Azure in 2022. A developer can create stateful functions in a serverless computing environment using Durable Functions, an enhancement of Azure Functions. Additionally, this extension enables the developers to create stateful entities and stateful workflows utilising entity functions written in the Azure Functions programming language [20]. By introducing code durability, these functions are added to achieve durability in software. Durable codes are also trustworthy codes.

Historically, *Microsoft's* products have arrived with default behaviour aimed at giving a completely open environment, utilising all of the operating system, service, or application's user-friendly capabilities. Nonetheless, the network administrator must maintain vigilance in terms of security. The network security manager must keep in mind that the cost of breaching security must be greater than the value of the assets being protected. Microsoft is now willing to assist with security and durability, which was not always the case. The "Security Configuration Manager" tool package from Redmond is the best example. A Security Configuration Manager is not a single application, but a collection of tools that specify the security configuration and make it easier to enhance the life-span. These are some of them:

- Security templates, which contain a security as well as durability policy. These templates can be used in a group policy or on a single machine. Windows Server 2003 includes several sample templates that you can use as-is or modify to meet your requirements [17].
- The group policy security settings extension allows you to quickly and simply update specific security settings on a domain, site, or organisational unit [17].
- Local security policy capabilities on your local PC for specific security settings [17].
- Secedit command is a command-line interface that allows security configuration procedures to be automated [17].

When the policies and templates make working with security, privileges, rights, and trust easier, figuring out why the software behaves in a certain way can be a daunting endeavour [17].

The extended Microsoft security development lifecycle, which includes privacy development practises, is one of the most well-known outputs of extended trustworthy computing integrated with the durability concept as shown in Fig. 2 [17]. The security development lifecycle was implemented as a company-wide, required policy, including industry best practises and lessons acquired from Microsoft's earlier security push. "Instead of recreating the wheel, we were keen to tap into that knowledge as we formalised our own secure product lifecycle." This gave the product teams more time to focus on the actual implementation. Microsoft has also made progress in terms of security and privacy. Better instrumentation, such as windows error reporting, has resulted in fewer software crashes, more productivity, and less user annoyance. Microsoft was one of the first corporations to publish privacy standards for developers and to provide tiered privacy disclosures to consumers in the domain of privacy [17].

Microsoft recognises that trustworthy computing has never been more vital [15–16]. The PC-plus age, the new world of devices and cloud computing, and the role of governments in computing will be the emphasis of the next decade or so of trustworthy computing. To stay effective, security, privacy, and durability solutions must be developed. The software industry still has a lot of work to do to improve trustworthiness in computing. Everyone within Microsoft, as well as the broader computing ecosystem, plays a part.

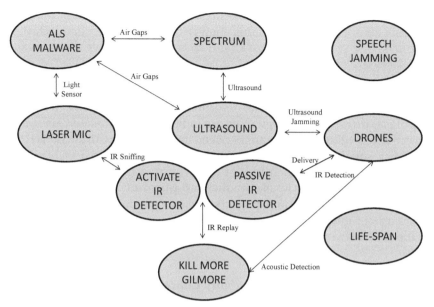

Figure 2: Extended Trustworthy Computing.

Pillar of Extended Trustworthy Computing

The Trustworthy Computing Initiative is divided into four main areas:

(a) Security

Data protection from unauthorised users is simply one aspect of information security. Information security involves guarding against unauthorised access to, use of, disclosure of, alteration of, or destruction of data [15]. Confidentiality, integrity, and availability (sometimes known as "CIA") are three commonly acknowledged characteristics of information security. Chapter VI contains information about security from a durability standpoint.

(b) Privacy

Personal information privacy refers to the protection of personal information maintained on computer systems [15].

(c) Durability

Microsoft presents durability in the content of trustworthy computing as more than just durability software for the expected life-span [15]. It entails, according to Microsoft, being a trustworthy business partner, keeping an open line of communication with the customers and industry partners, and soliciting feedback on how we may improve the software and services.

(d) Business Integrity

Developers should ensure that the interactions with clients, workers, suppliers, investors, and regulators are in line with their stated aims and objectives by filling up any gaps between their intentions and actions [16].

Microsoft has pledged to maintain the highest degree of business ethics. They've shared their idea of trustworthy computing and see it in action throughout their whole product line. Microsoft maintains a variety of corporate initiatives and projects aimed at maintaining the highest standards of integrity. Microsoft and other businesses maintain the core values of trustworthy computing through projects and programmes like these.

4.3.3 Robust Software in Durability Context

"Robust design" (which includes product and process design) refers to the creation of a product or process that can work properly under a variety of conditions. This definition, at least for corporate enterprise applications software [18], can be expanded to make it more prescriptive, which is the goal of this work. Our point is that durable software is "robust" software because it works as planned, expected, and wanted even when there are interruptions [18]. The components of a robust software development procedure from a durability perspective are shown in Fig. 3.

To estimate how close a signal is to an ideal output function, this method uses measurements performed in the product's functional space. As a result, its application in quality engineering or durable design necessitates a strategy for improving functionality to suit user wants (voice of the customer) and raising outcome prediction accuracy by employing measuring methodologies in both functional and multidimensional space. Each design feature or improvement presents a distinct engineering difficulty.

When specifying the function set of a new application, it is not necessary to explicitly indicate robustness or trustworthiness as features in either quantitative or qualitative terms. These features are inherent in the individual. Software is considered trustworthy if it performs the intended function set without error. As a result, it is long-lasting. The most critical need at this level is clarity in explaining the system's intended functions. Only the system's final users can give the necessary amount of transparency. Neither the buyers nor the managers of the software can

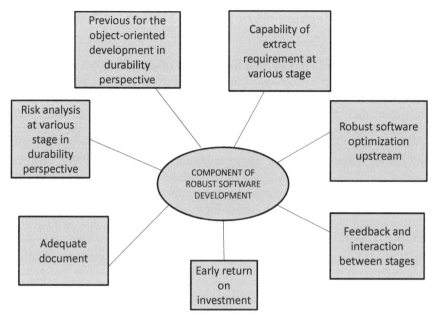

Figure 3: Robust Software Durability.

give precise feedback in this league. The demands of these organisations in terms of efficiency, performance, auditing, transaction recording, and so on must, of course, be met. The system's core functionality, on the other hand, must be stated by the active users. Getting this level of clarity has been a challenge since the dawn of computing. One of the early business application development rules of thumb was that the first time an application was computerised, it was just to automate the paperwork. That is, the computer's inherent power to modify or reengineer business processes was completely overlooked. The second rule was a logical extension of the first: Before an information system can truly benefit from the computer, it must be designed three times. It follows a three-step procedure.

- The purpose of software design is to satisfy the end user's functional requirements.
- The goal of product parameter design is to make it so that a product's performance is less affected by outside factors in its environment of use.
- Tolerance design is the process of making products or process parameters have tighter tolerances so that there is less variation in how well they work.

4.4 Tools and Techniques of Durable Design for Trustworthy Software

To address the problems related to software quality, the developers need to be more proactive when conceptualising and designing the software in its initial stages of a development cycle. The focus of software quality must shift from detecting and eradicating bugs during and after development to preventing bugs during implementation [19]. The idea of the software is that essential quality deployment takes place before a single line of code is written. This client-centric integrated technology can help you achieve breakthrough outcomes in terms of cost, quality, and delivery timeliness, while also meeting and exceeding consumer expectations. The authors describe the principles of the technology and how they might be applied to real-world software durability design problems. It helps in learning Durable and Trustworthy Software technology quickly so that one can put it to use quickly and successfully. The following aspects need to be reckoned with thoroughly:

- Plan, construct, manage, and enhance the durable software development system.
- Adapt best practises in quality, leadership, learning, and management to the specific software development environment.
- Listen to the customer's voice, then help them translate their aspirations into attainable, durable software.
- Refocus on customer service considerations like durability, availability, and upgradeability.
- Encourage design originality and innovation.
- Ensure software durability by validating, verifying, testing, assessing, integrating, and maintaining it.
- Look into the financial ramifications of poor software quality.
- Get ready for Durable and Trustworthy Software by preparing the infrastructure and leadership.

Whether you build in-house, outsource, consult, or give support, designing for trustworthy software can help you increase quality. It has ground-breaking solutions for all kinds of software and quality experts, from developers to project directors to chief software architects to customers.

4.4.1 The Eight Basic (B8) Tools

The term "eight core tools of quality" refers to a set of graphical techniques that have proven to be especially useful in diagnosing quality issues [11–14]. They are called "basic" since they're suitable for those with only rudimentary statistical knowledge and can be utilised to solve the vast majority of quality and durability related issues. The eight tools are as follows:

4.4.1.1 Flowcharts

A flowchart, often known as a process map, is a visual representation of a process. It's a graphical representation of a sequence of events in chronological order as shown in Fig. 4 [11]. It includes all of the operations, inspections, delays, and decision loops that occur during a process. A well-drawn flowchart highlights essential activities that may result in positive or negative process results. Identifying these activities and their causes can aid in the elimination or reduction of redundancies and inefficient processes, as well as the enhancement of activities that help designers reach process goals and provide value to their customers. A flowchart can also be used to communicate. As a result, it serves as the cornerstone for successful process improvement projects like Six Sigma. It also aids in the definition and improvement of the durable software development process.

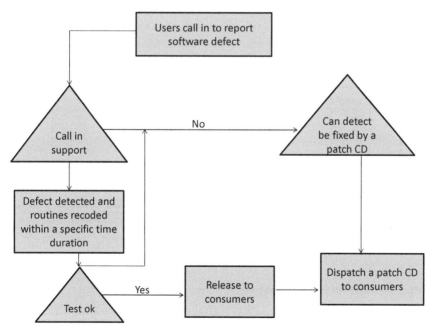

Figure 4: Flowchart of Trustworthy Software.

4.4.1.2 Pareto Charts

A Pareto chart gives information for prioritisation [11]. It organises and presents data to demonstrate the relative importance of various issues or causes of issues as shown in Fig. 5. It's a type of vertical bar chart that ranks items according to some observable effect of interest, cost, or time (from highest to lowest). Pareto charts help teams concentrate on a small number of crucial problems or their root causes. They are crucial for setting priorities since they clarify which issues or causes should be dealt with first. Comparing Pareto charts of a certain situation over time can also help figure out if a solution is working to reduce the number of times or costs of a problem or cause.

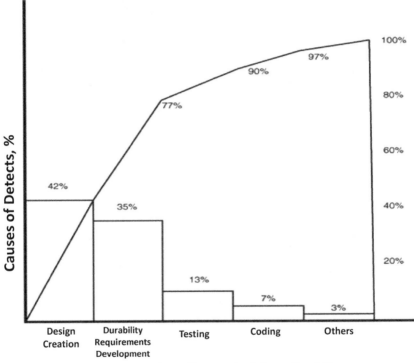

Figure 5: Pareto Chart of Trustworthy Software Durability.

4.4.1.3 Cause-and-Effect Diagrams

Ishikawa-san, a Japanese quality management guru, created the Cause and Effect Diagram, often known as the Fishbone Diagram [12–14]. This technique is relatively simple, but it is one of the most successful techniques and instruments for finding the fundamental causes of various production or project difficulties or flaws. The cause and effect diagram has become a widely used tool for analysing a wide range of organisational issues, not just quality-related issues as shown in Fig. 6. The fishbone diagram is a graphic representation of the cause-and-effect relationship. It resembles a fishbone. The problem is represented by the fish's mouth or head, while the numerous bones symbolise the possible root causes. Root-cause analysis is frequently carried out as a brainstorming session among team members. The team investigates each of the problems or defects, with the goal of determining the fundamental causes. This needs to be done in a planned way, and it's important to know all of the things that led to the flaw or problem.

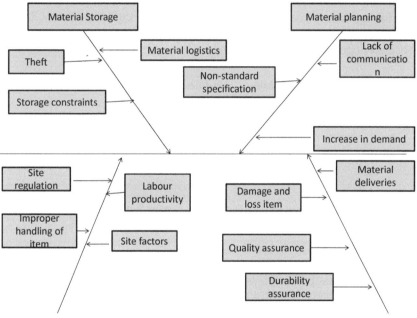

Figure 6: Cause and Effect Diagram of Trustworthy Software.

4.4.1.4 Scatter Diagrams

A scatter diagram presents two pairs of numerical data with one variable on each axis in order to find any links between them [13]. If the variables are correlated, a line or curve will be formed by the points. The relationship is stronger when the points touch the line closely. When examining the relationship between the X and Y axes with only one variable, a scatter diagram is used. If the variables are plotted on the graph as being connected, the point will move along a curve or line. A scatter diagram or scatter plot could provide insight into the relationship's nature. The correlation is perfect and equal to one if every dot in a scatter correlation diagram merges into a single line. The correlation is believed to be low if the scatter points are evenly spaced along the line. The correlation is referred to as linear if the scatter points are on or very close to a line.

4.4.1.5 Check Sheets

A check sheet is a piece of paper that contains a list of elements that must be measured, checked, and recorded as shown in Fig. 7 [14]. Because of the form's unique design, data collection is simple and uniform. Depending on the goal of the data gathering exercise, such as evaluating process variance, analysing types of defects, and identifying causes of faults, different check sheets are conceivable. Check sheets are frequently used in conjunction with histograms to see and utilise data obtained in the histograms. In the case of software, it makes sense to start with check sheets to see if the data collected is possible and useful.

Defect Type	Module#1	Module#2	Module#3	Total
A	III	II	IV	IX
B	II	III	V	X
C		VI	II	VIII
D	IV	I		V
Total	IX	X	XI	XXXII

Figure 7: Check Sheet of Trustworthy Software.

4.4.1.6 Histograms

A histogram is a visual representation of how the process data is spread as shown in Fig. 8 [15]. The normally distributed bell-shaped histograms, also known as Gaussian histograms, have different statistical features. Such uni-model curves are linked to predictable processes with predictable variance. Chance or natural variation is the term for such variance around the bell form. Variations that do not have a bell shape could be due to a variety of process flaws that can be traced back to specific and identifiable sources and are linked to unstable processes. Exponential, gamma, beta, Wei-bull, binomial, and Poisson distributions, for example, are not bell-shaped but are associated with steady and predictable processes. These and other statistically significant distributions are well-known.

4.4.1.7 Graphs

In mathematics, a graph is a visual representation or diagram that shows facts or values in an ordered way [16]. The relationships between two or more items are frequently represented by the points on a graph. There are

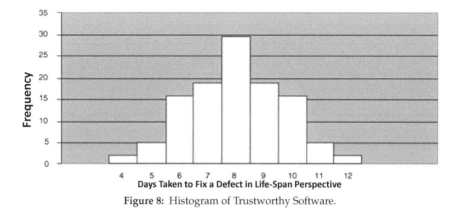

Figure 8: Histogram of Trustworthy Software.

a wide variety of graph types that can be used to create durable and long-lasting software. A pictograph is, for instance, a depiction of information using images. Each graphic entity represents a specified number of objects. The display of numerical data in a bar graph consists of rectangles (or bars) with equal widths and different heights. The distance between each bar is the same across the board. Bar graphs can be vertical or horizontal. Each bar's value is directly correlated with either its height or length. In a line graph, dots are connected by lines to depict changes over time. The circle graph is another name for the pie chart. It demonstrates the division of a whole into various sections. The relative size of each data set concerning the total dataset is displayed on the pie chart. To depict how much of the total each category takes up, percentages are employed.

4.4.1.8 *Control Charts*

A graph used to track a process' evolution over time is called a control chart. The data are displayed on a timeline as shown in Fig. 9 [17–18]. A central line, an upper line, and a lower line are always used to represent the average on a control chart along with the upper and lower control limits. These charts are built using historical data. Current data compare these lines to determine whether the process variance is predictable or unexpected (affected by special causes of variation). One of the seven basic quality tools that may be used by a variety of businesses is this adaptive data collection and analysis tool. Control charts are used in pairs for variable data. The average, or centre, of the data distribution from the procedure, is shown in the top graph. The distribution's range, or width, is shown at the bottom of the graph. If your data were target practise shots, the average represents where the shots are clustered, and the range represents how tightly they are clustered. Single control charts are used for attribute data.

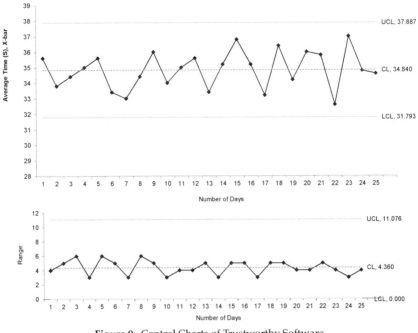

Figure 9: Control Charts of Trustworthy Software.

4.4.2 Financial Perspective

As is well acknowledged, banking applications are becoming more sophisticated by the day, with new functionality and features being introduced all the time, as well as an expanding number of channels and platforms available to reach a growing number of clients [19]. End-users in today's financial system are faced with a multitude of decisions: which banking applications will be secure and durable with trustworthiness? There is a list of qualities that continues to increase. Customers are very picky about what they buy, so every institution whether economic, financial, or academic should make sure the software they use have durability, quality, and no flaws. This makes durability, quality management, testing, and automation even more important.

4.4.2.1 Cost and Quality: Then and Now

The integrity, correctness, and efficacy of applications and services are more important than ever for financial institutions, which rely heavily on quality-centric service offerings [12]. Main components of cost of quality software services for an expected time line are shown in Fig. 10. Any improper use poses the danger of causing reputational harm, such

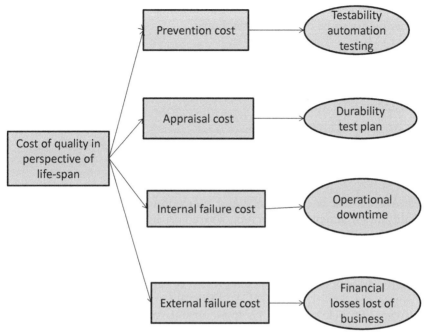

Figure 10: Cost of Software Quality.

as the loss of customer confidence. This raises the bar for trustworthiness goals above that of many other businesses. Software quality refers to two related but distinct notions:

- Functional quality refers to the degree to which software complies with or adheres to a specified design based on functional requirements or specifications. That attribute can also be viewed as a piece of software's suitability for its intended application or how it compares to its market competitors as a valuable product.

- Structural quality in software refers to the amount to which the correct software is generated, as well as non-functional criteria that aid in the fulfilment of functional needs, such as robustness and maintainability. It has a lot more to do with the software's capacity to do what it's supposed to do.

In today's culture, software is everywhere. Think about your smartphone. It's a mobile computing device that contains millions of lines of code. For example, the average iPhone app comprises 10–50 thousand lines of code, whereas Google's complete code base for all of its services has two billion lines of code [13]. The operating system for smartphones (for example, Android) contains approximately 12 million lines of code.

Software, as a product, is distinct from any other manufactured item. The following are some obvious distinctions:

- It has a high fixed cost structure and a reduced variable cost structure.
- It doesn't break down, but it does need to be maintained.
- In the future, it will be easier to offer additional value (i.e., vs. hardware).
- It's naturally more difficult.
- Because it is non-physical, it is more intangible and less evident.

4.4.2.2 Cost of Quality Tasks

The overall cost of compliance and nonconformance to the customer's quality requirements can be characterised as the cost of software quality (Co-SQ) as shown in Figure 11. It includes all direct and indirect costs associated with preventing, evaluating, testing, identifying, analysing, and correcting software flaws, as well as upkeep. Testing accounts for roughly 40% of software development costs, to eliminate errors and ensure appropriate quality [14]. Additionally, around 80–90% of the entire software life-cycle cost (LCC) is spent on software maintenance to correct, adapt, and add to the programme so that it can meet the changing and rising needs of users [15].

cost of performing quality tasks	= cost of conformance + cost of non-conformance
cost of conformance	= preventive costs + appraisal costs
cost of non-conformance	= cost of internal failure + cost of external failure
cost of internal failure	= cost of upstream internal failure + cost of downstream internal

Failure

The goal should be to stop this from happening. The majority of durability-quality costs should be spent on prevention, with a few dollars spent on appraisal, a few dollars spent on upstream and downstream internal failures, and almost no money spent on external failures. As a result, the software developer should first try to minimise external failure costs to zero by investing in preventive and assessment operations to create bug-free durable software. Then, if there are any sources of design or code failure, he or she should identify them and take corrective action. As quality improves, failure costs drop, and with a shift in emphasis to

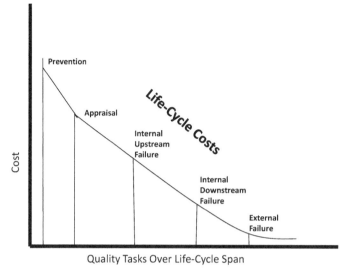

Figure 11: Life Cycle Span of Software Quality.

prevention efforts, the quantity of appraisal can be lowered. Finding the cost of quality is the first step in figuring out and getting rid of the main causes of failure.

4.4.2.3 Benefits of Cost-of-Quality Analysis

- The software team can focus on detecting and addressing the root causes of software faults with the help of cost-of-quality analysis.
- The project team can employ root-cause analysis to see how the development process can be modified to prevent more failures and hence increase quality.
- This visibility also makes it easy for all project-supporting functions to communicate with one another, regardless of how the organisation is structured.

Traditional cost-evaluation measures, which are typically used for manufactured products, have solely looked at "failure-related activities" [16]. They have concentrated on internal costs of rework, rejects, and returns. They emphasis inspection and cost reduction by implementing corrective actions after inspection. Although the need for corrective actions cannot be completely eliminated, an enlightened approach emphasis preventive intervention so that corrective measures are unnecessary or can be minimised in the first place.

4.5 Conclusion

All devices run software, and businesses rely on huge infrastructure software that is invisible to them to make daily decisions for us. Due to this, users' and developers' need for trustworthiness grows. The reliability of software is influenced by its durability and quality. The particular elements of a system's trustworthiness rely on the type of system, the standards of the industry in which it operates, and the repercussions of failures, just like all other system features. Hence trustworthy software with good durability is the requirement in this era.

This chapter described the relationship between trustworthiness and its importance in ensuring the durability of software. Further, a framework for durability with trustworthiness is provided for ensuring quality in software. Due to time-to-market constraints, certain software techniques and organisational cultures may produce software that lacks trustworthiness, durability, and quality. It is obvious that earlier stages in the research and product development lifecycle must be less expensive to validate the underlying engineering and scientific principles of the product with a "minimal feasible product", but every release should start by focusing on trustworthiness, dependability, durability, and quality.

Points to Remember

- Software trustworthiness is a crucial element that will enable a developer to gain access to software durability via the service life forecast in order to construct well-durable and dependable software.

- The chapter is a starting point for figuring out if a project is compatible with the software development that is needed, making sure that the basics of durability are met.

- The framework improves the durability and life-span of software for users and lets businesses and developers manage and evaluate the durability of software they make themselves and add code from outside sources.

- A growing variety of intricate technological systems are now controlled by software, including embedded controls in automobiles, factories, and aeroplanes, as well as Internet-based e-health and e-government applications.

- The degree to which we can trust software systems will determine how well they are deployed. Several initiatives have been launched by academia, the government, and the industry with the goal of presenting a perspective on software trustworthiness from software creation, evaluation, and analysis.

Review Questions

Objective Type Questions

1. .... is the First phase of the STGP model.
   - (a) Development Link
   - (b) Improvement Link
   - (c) Conception Link
   - (d) Application Link

2. A trustworthiness attribute that is responsible for performance consistency is:
   - (a) Availability
   - (b) Reliability
   - (c) Maintainability
   - (d) None of the above

3. Process map is also known as..................
   - (a) Flowchart
   - (b) Control chart
   - (c) Scatter diagram
   - (d) All of the above

4. Flowchart helps in identifying how a process is carried out.
   - (a) True
   - (b) False

5. Preventive cost + Appraisal cost =?
   - (a) Cost of conformance
   - (b) Cost of internal failure
   - (c) Cost of non-conformance
   - (d) None of the above

Short Answer Type Questions

1. What is flowchart?
2. Define Histogram.
3. What do you mean by check sheet?
4. What do you mean by security template?
5. What is local security policy?

Descriptive Questions

1. Describe STGP Model.
2. What is trustworthy software? What do you mean by various attributes of trustworthiness?
3. What are seven basic quality tools? What is the relationship in between cost and quality?

References

1. Software Trustworthiness Best Practices. 23/03/2020. https://hub.iiconsortium.org/portal/Whitepapers/5ece527ad2df3f001102b74e.
2. Mall, R. 2018. Fundamentals of software engineering. PHI Learning Pvt. Ltd.
3. Pressman, R.S. 2005. Software engineering: a practitioner's approach. Palgrave Macmillan.
4. Alberts, D.S. 1976. The economics of software quality assurance. In Proceedings of the June 7–10, 1976, national computer conference and exposition 433–442.
5. Data Breach Investigations Report - Executive Summary. 2020. https://enterprise.verizon.com/resources/executivebriefs/2020-dbir-executive-brief.pdf.
6. Staff, C.U. 2020. The biggest software failures in recent history. Computerworld https://www.computerworld.com/article/3412197/top-software-failures-in-recent-history.html.
7. Losavio, F., Chirinos, L., Lévy, N. and Ramdane-Cherif, A. 2003. Quality characteristics for software architecture. Journal of object Technology, 2: 133–150.
8. Jerman-Blazic, B. and Klobucar, T. (Eds.). 2013. Advanced communications and multimedia security: IFIP TC6/TC11 Sixth Joint Working Conference on Communications and Multimedia Security September 26–27, 2002, Portorož, Slovenia (Vol. 100). Springer.
9. Maza, S. and Megouas, O. 2021. Framework for trustworthiness in software development. International Journal of Performability Engineering, 17(2).
10. Nami, M. and Suryn, W. 2012, May. Software trustworthiness: Past, present and future. In International Conference on Trustworthy Computing and Services (pp. 1–12). Springer, Berlin, Heidelberg.
11. Hasselbring, W. and Reussner, R. 2006. Toward trustworthy software systems. Computer, 39(4): 91–92.
12. Thoughts on Software Trustworthiness Best Practices. 23/03/2020. https://blog.irdeto.com/software-protection/thoughts-on-software-trustworthiness-best-practices/.
13. At 10-Year Milestone, Microsoft's Trustworthy Computing Initiative More Important than Ever, https://news.microsoft.com/2012/01/12/at-10-year-milestone-microsofts-trustworthy-computing-initiative-more-important-than-ever/.
14. Paulus, S., Mohammadi, N.G. and Weyer, T. 2013, September. Trustworthy software development. In IFIP International Conference on Communications and Multimedia Security (pp. 233–247). Springer, Berlin, Heidelberg.
15. Introduction to TSFdn. 20/05/2021. http://www.tsfdn.org/.
16. Sarialioglu, B. 2012, July. A perspective of software trustworthiness based on finance industry. In 2012 IEEE 36th Annual Computer Software and Applications Conference (pp. 498–498). IEEE.
17. Celebrating 20 Years of Trustworthy Computing, Available at: https://www.microsoft.com/security/blog/2022/01/21/celebrating-20-years-of-trustworthy-computing/.

18. Hamzaçebi, C., Li, P., Pereira, P.A.R. and Navas, H. 2020. Taguchi method as a robust design tool. In Quality Control-Intelligent Manufacturing, Robust Design and Charts. IntechOpen.

19. Sahu, K., Alzahrani, F.A., Srivastava, R.K. and Kumar, R. 2020. Hesitant fuzzy sets based symmetrical model of decision-making for estimating the durability of Web application. Symmetry, 12(11): 1770.

20. What are Durable Functions? 2022. Available online at https://docs.microsoft.com/en-us/azure/azure-functions/durable/durable-functions-overview?tabs=csharp.

Useful Links

https://www.iiconsortium.org/pdf/Software_Trustworthiness_Best_Practices_Whitepaper_2020_03_23.pdf

https://hub.iiconsortium.org/portal/Whitepapers/5ece527ad2df3f001102b74e

https://cse.engin.umich.edu/research/research-areas/secure-trustworthy-reliable-systems/

https://hal.inria.fr/hal-01492828/document

https://ieeexplore.ieee.org/document/6616347

Chapter 5

Integrating Usability with Software Durability

5.1 Objectives

Usability is becoming an increasingly important factor in the success of durable systems. The end-users may reject durable systems that meet all of the functional requirements, but have usability issues. This Chapter, in particular, discusses the nature of software usability with durability. This chapter's goal is to clarify the basic evaluation of software usability for durability estimation, which will be revisited in future chapters. It will also do some domain analysis in the area of how long software lasts. Efficiency, effectiveness, contentment, and learnability are all regularly addressed aspects in existing software usability models and standards, according to our findings. Furthermore, developers lack the information necessary to select the most effective usability evaluation approach for a given area. On the contrary, the most commonly used approaches for evaluating software usability are user-based assessment, inspection-based evaluation, and model-based evaluation. The following objectives are kept in mind when creating a roadmap for this chapter:

- To define the fundamental principles of usability concerning durability;
- To discuss in detail the user-based evaluations; inspection-based evaluations; and model-based evaluations;
- To propose a unified usability management framework from the perspective of durability.

5.2 Fundamental Principles

5.2.1 The Evolution of Usability Concept

Evolution is a normal process in the life of software systems. Software evolution happens in incremental steps as a result of modifications in the environment, purpose, or use of the measured software system [1]. There may be an impact on the eventual durability of software if changes are made to a software system that affects its quality. This refers to aspects such as correctness, consistency, usability, and maintainability. The quality of evolving software should be preserved or even improved over time. Building, maintaining, and modernising software systems are all part of the evolution of software [2–3].

Evolution is crucial to the success of software systems since it permits the addition or improvement of different components of the system. Software evolution can be considered a continual process of change. Software systems can easily adjust to changes over time. Software that does not support the modification will gradually degrade over time [4]. New requirements can be added to software systems to meet the needs of stakeholders. All software development procedures state that the programme should be created in response to the need for it to adapt to the environment or to maintain user satisfaction [4–5].

Software management and developers must work together to understand the factors that influence software evolution and take proactive measures to make modifications easier and prevent software decay [6–7]. This will minimise software production costs and improve durability. Continuing for an extended period after origin is one effective attribute of software systems, including open-source ones. For software systems to survive in this high-paced world, they must adapt continuously. The dynamic behaviour of software systems is investigated by software evolution when they are maintained and upgraded over their lifetime [8]. Usability engineering establishes a goal usability level and guarantees that the software developed meets it and becomes durable for user satisfaction. Some experts on durability and usability came up with the word to describe how they design things to last and be easy to use.

- It's "a means of early in the development process of specifying usability attributes in terms of numbers and then measuring them as the project advances."
- Usability is an issue that can be handled from many different angles, which is why it is being studied by many different fields, including psychology, computer science, and sociology. As a result, there is a scarcity of standard jargon.

In fact, ISO 9241, Part 11, says that usability is "the extent to which a product can be used by specified users to achieve specified goals with effectiveness, efficiency, and satisfaction in a specified context of use." According to this definition, the usability of a system is tied to specific conditions, needs, and users. It necessitates determining certain levels of usefulness based on a system's essential features. According to [9–10], usability evaluation is a way to judge how easy it is to use a user interface and find problems with it. In this row, we will now discover the relationship between usability and durability in the following sections.

5.2.2 Usability Analysis into Durability Concept

The ability of a software system to continue serving its customers' demands over an extended period is referred to as software durability. The software's durability determines how happy the user is. For software to be effective over time, it must permit an organisation to make unplanned modifications to the software system to accommodate shifting business needs. The three factors that affect a software system's durability are its reliability, serviceability, and usefulness. As was previously said, the interaction design influences how usable a system is. So, when making software that will last, usability must be taken into account at every step.

Usability testing alone will never result in a product that is both simple to use and durable. For this reason, usability testing is frequently used by the developers at the end of the development process, when resolving significant usability problems would be extremely costly, if not entirely unfeasible. Because the process of creating a product must be iterative, every result must be evaluated as it is being developed. It is quite difficult to incorporate usability concepts into a waterfall method of durable software development.

Software usability and durability (SUD) have created additional difficulties for developers in the software development cycle [11–12]. SUDs have grown to be a crucial component of software development [13–15]. Though the developers put a lot of time and attention into solving security issues in the early phases of software development [16], they neglect to consider how long the software will last.

Software with poor usability and durability will fall short in a very competitive market. The concept of durability-usability should therefore be thoroughly understood by software development businesses. This chapter assesses the value of software usability attributes along with their importance in achieving durability. Usability cannot be boiled down to a single system feature. The answer varies based on the intended application of the system under development. Efficiency (the number of tasks accomplished per hour), for example, is negligible for this kind of system, but learning simplicity is crucial. A bank cashier's system, on the

Figure 1: Basic Usability Attributes.

other hand, would need to be extremely effective to help reduce customer waiting hours.

Because "usability" is too broad to be studied in depth, it is often broken down into the five categories shown in Fig. 1 [17–20].

- *Learnability:* How straightforward it is to grasp the functions of the primary system and get proficiency to complete the task. Learnability is usually calculated by comparing how much time a user spends working with the system to how long it takes an expert to do the same tasks. For first-time users, this is a critical feature.

- *Efficiency:* The maximum number of jobs a user can do in a given amount of time. We're looking for the best possible user task performance. If the system is more usable and durable, the user can accomplish more work and finish the work quickly.

- *Memorability:* System interfaces should be easy to remember so that casual users can use the system again after a break without having to learn everything all over again.

- *Error Rate:* This attribute harms usability. It has nothing to do with problems with the system. It is, on the other hand, concerned with the number of errors committed by the user while doing a task. A low error rate indicates that the system is easy to use. Errors hurt production and user pleasure. They can also be interpreted as a failure to instruct the user on how to perform something correctly.

- *Satisfaction:* This reflects how a user feels about the system as a whole.

When it comes to usability, there's a chance that these characteristics will clash. A person's ability to learn, for example, is frequently negatively correlated with their productivity. High learnability and efficiency are two objectives that must be met by well-designed systems. One common way to solve this problem is to use accelerators, which are a group of keys that do the same thing. To get at a user's perceived usability, all of these elements are combined. It's not just how many values each property has; it's how many values each attribute contains.

By further differentiating these traits, we may better serve our particular preferences for usability. The initial impression is one of several sub-aspects of efficiency, such as regular use and complex feature usage. As a result, we dissect the most important usability attributes to the proper level of detail when analysing the usability of a system. Usability is a phrase that encompasses more than just software interaction. There are also help features, user manuals, and installation instructions.

5.2.3 Durability and Usability Characteristics

This section is discussed in Chapter 2.

5.2.4 Systems, Software, Usability and Durability

Usability factors are crucial in creating software that is more durable and usable. The main goal of incorporating usability considerations into the design of a software system is to boost user effectiveness, contentment, and productivity. Usability techniques can thus assist the users in performing their tasks and any software system in achieving its goal of durability. Usability is also becoming more important in a world where consumers are less computer literate and can't afford to spend a lot of time learning how to utilise a system. The acceptance of a system by users depends heavily on its usefulness.

Users are less inclined to adopt a system if they don't think it will assist them in completing their tasks. The system might not be used at all or just ineffectively after deployment. If the developers do not sufficiently help them with their tasks, they are not satisfying the user's demands and are ignoring the core aim of designing a usable software system. A software development company runs the danger of losing market share in a cutthroat industry if usability isn't taken into account. This is because if the application is simple to use and durable, less money will be spent on hotlines, customer service, and other services.

Even though a system is in use, it does not always imply that users will find it easy to use. How a software product is utilised depends on a variety of factors, including the price, the choice, and prior training. As a result, in interactions between humans and computers, the human adapts to the machine rather than the other way around. On the other hand, forced adaptation to software that is difficult to use can negatively affect long-term viability, productivity, effectiveness, and user satisfaction. A software product's success depends on how usable it is and how long it will be.

5.3 Usability Evaluation: Durability Perspective

Users demand software that is simple to understand and use, as well as enjoyable and efficient. Furthermore, they value a system that rebounds quickly from user failures and can be easily memorised after a period of inactivity. A test should be done to see how well, efficiently, and effectively a certain group of users can use a software system. Several evaluation methods have emerged as a result of the growing relevance of usability in the software development process. Methodically assessing the usability of graphical software interfaces is the purpose of these approaches [21–22].

Usability assessment techniques are defined as "procedures consisting of a series of well-defined activities to collect data related to the end user's interaction with a software product to determine how the specific properties of a particular software contribute to achieving specific goals" [23–24]. During the software development process, these techniques are often used to make a useful product that meets strict quality and durability standards. As shown in Fig. 2, user-based assessment, inspection-based evaluation, and model-based evaluation are some of the most common methods for assessing software usability. Moreover, as shown in Fig. 2, each of these three software usability evaluation models has three sub-evaluation models, which are explained in detail in the sections below.

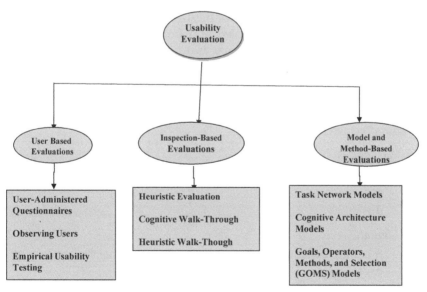

Figure 2: Common Methods for Assessing Software Usability.

5.3.1 User-Based Evaluations

Testing an application's usability using a representative sample of users performing a predetermined set of tasks is generally considered the most reliable and true estimate of durability. Measuring how well the programme aids its intended audience is the goal of usability testing, which can be done in a lab or on location. As part of the operational approach, the user-based approach for defining usability draws heavily on the experimental design tradition of human factors psychology. To measure performance, it uses task analysis, variables that have already been set up, and, in most cases, both quantitative and qualitative methods.

In a typical user-based evaluation, participants are asked to complete a series of activities using the technology. Depending on the evaluator's primary focus, the success and speed with which the user's complete tasks can be recorded. Surveys and interviews are routinely used to get information from users about their preferences and dislikes, or they may be requested to watch a section of their performance on video with the evaluator and describe their performance and opinions of the software durability in further detail as well. This way, it's possible to make measurements of effectiveness, efficiency, and customer satisfaction, as well as to find problems and suggest ways to improve durability.

User understanding and cognition concerns may necessitate the employment of concurrent verbal procedures in some situations, which may necessitate concurrent verbal procedures. Videotaping the entire encounter in a usability lab allows the researchers to go back and look at how transactions were handled and how well users navigated the site. On the other hand, less formal approaches are possible. Users and evaluators may interact with the system in an unstructured way to see what works and what doesn't in the durability design during user-based tests. Participatory approaches can be very helpful in the early stages of designing for durability, when it may be too early for traditional quantitative assessments.

(a) Advantages

- Most accurate estimate of usability.
- This can provide a clear record of the most critical issues in durability.

(b) Limitations

- It is time-consuming, expensive, and necessitates the creation of a prototype.

5.3.1.1 User-Administered Questionnaires

It takes considerable talent to create a pertinent questionnaire, quickly tabulate the responses, and then analyse the responses so they produce useful results. Contrarily, using a questionnaire allows you to gather information from many people without having to invest a lot of time or money. Testers can create questionnaires with open-ended or closed-ended questions (numerical and yes-or-no) (where users formulate their responses) concerning software durability. Although it takes less time and effort to analyse closed-ended questions, the findings might not be as meaningful as those from open-ended questions. Users are less likely to fill out the form since open-ended inquiries require more time to answer.

A smart tactic is to start with largely closed-ended questions and end with a few open-ended ones. User-based surveys are easy to design, practical for responders, allow for anonymity if necessary, and automate at least some of the tabulation. A major flaw in all surveys and many other forms of empirical evaluation is the fact that the researchers are merely soliciting people's opinions. Performance is not being observed or assessed in real time. Users are typically poor judges of both their skills and the documentation.

5.3.1.2 *Observing Users*

Users' real-world behaviour is observed by a small number of real-world consumers for user testing. With physical artefacts such as prototypes or systems, the experimenter observes and gathers empirical data on the users' actions and responses while they carry out the tasks in the experiment. The execution duration, the number of failures, and the level of satisfaction of the end user are all typical pieces of user testing information. The information acquired during the test is analysed, and the results are used to improve the program's usability concerning durability. The main goal of usability testing is to find out how the users interact with a piece of software to finish certain tasks for a long time.

The end users are approached and asked how they feel about the programme after it has been released for beta testing. Watching a group of people perform a specific job for a longer period while using an app is a form of usability testing. The test is usually recorded. This includes a breakdown of the problems that were found, as well as specific suggestions for a new design. To ensure the accuracy of the results, every step of the testing process, from design to execution, must be meticulously orchestrated. As a result, the following is an accurate description of effective user testing:

- *Defining the Goals of the Test:* If the goal is to make users happier and make the product easy to use, the evaluation goals could be broad or specific, like figuring out how well a navigation bar helps users find their way around, how well labels can be read, and so on.

- *Sample of Users Definition that will Participate in the Test:* The end-user community must be reflected in the test's sample size. Experts vs. novices in terms of application experience, age, frequency of application use, and experience with similar apps are all factors that can be utilised to characterise the test sample. Each test's objectives dictate how many participants are needed. Three users should be able to identify 50% of the most critical usability and durability issues. According to the other authors, involving five people is the best way to find 90% of usability problems.

- *Selecting Tasks and Scenarios*: When conducting a usability test, the tasks offered to the users must be based on real-world usage scenarios. If the results of requirements' elicitation aren't available, scenarios could be made to see if anything unexpected could happen.

- *Establishing How to Determine the Level of Usability of the System*: The parameters that will be used to evaluate the outcomes of the study must be determined before beginning the usability testing process. The use of subjective measures, such as user satisfaction and ease of use, the longevity of use in conjunction with objective and quantitative measures, such as task completion time, error number and typology, the number of successfully completed tasks, and the number of times users call for assistance, can yield valuable results (verbal, on-line help, manual). If their results are used in any manner, the participants will be told, but their identities will be kept private throughout the process.

In addition to thinking aloud, which requires the subject to state explicitly all of the actions she is attempting, the reason for her/his actions, and the expected outcomes; co-discovery (or collaborative approach), which requires two participants to complete the tasks cooperatively; and active intervention, which requires the experimenter to stimulate participants to reflect on the elicited data. It's worth noting that these methods exclude data collection on user satisfaction. Instead, survey methods based on questionnaires and interviews with users could be used after testing is done to get such a subjective metric.

- Organizing *the Needed Material and the Experimental Atmosphere*: The experimental environment must be organised by providing a computer and a video camera for recording user behaviours; specifying the roles of the members of the experimental team; and preparing any necessary supporting materials (manuals, pencils, papers, etc.). The test does not have to be conducted in a laboratory. Before the testing session, a pilot test must be done to check and maybe improve the test processes.

5.3.1.3 Empirical Usability Testing

It's a research-based approach to software development that prioritises the needs of the end user before anything else. While running tests on the system, it monitors the users' behaviour and demeanour. The system records both the user's behaviour and the system's response when naive users engage with it. In the testing process, a prototype or a final product might be used. A finished product's acceptability by users may be tested, whereas improvements can be made to a prototype system to assure the product's success and its durability as well. As a result, a system can be discarded if necessary.

5.3.2 Inspection-Based Evaluations

Conducting user testing for research users while utilising prototypes, is encouraged. This action, however, is highly costly. Besides this, feedback must begin to flow preferably before the first piece of software or hardware is developed, and that too at the earliest possible stage. Because of these and other things, the developers now have tools that let them find potential usability problems before users do. An evaluation strategy known as usability inspection has emerged from past software engineering methodologies for troubleshooting and improving code. Evaluators use these techniques to look at an application's usability in terms of how well it sticks to generally accepted principles of usability. They do this so they can make suggestions to the software's durability designers about how to improve the design of the software's durability.

Usability experts can be designers or engineers who have had special training in the field (for example, they know about certain domains or standards). The implementation of these approaches relies on an in-depth knowledge of usability and durability principles and how they apply to the particular application under investigation, as well as the ability to recognise crucial instances when principles have been violated. Since the question of cost efficiency began to guide methodological work on usability evaluation [25–26], usability inspection approaches have been presented.

The cost of user research and laboratory tests has become a major concern. As a result, various ideas for usability evaluation approaches based on the engagement of experts to supplement or even replace direct user testing have been offered [27]. An application can be inspected using a variety of approaches. We can use heuristic evaluations to see if an application's properties are in line with the established rules of usability, and cognitive walkthroughs to see if the application's functions are efficient for users, as well as to see if the application leads them to the next correct actions.

(a) *Advantages*
- Inexpensive
- High-Speed

(b) Disadvantages

- Due to expert-variability, the outcome may be inaccurately predicted
- May exaggerate the genuine number of issues

5.3.2.1 Heuristic Evaluation

When making a durable design decision or analysing an existing one, heuristics can be used as a general rule of thumb, general principle, or guideline. In the 1970s, Jakob Nielsen and Rolf Molich created a method called heuristic evaluation to aid researchers in determining what to say about various systems using a set of basic and universal criteria [16]. Heuristic evaluation is based on the idea that many evaluators independently study a system to discover potential usability flaws. It is vital that a large number of these assessors be present, as well as that the evaluations be done independently.

According to Nielsen's experience, about five employees are responsible for discovering about 75 percent of all usability concerns. The assessors are given a set of heuristics to aid them in spotting usability issues and developing ideas while evaluating the system. An example of a heuristics list is as follows:

- When something happens, the system should offer immediate feedback so that users are kept informed.
- Instead of system-specific jargon, the system should use user-friendly terms, concepts, and ideas. When it comes to data organisation, it's critical to stick to industry standards.
- Users frequently pick system functions by accident, necessitating the usage of an "emergency escape" to exit an unpleasant condition without having to engage in a lengthy argument with system administrators. The functions of undo and redo are available.
- Users should not have to make educated guesses about the meaning of particular phrases, situations, or actions. Pay attention to the platform's conventions.
- Smart design that stops problems from happening is often better than clear error messages.
- All objects, actions, and options should be displayed simultaneously. It should not be necessary for the user to remember information from one dialogue segment to the next. Instructions on how to use the device should be displayed or easily accessible whenever possible.
- Accelerators, which are imperceptible to the novice user, frequently considerably speed up the interaction for the expert user, allowing the

system to manage both inexperienced and experienced users. It's vital to give clients the ability to customise their everyday routines.

- There should be any need to include irrelevant or only occasionally required material in interactions. When more information is added to a conversation, it competes with the important information and makes it harder to understand.

- While it is preferable if the system can be used without documentation, assistance and documentation may be required in' some cases. It should be easy to find, focused on the task the user wants to complete, have a list of easy-to-follow actions, and not be too large.

It's important to remember that the heuristics are meant to help evaluators find usability problems, not to limit them to only those that the heuristics can explain.

5.3.2.2 Guideline-Based Methods

"Guideline reviews" [25] are inspections of an interface for compliance with a comprehensive set of usability standards. Guidelines are routinely established using freely available books, studies, and articles. They usually aren't company-specific and instead cover the entire field of user interaction design [26]. As a result, usability experts must routinely adapt recommendations to meet their organization's structure and product focus. While some guidelines can be evaluated using only a few heuristic concepts, many guideline volumes contain thousands of rules spread over hundreds of pages. The majority of guideline reviews are undertaken using a custom set of domain-specific rules. Guidelines are typically reviewed by several members of the design team, but they can also be completed by one person for smaller development projects.

(a) Guidelines' Advantages

The primary advantage of guideline reviews is that they give the evaluator a systematic way to evaluate the user interface in accordance with the durability designer's guidelines. They also offer the benefit of allowing the evaluator to quickly examine the design without having any prior understanding of the process.

(b) Guidelines' Weaknesses

According to the majority of studies, durability designers and evaluators should not rely only on guidelines. Rules might be complicated, inconsistent, and require trade-offs between competing goals, and they're rarely translated into explicit design principles that can be applied quickly. Many durability designers have constructed their lists of essential principles that they store in their working memory for reference because it is hard to keep track of all interface design standards. Aside from that, durable design ideas quickly become out of date because there isn't enough evidence or theory to back them up.

5.3.2.3 Cognitive Walk-Through

A cognitive tour is a method of analysing the user interaction of a working prototype or completed product. It's used to determine how simple the system is to grasp. When dealing with a system, a cognitive walkthrough can help you comprehend how a user thinks and makes decisions, especially if you're a first-time or infrequent user [27].

- *Learnability:* Refers to how straightforward the consumers think it is for them to accomplish simple tasks after viewing the design.
- *Efficiency:* Refers to how quickly can the consumers complete the tasks once they have become familiar with the design.
- *Memorability:* Refers to, how quickly the users learn to use the system once they start reusing the system after sometime.
- *Errors:* Refers to how many mistakes do users make daily. What is the severity of these errors, and how easily can they recover from the errors, are the questions?
- *Satisfaction:* How easy is it to navigate through the design?

One or more assessors complete activities and rate the user interface's understandability and ease of learning on a scale of 1 to 10 in a cognitive walkthrough. The user interface is frequently demonstrated as a paper mock-up or a functional prototype, but it can also be demonstrated as a fully constructed interface. The user profile, including the user's understanding of the task domain and interface, as well as the task cases, are all inputs to the tour and are used to lead the user through it. The evaluations may be conducted by human factors engineers, software developers, or workers from marketing, documentation, and other departments. This strategy is most effective when employed during the development process's design phase. It can be used during the development, testing, and deployment phases as well.

5.3.2.4 Heuristic Walk-Though

Heuristic walkthroughs combine heuristic evaluation, cognitive walkthroughs, and pluralistic usability walks into one inspection. The heuristic walkthrough uses a two-step process to discover problems. The first step is to evaluate a product by completing a set of tasks and answering the questions that go along with them. The product is then evaluated by using a set of heuristics in the second stage [6]. Multiple assessors can participate in the walkthrough, but each evaluator should give each obstacle a unique rating. After that, the ratings are compared, and each task is assigned a single score.

(a) *Advantages*

- Detection of both serious and minor issues.
- It identifies issues that are both global and local in nature.
- Both user tasks and usability principles are utilised in this evaluation.
- Task knowledge assists evaluators in narrowing their focus to the most significant issues.
- Evaluators require little or no training. It is quick (and cost-effective, as there is no formal lab process).
- It is likely to aid in the determination of the tasks to be tested in formal tests.

(b) *Limitations*

- Evaluators with specialised knowledge may be required (product-dependent).
- There is a direct correlation between the number of problems that are discovered and the number of tasks chosen for the walkthrough.
- Some major problems may be overlooked if a critical task is not completed.
- If the set of heuristics used to find problems is different from time to time, the results could be off.

5.3.3 Model-Based Evaluations

By modelling how a person would interact with a software system, model-based evaluation simulates or calculates expected usability measures. In some cases, these projections may be used in place of or in addition to empirical data gathered from user testing. But that's not all: The model's content provides helpful information on the interactions between the system's durability design and the user's task. Before a prototype is produced or put to use on real people, it is evaluated using models to assess how usable it is.

The method integrates the interface design with a model of the human-computer interaction situation to produce expected interface usefulness metrics. Due to their applicability, these models are frequently referred to as "engineering models" or "analytical models". The model is founded on exhaustive task analysis and a clear explanation of the suggested design. It shows how users will interact with the suggested interface, and it uses parametric data and psychological theory to predict how easy it will be to use.

After the model is built, predictions about usability can be generated quickly and easily by using computation or simulation. Additionally, by appropriately altering the model, the consequences of design variants can be quickly evaluated. It is easy to swiftly complete a circuit around the revise/evaluate iterative design loop following the first investment in model creation because the majority of changes are modest. Iterations, as opposed to user testing, grow quicker and simpler as the design gets better. The model also gives an overview of the design, which can be used to figure out how it helps or hurts the user to finish their task.

Depending on the type of model, parts may be reused not just in subsequent iterations of the system under development but also in other systems. In addition to enhancing our scientific understanding of human-computer interaction, the characterization of such reusable model components captures a stable characteristic of human performance, task architectures, or interaction tactics. This section examines three innovative methods for simulating human behaviour that are particularly helpful for assessing the usability of interfaces and model-based systems. Models like task network models, cognitive architecture models, and GOMS models are included in this category.

5.3.3.1 Task Network Models

A network of processes that resembles a PERT chart serves as the task performance representation in task network models. Each process has an assumed completion time distribution that is specified in the protocol, and it begins after the previous ones have finished. By including arbitrary calculations to estimate completion time, as well as symbolic or numeric inputs and outputs, this fundamental paradigm can be further developed. Although the actions are frequently referred to as "tasks", robots can also carry them out.

A process may also be associated with other data, such as workload or resource parameters. By executing a Monte Carlo simulation of the model activity, where the triggering input events are either provided by random variables or by task circumstances, performance forecasts can be generated. This method makes it simple to produce a variety of statistical results, such as workload or resource utilisation aggregations. Two examples are the conventional SAINT and the for-profit MicroSaint tools [22–25]. These systems are made using systems engineering and applied human factors. They can be frequently used in system durability design, especially in the defence sector.

5.3.3.2 *Cognitive Architecture Models*

Byrne researched thinking or cognitive architecture systems. Each of these systems consists of a set of hypothetically interconnected perceptual, cognitive, and motor components whose properties are based on empirical and theoretical discoveries from psychological and related research and which are believed to exist in the human brain. A computer programme that constructs a virtual person performing in a virtual task environment and delivers inputs (stimuli) and responds to the virtual person's outputs is run in order to achieve this. This is done by having a fake person do a fake task (and give a fake answer) in a fake place.

Tasks are initially modelled by programming the cognitive component in accordance with a task analysis, and then by running the simulation using predetermined scenarios to produce the task's input events. This process provides performance estimates for the task. These systems are sincere attempts to represent a theory of human psychological processes, making them typically challenging and rarely used in practical design situations. Because of this, there haven't been many experiences using them in actual design situations.

5.3.3.3 *Goals, Operators, Methods, and Selection Models*

Objectives, operators, and techniques are all used in programming. The ground-breaking study established the Goals, Operators, Methods, and Selection (GOMS) models as well as the model-based assessment methodology as approaches for designing user interfaces. In a card format, the psychology of human-computer interaction is explained. The ideas of human skill acquisition and problem-solving were used to develop the GOMS concept. GOMS models consider the procedural knowledge that a system user needs to operate the system. Here is a brief explanation of the process and abbreviation:

The system makes it simple for the user to accomplish some goals (G). Operators perform the fundamental tasks of the system, such as pressing a key or finding an icon on the screen (O). Selection rules (S) define which strategy should be applied in which circumstance when there are several options to accomplish a goal. The terms "methods" and "selection rules" are used to describe which technique should be employed in which circumstance to accomplish a goal when more than one approach is available.

Writing down the strategies for achieving the task goals of interest is the first stage in creating a GOMS model. Next, projected usability metrics are calculated using the method representation. It is known as the method representation phase. Many unique forms of GOMS models have been systematised by [18–21]. In addition to other things, these models provide explanations of processes at different levels of depth, with computations ranging from straightforward calculations to comprehensive simulations. The findings demonstrate that the various forms are based on condensed cognitive architectures. As a result, the models are simple to utilise for typical interface design concerns and spare the model developer from having to consider numerous challenging theoretical issues.

More than any other model-based strategy, GOMS models have a long and well-established track record of efficacy in user interface design despite their simplicity and a record that validates their use. Although GOMS models are still in the early stages of academic study, they are covered in this chapter since in some versions they are a "ready to use" modelling methodology. The reader can find more information in [22–25].

(a) Advantages

- Produces a rigorous estimation of the usability criterion.
- It is possible to conduct operations on interface specifications.

(b) Disadvantages

- Only one component of usability is measured.
- Only a few tasks can be performed using this tool.

5.4 Usability Management Framework

To acquire a better understanding of the proposed established process for the usability management framework of durable software, it is critical to grasp each stage of the suggested established process. Keep in mind that the scope of the project is not meant to be limited in any manner. Changes to the system shown and different ways to use the development's ideas are things that a professional in the field this development belongs to would usually think about.

The preceding simple description and the following extended explanation are meant to be descriptive and informative of the process rather than limiting, as those knowledgeable about the art will recognise. An embodiment with a thorough description of the recommended technique is shown below, with appropriate reference to the picture. Figure 3 shows the whole suggested method, which is made up of three main processes and different smaller processes that work together in a unique way to make a software usability management framework with a perspective on durability.

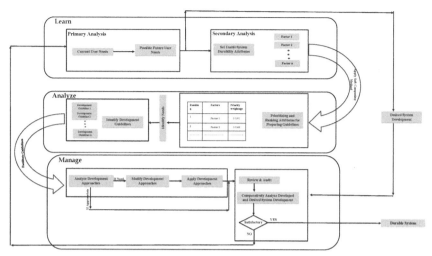

Figure 3: The proposed unique processes.

These three major and different smaller processes include fundamental components such as learning, analysing, and managing. The proposed snake model's method begins with learning. As the first small step in this big step model, analyse and write down what users want now. Then, as shown in Fig. 4, predict what users will want in the future so that the system can be used in a systematic and long-term way from the start.

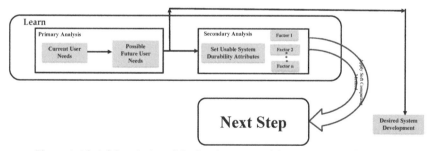

Figure 4: A brief description of the first learn step of the proposed snake model.

It's time to move on to the second minor stage of the model's anticipated main phase, which involves defining and establishing qualities of the necessary system that are crucial to its development and long-term usability. The suggested model also includes a step (shown in Fig. 5) that entails developing a desirable system development and functionality demonstration based on user requests, which will be used in succeeding phases once the needs of current and possible future users have been assessed. This is a one-of-a-kind form of treatment.

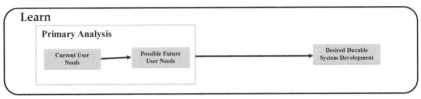

Figure 5: A descriptive demonstration of an additional step in the preparation of a copy of a desired system design.

Thereafter, in the model's second analysis phase, which comes after the successful collection of attributes in the model's first main phase, the approach uses a soft computing method to prioritise and rank those attributes (Fig. 6).

This makes items easier for durability designers to understand and use based on their ranking. This level also includes a unique rating idea that serves as a solid foundation for the system. In addition, based on

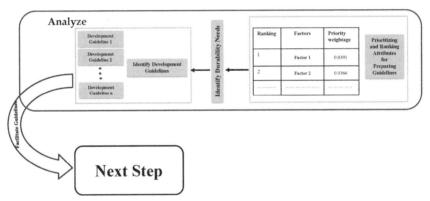

Figure 6: An idea of the second analysis step, in which the suggested model evaluates system requirements using soft computing techniques.

the evaluated features and their ratings for systemic compatibility in terms of durability and usability, the next step in this primary phase is to define durability demands. As shown in Fig. 6, the procedure generates or defines the guidelines for system development based on the outputs of the preceding processes after identifying the appropriate durability demands of evaluated attributers. So, once the guidelines have been made in the second phase of the model (shown in Fig. 6), the process moves on to the third and final phase (shown in Fig. 7) through a step called "apply guidelines".

During this step, these principles are included in the development process, and the first step of this phase is a durability and usability analysis of the recommendations that have been implemented. If the

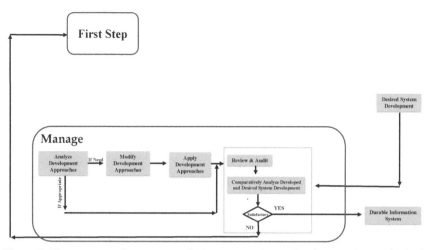

Figure 7: The processes of management for long-term software development in a methodical manner.

analysis results are satisfactory, the procedure will proceed to the final stage, which is the second minor step of the final phase. If, for example, an analysis report identifies a problem with the implementation of guidelines in development phases, a model directs the process to a phase where the development approach is changed, after which it applies the modified development technique. The second step of the final review and audit phase is to correlate specific, unique methods and comparison concepts with one another to promote better field development. It's crucial to compare the generated system and its functionality to the demo copy of the desired system and its functionality, created during the model's first phase and completed during the final phase. Figure 8 illustrates this.

This type of step allows for more dependable system management and provides the designer with the ideal technique for controlling durability and usability at the same time. There is now a decision-making step during the review and audit stage that asks if the review and audit find everything good and acceptable based on the currently built and intended comparison, allowing the model to generate durable software. If any aspect of the review and audit report is judged to be unsatisfactory, the model returns the process to the first phase. The recommended design model loop power is delivered by this type of cycle process.

5.5 Hierarchical Usability Model

When the degree to which software is quickly and comfortably accessible to various types of clients is assessed, it is referred to as usability. More than a dozen researchers [26–27] have looked into usability in various

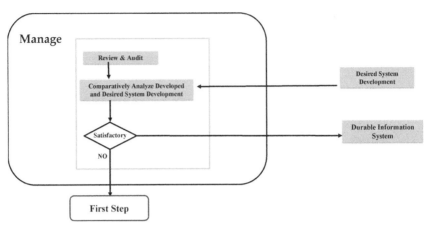

Figure 8: A brief description of the last step review and audit which incorporate comparison.

approaches. However, no single explanation can encompass all of the crucial aspects of software usability. Usability is determined by five factors, according to this study: efficiency, effectiveness, learnability, satisfaction, and productivity. We discovered three factors: efficiency, efficacy, and learnability. As numerous experts have pointed out, the outcomes of this study presented a full taxonomy of all principles, variables, and qualities that influence software system usability with respect to durability. Table 1 shows the taxonomy in further detail. The model is set up in a hierarchical way and takes a number of usability factors into account.

5.6 Conclusion

A vast number of primary studies on software usability were uncovered. This study looks at how existing software usability models and standards address some of the most common issues. The chapter outlines the most common approaches for assessing programme usability concerning durability. The review identifies several metrics for measuring usability. The study also reveals the stages during which software usability issues are most commonly solved. The study also considers how software usability difficulties might be applied in other fields. The following are some of the most important findings from selected primary studies:

- Different software usability models and standards often look at how efficient the software is and how easy it is to learn.
- The most common ways to measure how easy it is to use software are through usability testing, heuristic evaluation, and questionnaires.

Table 1: Taxonomy of model.

Factor	Sub-factor	Description
Efficiency	User effort	How readily will participants be able to complete the assignment once they have gained an understanding of the interface?
	Time-effective	
Effectiveness	Operability	When users return to the prototype after a period of time in which they have not used it, how quickly do they recover their skills?
	Scalability	
	Extensibility	
Learnability	User Interface	Individuals' ability to execute fundamental activities the first time they encounter an SRE technique is dependent on how straightforward the strategy is?
	Training	
	System structure	
Satisfaction	Convenience	How good is it to utilize the SRE approach?
	Likeability	
Productivity	Useful output	When it comes to implementing SRE in software development companies, how easy is it for software designers?
	Cost-effective	

- Usability-related issues are the most heavily weighted in the web-domain. Other fields where usability issues are being investigated include aviation, finance, industry and research, medical, mobile, and navigation maps.

Several research practitioners have yet to reach an agreement on software usability models with respect to durability. As a result, a non-redundant and uniform consolidated model for usability and durability is necessary. Such a software usability paradigm might be easily applied by software durability developers and designers without a background in durability engineering. According to the research practitioners, usability-durability-related concerns must be addressed at all stages of software development, including implementation. As a result, a uniform, well-defined framework is required to enable the integration of usability and durable software engineering. Methods for testing usability and durability can also be used to test smart gadgets, wearable devices, and systems that are built in.

Points to Remember

- Websites, software, devices, and applications are all examples of products or systems whose usability is determined by the quality of the user's interaction with them. The main goals of usability are to improve the user's effectiveness, efficiency, and general happiness.

- Effectiveness and learnability. There are now a lot of usability models and standards for software, and they often focus on how satisfied and effective users are.

- User-based assessment, inspection-based evaluation, and model-based evaluation are the most commonly used approaches for evaluating software usability. Furthermore, these software usability evaluation models incorporate three unique sub-assessment procedures.

- You can quickly detect the problems and issues in a user interface design by using heuristic evaluation in a cost-effective and straightforward approach. The evaluators employ usability principles or heuristics to help them through the implementation phase.

- The user interface is assessed by specialists using the Cognitive Walkthrough technique, who take into account the users' perspectives and experiences when evaluating the interface. It assists in determining what has to be done to resolve user interface issues.

- Task Network Models (before detailed design), Task Network Models (after detailed design), and Task Network Models (after detailed design) are the three types of model-based evaluations (after detailed design). Cognitive architecture models involve package restrictions, but GOMS models are simple and effective.

Review Questions

Objective Type Questions

1. .... is a model-based evaluation?
   a. Task Network model
   b. Cognitive planning model
   c. Usability task models
   d. None of the above

2. .... is not a Usability attribute?
   a. Learnability
   b. Efficiency
   c. Satisfaction
   d. Durability

3. Which one of these is the usability evaluation method:
   a. User based evaluation
   b. Inspection based evaluation
   c. Model based evaluation
   d. All of the above

4. Which one of these is the advantages of the heuristic walk through method of usability evaluation:
   a. Uncovers both major and minor problems
   b. Uncovers both global and local problems
   c. Relies on the use of both user tasks and usability principles
   d. All of the above
5. Usability is a problem that may be approached from a variety of perspectives, which is why many different fields are attempting to address it, including
   a. Psychology
   b. Computer Science
   c. Sociology
   d. All of the above

Short Answer Type Questions

1. Write advantages and disadvantages of Inspection based usability evaluation.
2. Define the cognitive walk through method of usability evaluation.
3. Define learnability, efficiency, and memorability in brief.
4. Design the first learn step of the proposed snake model.

Descriptive Questions

1. Design and explain in detail the usability management framework.
2. What are the characteristics of good usability testing?

References

1. Madhavji, N.H., Fernandez-Ramil, J. and Perry, D. 2006. Software Evolution and Feedback: Theory and Practice, John Wiley & Sons: Hoboken, NJ, USA.
2. Reussner, R., Goedicke, M., Hasselbring, W., Vogel-Heuser, B., Keim, J. and Märtin, L. 2019. Managed Software Evolution; Springer: Berlin/Heidelberg, Germany.
3. Sousa, B.L., Bigonha, M.A. and Ferreira, K.A. 2019. Analysis of coupling evolution on open source systems. In Proceedings of the XIII Brazilian Symposium on Software Components, Architectures, and Reuse, Salvador, Brazil, 23–27 September 2019; pp. 23–32.
4. Mens, T. and Demeyer, S. 2008. Software Evolution, 1st ed.; Springer: Berlin/Heidelberg, Germany.
5. Neamtiu, I., Xie, G. and Chen, J. 2013. Towards a better understanding of software evolution: An empirical study on open-source software. J. Softw. Evol. Process. 2013, 25: 193–218. [CrossRef]
6. Trenner, L. and Bawa, J. 1998. The Politics of Usability, Springer-Verlag, London.

7. ISO. 1998. Ergonomic Requirements for Office Work with Visual Display Terminals, ISO 9241-11, Geneva.
8. Good, M., Spine, T.M., Whiteside, J. and George, P. 1986. User-derived impact analysis as a tool for usability engineering. Proc. CHI Conf. Human Factors in Computing Systems, ACM Press, New York, pp. 241–246.
9. Hix, D. and Hartson, H.R. 1993. Developing User Interfaces: Ensuring Usability Through Product and Process, John Wiley & Sons, New York.
10. Ferré, X., Juristo, N., Windl, H. and Constantine, L. 2001. Usability Basics for Software Developers, IEEE Software.
11. ISO/IEC 9241. 1998. Ergonomic Requirements for Office Work with Visual Display Terminals (VDTs).
12. Abrahao, S. and Insfran, E. 2006. Early usability evaluation in model driven architecture environments. pp. 287–294. *In*: Proceedings of the Sixth International Conference on Quality Software. IEEE Computer Society, Washington DC.
13. Aquino, N., Vanderdonckt, J., Condori-Fernández, N., Dieste, Ó. and Pastor, Ó. 2010. Usability evaluation of multi-device/platform user interfaces generated by modeldriven engineering. *In*: Proceedings of the 2010 ACM-IEEE International Symposium on Empirical Software Engineering and Measurement, ESEM 2010, pp. 30:1–30:10. ACM, New York.
14. Fernandez, A., Insfran, E. and Abrahão, S. 2009. Integrating a usability model into modeldriven web development processes. pp. 497–510. *In*: Vossen, G., Long, D.D.E. and Yu, J.X. (eds.). WISE 2009. LNCS, vol. 5802. Springer, Heidelberg.
15. Gómez, J., Cachero, C. and Pastor, O. 2001. Conceptual modeling of device-independent web applications. IEEE MultiMedia, 8(2): 26–39.
16. Nielsen, J. and Molich, R. 1990. Heuristic evaluation of user interfaces. pp. 249–256. *In*: Proceedings of the SIGCHI Conference on Human Factors in Computing Systems: Empowering People, CHI 1990. ACM, New York.
17. Seffah, A., Donyaee, M., Kline, R.B. and Padda, H.K. 2006. Usability measurement and metrics: A consolidated model. Software Quality Control 14: 159–178.
18. Ammar, L.B. and Mahfoudhi, A. 2013. An Empirical Evaluation of a Usability Measurement Method in a Model Driven Framework A. Holzinger et al. (Eds.): SouthCHI 2013, LNCS 7946, pp. 157–173, Springer.
19. Song, L., Zhang, J. and Mukherjee, B. 2007. Dynamic provisioning with availability guarantee for differentiated services in survivable mesh networks. IEEE J. Sel. Areas Commun., 25: 35–43. [CrossRef]
20. Kieras, D.E. Model-based evaluation (in press). *In*: Jacko, J. and Sears, A. (Eds.). The Human-Computer Interaction Handbook (2nd Ed). Mahwah, New Jersey: Lawrence Erlbaum Associates.
21. Sagar, K. and Saha, A. 2017. A systematic review of software usability studies. Int. j. inf. Tecnol[Springer], DOI 10.1007/s41870-017-0048-1.
22. John, B.E. and Kieras, D.E. 1996a. Using GOMS for user interface design and evaluation: Which technique? ACM Transactions on Computer-Human Interaction, 3: 287–319.
23. Newell, A. 1990. Unified theories of cognition. Cambridge, MA: Harvard University Press.
24. Laughery, K.R. 1989. Micro SAINT - A tool for modeling human performance in systems. *In*: McMillan, G.R., Beevis, D., Salas, E., Strub, M.H., Sutton, R. and Van Breda, L. (Eds.). Applications of human performance models to system design. New York: Plenum Press. 219–230. See also the web site of Micro Analysis and Design, Inc., http://www.maad.com.
25. Madan, A. and Dubey, S.K. 2012. Usability Evaluation Methods: A Literature Review, International Journal of Engineering Science and Technology (IJEST).

26. Alhakami, H., Abdullah Baz, Wajdi Alhakami, Abhishek Kumar Pandey, Alka Agrawal and Raees Ahmad Khan. 2022. A usability management framework for securing healthcare information system. Computer Systems Science and Engineering, 42(3): 1015–1030.

27. Abushark, Y.B., Khan, A.I., Alsolami, F.J., Almalawi, A., Alam, M.M., Alka Agrawal, Rajeev Kumar and Raees Ahmad Khan. 2021. Usability Evaluation Through Fuzzy AHP-TOPSIS Approach: Security Requirement Perspective. CMC-Computers Materials & Continua, 68(1): 1203–1218.

Useful Links

https://en.wikipedia.org/wiki/Usability
https://www.usability.gov/what-and-why/usability-evaluation.html
https://www.usabilityhome.com/FramedLi.htm?CognWalk.htm
https://www.usabilitybok.org/heuristic-walkthrough.

CHAPTER 6

Integrating Security with Software Durability

6.1 Objectives

Security is a crucial quality feature in software engineering. The security of software should be assessed by using its security considerations. This can be done effectively with the help of security factors, models, and measurements. More so, estimating and implementing security should be an integral component of the mechanisms used to organise and produce excellent software. It should be noted that the quality of security factors can be improved during the design development process by examining damages, determining vulnerabilities, and identifying attacks. In this league, the present chapter enlists and describes the group's security and durability features that are easy to use. Durability is a security attribute that refers to software's ability to complete a task on time. Software security qualities, as well as longevity, have an impact on software security. In terms of software security, we conclude that researchers have yet to establish a consensus. For this, the objectives of the chapter that have been set forth are:

- Establishing the inevitability of engineering durable security for designing high quality software as Human trust, reliability, and trustworthiness are all regularly addressed aspects in the existing software security frameworks and standards, according to our findings.

- Enlisting the key attributes for effective evaluation of security-durability because the developers lack the information necessary to select the most effective security evaluation approach for a given area.

- Security-durability traits and security management frameworks are the most common ways to measure how long software will last. Hence, the researcher aims to explore the possibility of developing a common framework for the same.

6.2 Fundamental Principles

When it comes to managing security risks in the current world of big data, scholars and developers alike have a responsibility to do it effectively [1]. When it comes to security, risk management is the most important component. As observed by the experts, security is an afterthought rather than a primary concern throughout software development. The writers make a point of emphasising the importance of considering security at the very outset of the development process. As a result, it will be easier to create software that is self-protective and doesn't require a third-party application security package to keep it secure.

6.2.1 The Evolution of Security Concept

In the present scenario, dependency on software is so high that life cannot be imagined without it. However, with the overall benefits of software and its security design, there are also grave concerns. Fear of being insecure, fear of being hacked, or worse, fear of being traced or spied upon continues to haunt the users. Software security considerations during development thus emerge as a user-friendly solution. Software security is a branch of software engineering that aims at preventing security problems by building software without security holes [2–3]. G. McGraw says that software security is about making software that is secure [2]. This means designing software to be secure, making sure it is secure, and teaching software developers, architects, and users how to make secure software.

With the widespread use of, information systems in recent years, software security has emerged as a critical component of the software engineering process [3]. Software security is one of the most important aspects of the software development process, and it deserves the highest level of attention from engineers at all levels. Indeed, software faces danger from a wide range of possible hostile adversaries, with the number of these adversaries increasing daily. Some of these threats come from PC apps that can connect to the web, and others come from complicated media communications [4].

These dangers can present a significant challenge to software engineers when it comes to developing risk mitigation strategies as part of their risk management efforts, as well as developing the proper security standards and regulations. This is due to the degree of subjectivity in how security is viewed and the fact that varying levels of worry are expressed about different aspects of security. Moreover, a lot of software products are made without taking security issues like privacy, integrity, access control, and non-repudiation into account.

6.2.2 Security Analysis into Durability Concept

The primary goal of innovation development is to benefit mankind by contributing to societal upliftment and protecting the customers from harmful attacks. Paying close attention to the security of the software during each point of the development life cycle can result in higher reliability and enhanced user satisfaction [5]. In many cases, the security of software improves the overall quality of the software's capacity to meet business needs. As security experts point out, the process of identifying security aspects is carried out at the same time as that of security evaluation.

During the early stages of software development, practitioners must accord high priority to security. Although it is not always practicable, this is the case [6]. It is getting increasingly challenging for security developers to provide longer-term security throughout software development [7]. In addition, security considerations must be taken into account, which include security traits, classifications, and security measurements, among other things. At every stage of making software, security needs to be seen as an important tool that needs to be used.

Security attributes are an extremely important component of security engineering. When security traits are identified, they can be used to increase security during the software development process [8]. These characteristics position them to play an important role in the field of security. Furthermore, security features are added so that strong cryptographic arrangements can be made and so that a way can be found to set security requirements to improve security throughout the software development life cycle [9].

The ability of software to secure itself for the expected life-span

or

The ability of software to withstand attacks for the expected life-span

Software security affects the life of software [10]. This statement reaffirms the requirement for a security-related feature, namely, durability. Durability should be seen as a supporting quality of security in this regard. In terms of software, durability refers to the period throughout which the software performs its functions [11]. So, it seems like the focus has moved away from security towards making the software last longer.

Security is inextricably linked with the product's administration life, whether directly or indirectly. Durability is also a factor in software security, either explicitly or implicitly, and conversely [12]. This research aims to collate the theoretical and empirical facts about security durability through assessment. Most commercial software has some kind of obvious feature, which gives them an advantage in the market over security measures like confidentiality, integrity, availability (CIA), and other less obvious features [13].

6.2.3 Security and Durability Characteristics

This section has been deliberated in Chapter 2.

6.2.4 Systems, Software, Security and Durability

Security specialists are dealing several concerns from the outset of software development to comprehend the new security challenges. To improve financial performance, developers are constantly under pressure to maximise development while minimising security costs and time. The essence of progress is becoming increasingly muddled, and the need for security is expanding across the board. Evaluation and control of CIA during software development are significantly superior to the alternative techniques for generating more secure software [14]. Security must be built into software from the beginning of the development process, and it must be kept up until the software is used.

When security is consolidated in the face of better security, development costs and effort are reduced. It should not be disregarded or handled late in the software development process by security specialists once the software security development is complete. According to technical research conducted by a Software-as-a-Service (SaaS) operations and management company [15], more than 73% of firms anticipate shifting virtually all of their applications to SaaS by 2025 and optimising service lifecycle management. The New Data study came up with nearly identical results [16]. By the end of the current year, 59% of the cloud workflows will be delivered as SaaS, and companies will put a lot of money into software lifecycle management.

Veracode commenced operations in April 2018 [17] and tested their clients' software for a year. They scanned almost 400,000 numbers. They found 12.8 million errors in these scans. According to the report, stakeholders that used the antivirus software to analyse security improvements found at least one vulnerability during the initial scan and improved security services as a result [5–7]. Around one out of every eight people discovered a *high-or very high-severity vulnerability* related to long-term security services. The picture of software security becomes murkier and more dismal as a result of these examinations. According to the report, only 58% of vulnerabilities were patched in 2016 [18], the year they were reported. Moreover, the number of companies that passed vulnerability testing against the OWASP Top 10 list for software made in-house has dropped from 39% last year to 35% this year.

Third-party code, which contains additional vulnerabilities, fared even worse year over year, with only 23% passing the top 10 assessment, down from 25% the year before [12–15]. The data shows that businesses all across the world are avoiding danger and undertaking regular security tests [16]. There is, however, something missing. For the time being, secure software appears to be a dumb idea. Security, like safety and other software quality characteristics, is in high demand [17]. Developers are focusing on security and other quality attributes since customers' priorities have switched to security and other quality attributes. Businesses' concerns about software security are growing as more information about an organization's assets is processed through the software.

Organizations must recognise and handle the various types of security attributes that influence the security service life span directly or indirectly to assess and improve security [18]. Developing security could be improved by combining other quality attributes, such as CIA, into the current attributes. Furthermore, organisations must upgrade security to extend the life of software security [2]. It is not a straightforward way to achieve software security for a long length of time (duration). It consists of key exercises that engineers and analysts must complete. One of the most important things you can do to make security last longer is to improve it early on in the software development process [3–4].

The following research is carried out to achieve the study's aims, based on the prior discussion and even looking at the subject of security. It has been found that the total time spent on software maintenance is more than the time spent on development; for example, 80 percent of the time spent on development [5–6]. Why is software maintenance such a huge issue? Software and its security, unlike physical objects, exist exclusively in digital form, which means they are not subject to wear or decay. So, in theory, a piece of software or security could work without being changed for years.

In actuality, this is rarely the case. Software and its security are similar to biological creatures in that they must adapt to changes in their environment. Adaptive maintenance aids in the adaptation of security changes [7–8]. This is beneficial, but if companies spend more time maintaining software than developing it, security concerns will shift from development to maintenance. As a result, there is a need to be concerned about this issue and strategies to deploy software with security that does not require more maintenance time or money [9–10]. The cost and time spent on maintenance are reduced when this problem is addressed.

6.3 Previous Models/Frameworks

A programme that can be accessed via a web browser over a network, such as the Internet or an intranet, is known as software. Software applications have become increasingly popular as a result of the broad use of the browser as a client. The ability to install and administer mobile apps without deploying and configuring software on potentially thousands of client PCs is one of the key reasons for their attractiveness [3–6]. Software applications are used to power e-commerce, online banking, email, enterprise apps, and a wide range of other programs.

Today, software security is the most underappreciated aspect of enterprise security, and it should be a top priority for any company. Checkout processes, multimedia content, login pages, forms, and other software applications are increasingly being targeted by hackers. Insecure internet apps that can be used from anywhere on the globe provide hackers with easy access to back-end company records and allow them to conduct illicit activities on the websites they target. Developers must adhere to the highest performance and security standards to create high-quality applications. Designing security while working is the most straightforward technique to achieve application quality.

To tackle these issues, durability is used as a security attribute. Using an innovative approach, security risks are identified from a durability perspective, resulting in not just high evaluations but also a minimal supportability process for long-term security and reliability. This study assesses the present barriers that projects to relate durability research to safeguarding are facing, and it makes recommendations for how to proceed in terms of security going forward. Several studies in this field focus on long-term effects, especially the idea of long-term security, as well as problems with modelling long-term effects and security in general.

Further, researchers have found from the literature review of security durability that although there has been a little research work where security and durability have been addressed separately, there has been no significant study that highlights the researcher's perspective of security and durability simultaneously. This presents the critical need for research on these two contrasting factors. Security and durability have been addressed independently by various foreign researchers in different fields. Some of the available literature has been cited below:

Alfakeeh, A. S. et al., [4]
The authors have devised a method for assessing the usability and security of both internal and external e-banking assets. It has been shown that the existing security-usability models are insufficient. The authors suggested their framework to analyse five large banks. The findings of the said research clearly show that banks have many security and privacy flaws.

Kumar, R. et al., [5]

The author discussed the security and durability of the phase change memory (PCM) allocation method. According to the findings of this study, a well-designed PCM must address both security and durability concerns at the same time. Pre-design security durability analysis of PCM can protect it from malicious attacks and unexpected threats. The research outlines an innovative technique for security refresh to increase durability and maintain security. In addition, it used the Security Refresh technique to analyse the wear-out distribution. As a result, the data placement will be more uniform and, therefore, last longer.

Attaallah, A. et al., [6]

The authors looked at the relationship between software and durability. In software development, four characteristics are most important: trustworthiness, human trust, dependability, and software usability. To address these attributes, software engineers examine the precise application serviceability criteria that must be met to meet these durability requirements. With this research, they sought to explore the interplay between application and durability features.

Attaallah, A. et al., [8]

Version 1 and version 2 of two domestically created application systems were evaluated for security durability. The mixed fuzzy analytic hierarchy process (AHP) decision approach was used by the authors to examine the durability of security. It has been determined that security durability has a significant impact on the other aspects of a product. The researchers' findings include a security durability assessment. They suggested that developers should look into the security life cycle of software applications and make changes based on what they find.

Alenezi, M. et al., [9]

The authors argued that accepting partial compliance with security requirements while it is allowed is preferable to ignoring or deferring compliance in the near future. They devised a goal-based methodology that allowed them to prioritise and partially allocate security criteria in accordance with security objectives. The solution they devised minimises the number of unmet security criteria, which in turn reduces the negative consequences of failing to meet security requirements in applications.

Kumar, R. et al., [11]

The authors proposed a methodology that can help the programmers to create secure software that doesn't require external security measures. Because of this, it is essential to take security threats into account when developing software. To measure the risks associated with expanding software security durability, the researchers used a hybrid Fuzzy AHP methodology. Furthermore, software durability was used to assess the e-component of security risk. Their discoveries could help improve the security and long-term viability of software.

In this row, software engineers should focus on security and durability concurrently throughout software creation to extend the life span of security as well as software. An extended security life cycle was also advocated for by Parker D. B. in 1992 [12] to increase user satisfaction with data security. It's not uncommon for practitioners to focus on long-term security design due to the high expense of security upkeep. IBM's OS/360 operating system was developed over four years and cost the business more than half a billion dollars, according to Nathan Ensmenger, who worked on the project in the early 1960s [19]. This was IBM's largest single investment ever.

To address these issues, it is critical to consider security durability throughout programme development. It is critical to use quantitative tools for tackling, assessing, and resolving problems. One of the most important aspects of software development is the consideration of security. Numerous factors influence both security and durability, including the CIA. Security and software design approaches and logic differ from organisation to organisation.

Although various authors have done extensive studies to improve application quality in the context of long-term security, there is a lack of an adequate method that is expressly built to provide long-term security. As a result, this work proposes new security-durability blueprints for developing reliable and high-quality applications. Early on in the process of making software, the suggested Security Durability Blueprints make sure that security features will last.

6.4 Challenges for Security-Durability Modeling

As the twenty-first century dawned, software development posed new difficulties for everyone, including security [1–3]. Development techniques show that the security of software is still not as resilient as it should be. Software development organisations invest a comparatively large amount of money and energy in correcting security concerns throughout the late stages of software development. They do not care about the durability of the security assets or features. The durability of software is one of the concerns that has gained a lot of attention in recent years.

Durable security is defined as the longevity or timeliness of security for a given time. Without ensuring the durability of security at the time of software development, the software may start failing after deployment (immediately or after some time) [4–6]. Durability can influence the security expiration time. Software security with low durability is likely to fail in a fiercely competitive environment. So, companies that make software are paying more attention to making sure that secure software will last.

From the above discussion, it can be seen that the instrumental role of durability in the development of secure software can't and mustn't be ignored [7–9]. Today, enterprises increasingly need secure software within expected durability that can support business-critical activities across departments, business units, and world regions. Software security is not built; it is developed phase-by-phase. It requires the consistent application of methodologies that include security attribute identification and application, vulnerability removal, trustworthiness, and dependability. Overall, the goal is to make secure software and retain the trust of the customer or user.

A literature survey in this area has revealed that the identification of security attributes is quite an effective way to maintain the trustworthy and secure design of the software. The literature survey also adds a new security attribute, i.e., durability. The durability of a security solution depends primarily on its architecture or design and on how the security has been designed and engineered. The equation is simple: the more durable security software will provide a greater service life than an unsecured system. Software now has private, valuable information like a company's important databases or a user's personal information.

The number of individuals who need access to software applications has increased noticeably [10]. Unsecure software makes it more vulnerable to attacks and provides a way to enter the system. Identification of security attributes may help to reveal vulnerabilities and mitigate security risks at the early stage of software development [11–13]. Durability is a significant attribute of security; without its consideration, security cannot be improved. Many attributes of durability affect the security of software. Among all of them, dependability, human trust, and trustworthiness are considered sub-attributes of durability. Figure 1 shows how the relationship between security attributes and security challenges affects security while making software that will last.

It makes designing security more challenging during secure software development. To find solutions to these challenges, it is important to maintain durability at the development level for a longer working life of secure software. Several experts now offer decision support systems to address security risks in security design. This method could also help improve security in the future by making it easier to find and deal with new security risks.

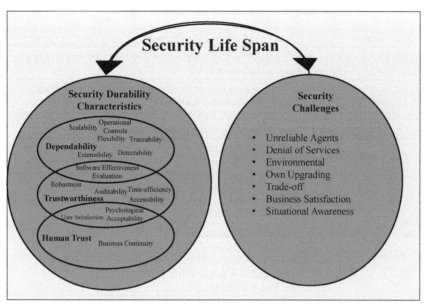

Figure 1: Durability with Respect to Security.

6.4.1 Types of Information Loss

Identifying the most potent security threat is one of the most challenging components of cognitive impact assessments for long-term security. The increase in qualitative qualities and the difficulties in interpreting them make this more complex. There are benefits and drawbacks to any security threat in terms of technology, economics, the environment, and other factors; these factors collectively define a set of boundaries. A comparative investigation is necessary to reach a corroborative solution that would be both scientifically valid and adequately supported. Multi Criteria Decision Making (MCDM) is an advanced way to make decisions that consider both objective and subjective factors [14–15].

In recent years, several MCDM approaches and technologies have been put forth in an effort to find the optimal answers. Given that there are just too many factors to take into account, evaluating the effectiveness of development services is challenging. Since each provider, client, and payer uses their standards to gauge effectiveness, there are no standard performance measures for this sector of the economy. The main criteria were created by utilising in-depth literature reviews and professional opinions. The institutes that were found to make specific recommendations for the

Table 1: Various Information Loss (IL) Types.

Alternatives	Description
Collective loss (S1)	The simultaneous loss of confidentiality, integrity, and availability is referred to as a "collective loss".
Confidentiality loss (S2)	It is deemed a violation of confidentiality when a user's sensitive data or information is shared with a third party without the user's knowledge or agreement. Individuals may suffer financial harm even if most breaches of confidence are unintentional.
Integrity loss (S3)	Data or an information system has been altered or deleted by unauthorised personnel, resulting in the loss of integrity. A change in the system's settings or the record could be the cause. When a file is infected with malware, for example, the integrity of the file is jeopardised. In the same way, an email's integrity is put at risk if its content changes while it is being sent.
Availability loss (S4)	Data and system availability ensure that they are available when needed. "Loss of availability" occurs when data or a service is unavailable when a user seeks it. For example, if a web server becomes unavailable when a visitor tries to make a payment, the server is no longer available.

choice of various security threat assessment criteria were also found to do the same for the choice of various security risk assessment criteria [16–17]. The various types of data loss that might occur when security is a concern are shown in Table 1 [10].

6.4.2 Security Challenges: Durability Perspective

The primary purpose of technological advancement is to benefit humanity in terms of social advancement and software engineering security. At each point of the software development life cycle, paying attention to the product's security can promote both, the users' satisfaction and better reliability. The security of software improves its quality to satisfy business requirements. According to a study conducted by security professionals, the identification of security variables is performed during security evaluation [4–6]. Researchers and developers must prioritise security at the early stages of software development, despite the fact that absolute security is not achievable. The development of secure software has grown increasingly complex for programmers. It requires delicate security measures, including security measurements, classifications, and security features.

At every step of software development, security attributes must be seen as an essential instrument. Security engineering recognises security qualities as a crucial environment. Identification of security attributes

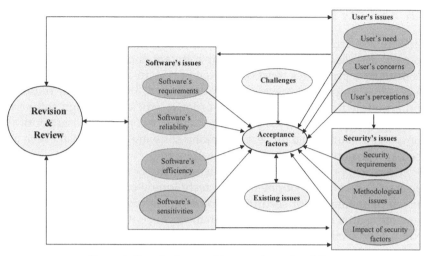

Figure 2: Security Issues with respective to Durability.

enhances software development security. These characteristics prepare them for a crucial role in the field of security. Not only are security attributes required to produce robust cryptographic solutions, but they must also discover a means to supply secure design needs. Software security is affected by the duration of a program's useful life. This phenomenon emphasises the notion that there must be a characteristic linking durability and security. Durability should be regarded as a security attribute in this situation. Durability, as it pertains to software, is the length of time till which the software provides services. It appears that the emphasis has shifted from software security to software durability. Secure software is stable and durable. Further, Fig. 2 shows the security issues and challenges with respect to durability.

This research is dedicated to completing theoretical information for security with respect to durability. Commercial products typically have a set of visible features, which give them a market advantage over harder-to-measure security such as CIA and similar less desirable attributes. The primary purpose of this contribution is to reduce the amount of effort required to manage security by leveraging durability. Research on durable security shows that security needs optimal maintenance. It is evident that to be durable, software must be maintainable. Hence, durability must be considered as one of the parameters of perfect and secure software. Based on what has been said so far, making secure software last longer will be a new problem for the software industry.

6.5 Security Durability Risks at the Design Phase

Security is a crucial aspect of the software development process. In this context, assessing the security risk of software is critical. To reduce the security risk, properties must be evaluated [15]. In addition, security risk management operations are revised, developed, implemented, tracked, and scheduled on a regular basis in order to efficiently design software security. Software security risk management must be regarded as a critical component. During the process of making software, security isn't seen as the key locus but it is more like an afterthought.

Researchers must guarantee that security is considered from the onset of software development. This technique would aid in the design and implementation of security measures in software that is capable of combating attacks on its own, rather than relying entirely on the product's external protection. Furthermore, the security risk variable is measured in terms of software security-durability and vice-versa. As a result, the findings of our research will be valuable in increasing the long-term stability of a variety of software programmes.

6.5.1 Risk Scenario of Durable Software

Cybercriminals can now access a huge array of customer data via the industry's digitization as a whole to extort or sell to clients. Hence, it is important to introduce the basic risk plots and attack conditions to have a better understanding of the underlying problems that need to be addressed for achieving the desired level of durable security of software. It would be easier to find appropriate answers if we knew everything about how attacks are now taking place.

The attack ratio of penetrators and hacking occurrences in organisations is predicted to climb by 25% by 2020, according to the analysis [10]. In 2020, according to another study on attack source classification for businesses, there would be 642 data breaches, with hacking and vulnerability exploitation in software application platforms accounting for 66.82 percent of breaches [10]. Figure 3 depicts how incidents and their causes can be explained simply and understandably.

Vulnerability exploitation is the biggest cause of security breaches and issues in enterprises, according to the data above. The importance of a standardised mechanism or technique for controlling the security of digital platforms is highlighted in this visual representation of 2020 statistics. According to a survey of business cyber security concerns [10], 125 billion dollars will be spent on security services and hardware by 2025. This massive investment forecast highlights commercial and security concerns in the region. As a result, the importance and demand for digital

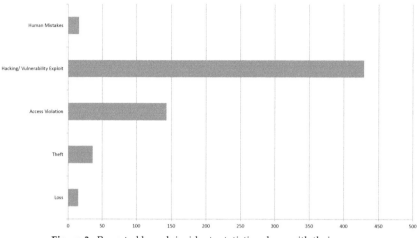

Figure 3: Reported breach incidents statistics along with their source.

platform security management cannot be overstated. During the design phase, this can be done more fully.

To address this problem, the work employs a basic and practical tactic that may be tweaked by researchers to increase the software's security and durability; similar issues have been discussed in the following sections. Because risk management involves specialised knowledge, the design manager is not always the best person to undertake a risk assessment. A thorough understanding of the economic repercussions, including legislation and regulation, as well as the software-supported business model, is required for a full risk assessment. At a decent level, risk and protection experts aid software designers and developers in putting their ideas about what is best for their systems and how to defend them against threats to the test.

Successful risk analysis methodologies offer a variety of benefits and drawbacks, but when it comes to advanced software design, they all share similar strengths and weaknesses. This is the capacity to apply traditional risk principles to application design and then create special mitigation variables that set a large-scale risk assessment apart from a typical software assessment. A tricky method for flexible risk analysis would be fully built into the process of making software.

Software security threat management has become a key duty. Software security is critical in the twenty-first century for anything from basic education to foundational engineering [12]. Because customers place such a high value on software development, software applications must be extremely secure. Figure 4 shows how a software development project will handle security risk management.

Figure 4: Security Risk Management Process.

Software development process designers should fully comprehend the source of the security concerns in question, as they have a significant impact on time and costs. Early recognition of security concerns and their root causes can assist programmers in putting in place the appropriate safeguards and measures to combat these risks. Looking at security concerns in software through computers has been discovered to be a wonderful technique to improve software security in the long term.

6.5.2 Security Risks Identification at Design-level

Around the world, technology is now used by the majority of service providers. Its application in virtually every area has grown significantly. This emphasises how crucial it is to find solutions to security issues because compromised security could endanger human lives. Gary McGraw asserts that no programme can be protected after it has been created; security must be evaluated during the creation process [2]. This approach may make it simpler to create apps that actively combat attack vectors rather than depend on software protection (like antivirus) [3–5]. Defects found in the finished product are the main cause of the high rate of security breaches. These difficulties can be lessened with the early identification and correction of these inconsistencies. In general, the design process aims to stop mistakes from being put into practise [6].

Therefore, design-stage security vulnerabilities in the software development life cycle must be addressed in order to reduce the frequency of security breaches. By identifying the safety problems that can be fixed in the initial stage, the application can be made safer by "installing" protection. The majority of experts now emphasise the need to address safety concerns early in the life cycle of software development. Current security issues in app development can be resolved with the help of effective vulnerability detection and patching. According to Kumar et al. [14], security concerns should be taken into account at every stage of the development life cycle. The authors have also suggested that the requirements and design processes be made better so that the focus can be moved to the early stages of development.

Baker et al. have called attention to the lack of a trustworthy method for figuring out how effective the security measures are. Instead of a lack of security approaches, what prevents the development of secure software is a lack of the essential tools to assess how secure software is [15–16]. M. Alenezi et al. [9] have explored the notion of incorporating security into the development process. The authors also assert that the only approach to support the creation of secure software is to alter the development life cycle. According to S. Alfakeeh et al. [10], risk management practises should be incorporated early in the software development process. The researchers believe that late risk management in itself poses to be a potential problem because late detection of vulnerabilities not only incurs extra time and costs in resolving the issues during the design phase, but also hampers the overall efficacy of the end product. The study insists on taking well-timed action and working out the best ways to deal with risks and weaknesses.

6.5.3 Need for Identification

It is commonly acknowledged that two essential elements of security are the employment of appropriate countermeasures and effective risk management [16–18]. The function of risk assessment in the risk management process is widely understood. The risk assessment process is divided into numerous steps, including the identification of hazards; evaluation of vulnerabilities; detection and mitigation of threats; creation of a corrective action plan; and review and monitoring. Because identifying the risks is the initial step, defining the risks becomes essential. The main goal of risk assessments is to figure out how much security a system needs by rating risks based on how bad they are for the system as a whole.

It helps to prevent potential latencies that could endanger the system's security by identifying various security issues during the software design phase. When the design is geared toward quantifying security risk, it will help to reduce the cost and time spent on software security implementation. It was found that finding and fixing issues after manufacturing is 100 times more important than doing so at the design stage [17]. Because of this, the security issues need to be fixed as soon as possible during the software development process.

6.5.4 Major Security Risks in the Design Phase

Based on the security concerns that are posited, the researchers chose the significant dangers. Confidentiality, access control, authentication, integrity, and other security considerations have become requirements for secure software development [19]. In the current environment, where everyone is concerned about the security of their personal data, it is the responsibility of software developers to successfully handle these concerns and ensure that their products meet the expectations of their consumers. Because of this, the authors of this work used the Common Weaknesses Enumeration (CWE) list to filter the security risks that could enter software throughout the design phase. To facilitate the creation of secure software, the CWE community has created a list of every potential software flaw. It is a security tool since it establishes a standard for identifying and resolving software issues. Table 2 [3] displays the main design-level security issues that the researchers found, along with the security variables and how the risks are defined.

6.5.5 Relation between Security Risk and Security Characteristics

When a danger exploits a vulnerability, risks refer to the potential for loss or damage [3]. The dangers that jeopardise the software's security are classified as "security hazards". The authors explain why the detected hazards are referred to as "security risks", and the relationship between the identified security risks and their corresponding security elements is shown below:

- Access to Critical Private Variable via Public Method (ACPVPM): It is possible for any public method to gain access to any critical attribute (variable) that has been marked as "private". This may occur if appropriate access control mechanisms weren't utilised at any point throughout the design process. As a direct consequence of this, there is a chance that the assumptions made in various other sections of the code will not be honoured. In addition, sensitive information may be divulged if an attacker is successful in gaining access to any private variables. As a direct consequence of this, the security of the code has been breached.

- Password in Configuration File (PCF): Developers use configuration files to alter settings without recompilation, while administrators use configuration files to specify policies for multiple programmes operating on a computer system. The software should not save any form of password in the configuration files, according to the designer. This could result in a security compromise if a non-legitimate user obtains the password, compromising authentication. This vulnerability also puts access control at risk if the attacker changes the password.

- Critical Variable Declared Public (CVDP): The disclosure of any crucial parameter or field that must be treated as private in accordance with security standards constitutes a security risk (for example, a password). When a non-authorized user reads information linked

Table 2: Selected Security Factor and Security Risks.

S. No.	Security Risk at Design Phase	Description	Related Security Attribute
1.	Access to Critical Private Variable via Public Method (ACPVPM)	Defining a public method that has the ability to read or alter a private variable is the responsibility of the software.	Access Control; Integrity
2.	Password in Configuration File (PCF)	Because the password is saved in the configuration file, it is vulnerable to being misused by anyone who has access to the file.	Authentication; Access Control
3.	Critical Variable Declared Public (CVDP)	Whenever a vital variable or field is defined as public, even when the intended security policy requires it to be private, the security policy fails.	Confidentiality; Integrity
4.	Unverified Password Change (UPC)	In the process of creating a new password for a user, no authentication mechanism is utilised.	Authentication; Access Control
5.	Race Condition within a Thread (RCT)	If more than one resource is being utilised at the same time, there is the chance that resources will be accessed when they are invalid, resulting in the execution state becoming undefined.	Integrity
6.	Untrusted Search Path(USP)	For crucial resources, an externally supplied search path is being used, which has the potential to point to resources that are not under the direct control of the programme.	Confidentiality; Integrity; Availability; Access control
7.	Download of Code Without Integrity Check (DCIC)	An executable source code is downloaded from any remote location without any verification of the code's origin or integrity.	Integrity; Confidentiality
8.	Concurrent Execution using Shared Resource with Improper Synchronization ('Race Condition') (RC)	A code sequence needs temporary exclusive access to a shared resource when it can run concurrently with other code. There is a temporal window, though, in which another code sequence that is simultaneously active at the same time may update the shared resource.	Integrity; Confidentiality
9.	External Initialization of Trusted Variables or Data Stores (EITV)	Using inputs that can be manipulated by suspicious actors, the software initializes crucial internal variables or data stores.	Integrity
10.	Improperly Controlled Modification of Dynamically-Determined Object Attributes (ICMD)	Vulnerability can occur if an object contains properties that were solely meant for internal usage, and their unexpected modification results in a vulnerability.	Integrity

to this kind of attribute, it could endanger both confidentiality and integrity if the attacker goes on to change the information.

- Unverified Password Change (UPC): Authentication and access control may be jeopardised if passwords are changed without verification. If the software does not ask for a previous password or any other sort of authentication while setting a new password, authentication is thought to have been neglected. As a result of the failure to evaluate the authentication factor, an access control vulnerability exists. If a non-legitimate user changes the password, it may prevent the genuine user from accessing the information. While the software should double-check the modified password, it should also verify whether the password is being changed by an authorised user.

- Race Condition within a Thread (RCT): When two or more threads attempt to access and change a shared memory location at the same time, this condition is said to occur. If any current value is changed by another piece of code at the same time, it may compromise the application's integrity. This type of risk is thought to have a 'locking' mitigation scheme. A good locking mechanism should help by preventing the use of the same shared memory location at the same time. The use of flags or signals may also be beneficial in this situation.

- Untrusted Search Path (USP): When the application allows access to essential sources by any externally specified search path, this type of vulnerability can arise. For example, if any search URL contains the primary key (such as User ID), simply changing it allows the user to view another user's profile without their permission. If the attacker tries to change the content, the system's integrity may be jeopardised. The application's availability is jeopardised if the attacker directs it to incorrect files or forces it to crash or hang. When a query's result is directed at a non-legitimate user, confidentiality is said to be compromised. As a result, this risk directly jeopardises the software's confidentiality, availability, access control, and integrity.

- The download of Code without Integrity Check (DCIC): the software may permit code to be downloaded from any remote address without verifying the source's legitimacy. The developers are under pressure to reduce the time-to-market phase for the end product. This increases the likelihood of software updates via mobile code. As a result, it should be the first condition to check the source's validity. The failure to verify the source's legitimacy may jeopardise the application's confidentiality and integrity. Integrity is jeopardised if the malicious code downloaded from an unknown source alters the software's operation, and confidentiality is jeopardised if important information is disclosed.

- Concurrent Execution using Shared Resource with Improper Synchronization ('Race Condition') (RC): The 'Race Condition' is said to occur when a piece of code in an application can run concurrently with another code section. It should be carefully enforced that no two processes can share the same memory address unless all of them only need to read the data from that location and none of them need to update it. When shared code involves access to a critical resource, there is a security risk due to a race condition. In such a circumstance, the intruder may get access to or overwrite key data, jeopardising the data source's integrity and confidentiality.

- External Initialization of Trusted Variables or Data Stores (EITV): The developers need to be very aware of the fact that if a variable is set from outside the program, it may be set incorrectly, which could make the software less secure. The unexpected initialization may lead to an abrupt response from the software. Similarly, the blind input to the data stores may also introduce flaws. So, it's secure to say that this security risk is a direct threat to the software system's integrity.

- Improperly Controlled Modification of Dynamically-Determined Object Attributes (ICMD): The inputs to any object's attributes may be governed by an upstream component. This situation could lead to serious security flaws like mass-assignment, object-injection, and so on. Two ways to deal with this type of risk are to separate the accessible and protected attributes of an object, or to add an authentication code to the deserialized data when it is stored.

The classic adage "prevention is better than cure" effectively defines the core topic under discussion. If security issues are addressed while they are still in the early stages, it will substantially aid in the reduction of security violations. It is critical to prioritise a proactive approach for creating secure software. If any flaws are discovered early on, it will lead to stronger and safer software.

6.6 Managing Software Security Risk: Durability Perspective

When it came to boosting the application's security, the software development team is faced with several challenges. Software companies are constantly on the lookout for a viable software security solution. Scientists and developers adjust their strategies in these circumstances to ensure that the device's security is maintained. Risk is a challenge that has the potential to derail well-defined plans with specific goals [1–3]. Risk management is used to reduce the risk while also enhancing efficiency by preserving the software product. The risk management security strategy is a theoretical framework for monitoring the risk mitigation security program's progress. Risk, control, and security management are all interconnected methods embedded into the protective design for secure software manufacturing. Throughout the software development process, risk management technology helps with risk reduction activities [4–6].

The best risk management protection system also includes several other concepts with distinct qualities. Risk management for security has been the subject of a significant study [7–8]. Software security risk management and compliance are essential for dealing with a wide range of security threats. All systems must be updated to attain better results. Threats are established and decreased throughout the life cycle of a software product, which is beneficial for managing strategic risk. Depending on the policy and supervision involved in the security evaluation, the emphasis on risk management and control systems varies. It's not only the results of criteria like costs and plans, even though they're important aspects of safety risk management.

This point of view had not previously been explored, but the concept of integrated protection is vital to implement right now. Risk identification and security management systems are two techniques for security performance evaluation that are better and simpler. Integrated risk assessment uses both rules and procedures to provide realistic protection. Computer security is crucial in the twenty-first century for everything from primary education to intrinsic engineering [9–10]. Software must be very secure everywhere because it seems like more and more people are using and depending on it.

We've been working to improve application security over time to increase transparency and assess how and to what extent technological and system developments make our apps safer. "Design compromise" has been identified as one of the most critical security vulnerabilities in the majority of cases. Engineers strive to minimise "time-to-market" by speeding up the design process and ensuring that protection is not built into a gadget but rather squeezed in from the outside. As a result, security must be taken into account early in the software development process. According to Gary McGraw [2], the three pillars of application security are risk management systems, contact points, and expertise. As a result, if one wishes to improve security, risk management is one of the most critical areas to focus on. If a danger weakens vulnerability, the risk is defined as the chance of failure or injury. Without good frameworks, the development team has to rely on its knowledge and experience to handle risks.

6.6.1 Development Risk

Risk management includes the creation, analysis, planning, implementation, control, and monitoring of applied procedures and security requirements. It is the process of establishing and maintaining adequate management controls, including policies, procedures, and practises, to minimise risk to a bare minimum. Risk management principles can be used to both mitigate undesirable outcomes and achieve desired outcomes. Risk management is the process of making sure that an organization's information and knowledge assets are secure from threats like unauthorised access, use, disclosure, disruption, change, perusal, inspection, recording, or destruction.

The practise of managing the risk associated with information assets is referred to as "Information Risk Management". Furthermore, information risk management employs the general risk management methodology to ensure the integrity, availability, and confidentiality of information assets and the information environment. Every company's day-to-day operational decisions should include information risk management. Information risk management includes the usual processes of analysis, assessment, audit, monitoring, and management.

Secure software increases the vulnerability of software to external attacks and gives a way into the system. Identification of security traits could aid in the early detection of vulnerabilities and mitigate security risks in the development life cycle [11]. Keeping software secure is a never-ending process. Software security elements must be built at every stage of development. Developing and designing secure software is a difficult task. While developing software, security factors are recognised and integrated. As a result, security variables have an impact on both the security and the quality of software. Durability also refers to the guarantee that security will continue and be durable after the software has been notified of success. When the intended security is back, it will be hard to tell how long the software will last, so it will be recycled until there is no reason to manage it anymore.

6.6.2 Development Environment

The early twenty-first-century software development environment has posed significant obstacles for everyone, including the developers. On one hand, the exponential increase in catastrophic software security attacks has forced the requirement for security to be built in from the start, while on the other hand, a large investment in software has posed the demand for long-lasting software to justify returns on the investment that was made [12–15]. Because of this, both software security and software durability have become important factors in making new software. The lifespan of software security might be defined as durable security. From a security point of view, software development includes security traits, a security strategy, security design, security testing, and security management.

Previous practises have revealed that software security is not as high as it could be. The reason for this is that, in addition to the growing demand for secure software, developers are confronted with new obstacles in meeting the needs of consumers while designing software. Furthermore, organisations impose development limits owing to cost, time-to-market needs, productivity implications, and customer satisfaction concerns, among other factors. Because of this, software that wasn't made well has a low level of security in the long run.

6.6.3 Program Constraints

Software connects almost every aspect of life, including medical, engineering, social, and other fields [16]. All software-related data must be kept secure. As a result, today's demand for secure software has skyrocketed. Software security is the concept of protecting software from hostile attacks and fraudulent people or hackers. Many experts have explored various aspects of security, such as security qualities, security administration, and security maintenance, yet something remains unsolved. Development organisations invest money and effort towards improving security maintenance to extend the life of software, but they have yet to achieve success.

6.6.4 Governance, Management, and Compliance

Businesses need a technique for identifying and managing important internal activities as they get more complex [7]. It is also necessary to have the ability to combine conventionally distinct management tasks into a single discipline that enhances the effectiveness of staff, operational procedures, technology, physical assets, and other crucial business elements. Governance, management, and compliance (GRC) achieve this by reducing traditional barriers between business units and requiring them to work together to achieve the organization's strategic goals. GRC was one of the elements of a well-managed organisation in the 2020s. [7] GRC, which stands for "governance, risk, and compliance", is an organization's plan for dealing with how the following three things affect each other:

- Corporate governance policies
- Enterprise risk management programs
- Regulatory and company compliance

Companies realised that coordinating the pool of people, procedures, and technologies that they employ to manage governance, risk, and compliance might benefit them in two ways; hence, GRC arose as a discipline in the early twenty-first century. A synthesised strategy would assist them in ensuring that their companies performed ethically. It would also assist the businesses in achieving their objectives by minimising the inefficiencies, misunderstandings, and other risks associated with a segmented approach to governance, risk, and compliance. GRC may be used by any sized company. In large organisations with complex governance, risk management, and compliance obligations, and where programmes to meet these needs frequently overlap, developing a GRC discipline is extremely crucial. The three GRC components are also defined as follows:

- Governance: Governance refers to how an organization's leaders administer it ethically and in accordance with approved business goals and strategies.
- Risk Management: Risk management is the process through which an organisation identifies, categorises, assesses, and implements strategies to reduce risks that would obstruct operations and control risks that would improve operations.
- Compliance: The level of adherence an organisation has to the rules, regulations, and best practises demanded by their business as well as related regulating bodies and laws is referred to as compliance.

Traditionally, these three activities were carried out in a more or less independent manner. Each of the three programmes continues to operate with and assist the other business activities in a GRC approach, but the benefits become apparent when the three programmes are combined.

6.7 Security Durability Blueprints

Cybersecurity has gone from being a pleasant feature to being a top priority for all kinds of enterprises. Despite organisations' best attempts to improve their defences, malicious actors still hack data and systems daily. A sound security strategy can assist organisations in fortifying their defences, achieving their objectives, and assisting clients in navigating the increasingly complicated security and technological landscape. The design must consider the technologies that work together to generate an end-to-end service, as well as security flaws and client maturity levels, to achieve this. A unique cyber management approach called the Secure Blueprint assists businesses in aligning their cybersecurity strategy with their financial and operational objectives. The Secure Blueprint compares a company's cyber capabilities with contemporary cybersecurity management theories to assess the maturity of its cyber programme [20].

It is necessary to build up the technological elements that make up a cybersecurity foundation. This strategy includes risk analytics; strengthening and reducing the attack vector; monitoring and reaction; mitigation solutions; and sophisticated defence against upcoming malware and ransomware attacks. Businesses can ask their security providers for managing the detection and mitigation services for continuous attack avoidance and threat tracking, which enables them to find unseen intruders in advance. With a single security solution, you can combine as many of these technological tiers as you like. By giving customers a single point of contact, the organisation is better able to meet their specific demands.

The CIA triangle is in charge of a company's cybersecurity procedures [20]. It represents availability, integrity, and confidentiality. The CIA triad components are three of the most important and essential cybersecurity requirements, although experts think that they can be improved. In this context, availability refers to the guarantee that the authorised individuals will consistently have access to the data, while integrity refers to the assurance that the data is accurate and reliable. Confidentiality refers to a set of procedures that restrict information access. The most crucial actions to take to guarantee an app is secure for a long period are shown in Figure 5 [20].

The CIA triad security architecture's significance is obvious given that each letter stands for a key cyberspace concept. The execution of

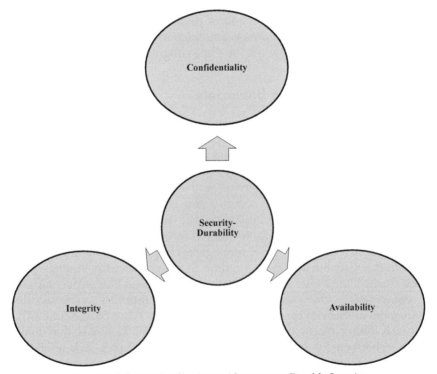

Figure 5: Software Applications with respect to Durable Security.

organisational security practises may be aided by considering these three variables as a "triad". When examining their demands and potential uses, the triangle enables the organisations to ask precise questions about how new goods and technology could assist in those three key areas. The Security Durability Blueprints for software include the elements shown in Fig. 6 and Table 3 [20].

6.7.1 Identify Goals

Goals serve as a logical framework for identifying, organising, and communicating software needs. Strategies are needed for the initial selection and creation of goals. Goal analysis and goal formulation are two alternative angles through which to view goals. Before summarising our findings and applying them to a sizable case study, we came up with a goal-oriented method. The difficulties that experts have when using a goal-based technique to specify system requirements are noted by the designers [19]. Every endeavour needs to have a goal at the very least. Most of them have several objectives in mind. These can also be called the project's goals or the main goal of the project.

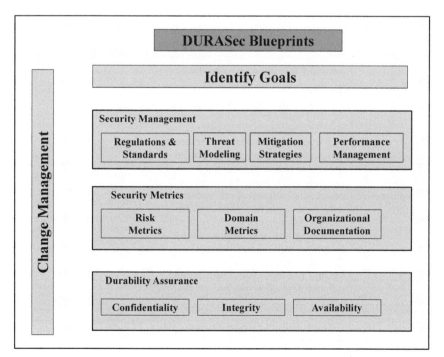

Figure 6: The Architectural Diagram of Security Durability Blueprints for Software.

Table 3: Durability Blueprints in Engineering Perspective.

Designing	Durability Perspective	Engineering Suggestion
Planning	The durability of a security system can be influenced by its design (e.g., trustworthiness). Security development, on the other hand, can improve durability attributes by removing security risks.	Monitor security complexity; Identify the change-prone parts of the security; Carefully manage basic security structures; Monitor durable security metrics.
Security Architecture	The growth of security architecture is frequently an expensive process. It has little direct impact on durability, but it poses significant security threats if the evolution process is opaque and poorly understood. To support specific software properties, security architecture evolution may be required.	Assess the stability of the security architecture; Understand the relationship between the security architecture and the business core; Analyse any security architecture change.
Security Requirements	Although the growth of security requirements has no direct impact on durability, ineffective management of the security requirements processes may allow unwanted modifications to enter the security system, compromising its long-term viability. On the other hand, as security requirements evolve, software durability may improve with time.	Classify security requirements according to their stability/ instability; Classify security requirements changes; Monitor security requirements evolution.
Software-based Security Design	Non-durability may arise as a result of software evolution. This is owing to the software resources' incomplete evolution. In order to register a new configuration for the software, the evolution of some resources (e.g., security) should be taken into consideration by other resources (e.g., live ware and system). As a result, resource interactions help to properly install new software and security configurations. Humans, on the other hand, can react to and learn how to deal with non-durable conditions, but constant changes in software setup may lead to a lack of security awareness. As a result, human-software interaction may become non-durable.	Acquire a systemic view (i.e., Software, Security Live ware and Environment); Monitor the interactions between resources; Understand evolutionary durability.
Secure Business	The evolution of an organisation should correspond to the advancement of software security. Untrustworthiness may result from a lack of coordination between security and organisational progress.	Understand environmental constraints; Understand the business culture; Identify obstacles to changes.

A vague goal will almost certainly result in a vague result. Two of the most important components of effective software project management are managing expectations and foreseeing dangers. The job's completion appears to be the project manager's sole goal. This is derived from the definition of a system design, which is defined as a unique, temporary undertaking with predetermined start and end dates that seeks to accomplish one or more goals while adhering to financial, time, and performance evaluation constraints. Even when a project's aim seems obvious, not everyone will always see it that way. Because of this, it is important to write it down and evaluate it for the development team.

The initial assessment and conceptual model design and development methods, as well as project planning skills related to assessing and documenting while utilising people management skills and knowledge of management, negotiation, and compromise, as well as communication and collaboration, have a direct impact on the project goal and scope. The first stage in the goal-driven method is to identify the application development goals and then break them down into smaller, more manageable sub-goals. It ends with a strategy for implementing clearly defined metrics and indicators to aid in achieving the objectives. It makes sure that the people who take notes and figure out what they mean are always held accountable for the goals, so they don't lose track of them.

6.7.2 Security Durability Management

The basis of effective software security management has long been acknowledged as being practical, adaptable, and transparent. A crucial element is the security of any application. When effective application security integration isn't implemented during the development phase, some programmes are outsourced. It's important to look into the growing demand for the application of security practises to be taken into account at every stage of the development process. By incorporating particular steps or practises into the development lifecycle, application security can be effortlessly included in the SDLC. These steps, which are meant to make the application safe [17–18], will be interesting for future users.

It seems that many businesses have started to address security issues early in their development cycle to reduce the risk of application security breaches. There is, therefore, still an opportunity for development. The field of application security is continually changing. Customers who outsource programmes must confirm that the IT services provider's application development methodology includes software security. Conversely, technological network operators need to ensure the validity of their SDLC application security requirements. If the service provider doesn't think these non-functional parts are important, the client loses.

6.7.3 Security Durability Metrics

To determine if a company's security programme is on track to achieve its goals and stay compliant, security metrics are frequently utilised. If businesses are aware of the successes and failures of their information security programme, they may make better judgments about regulations, tactics, and operational practises.

There are additional metrics that can be used to assess the quality of a security programme, even though risk reduction is a crucial KPI for assessing the overall efficacy of any security programme. Developers should select metrics that are quantifiable and affect behaviour and direction. To follow the architecture through time, it should be concentrated on continuing security operations. Metrics can be utilised to give management teams a clearer, more analytical way to receive data from security programmes. Using precise metrics and standards eliminates uncertainty and identifies problem areas fast.

Metrics can give information about how well the information security regulations are working, and about how well the employees and departments are managing security breaches that fall under their purview. Metrics can also be used to calculate the risk of not carrying out a set of mitigation measures, which can then be used to prioritise future resource allocation. Because they provide accurate data and a common language for discussing dangers, metrics may be used to ensure that everyone within an organisation is more aware of security.

6.7.4 Security Durability Assurance

Security Durability Assurance (SDA) is a method for figuring out whether or not an application satisfies particular requirements. To offer consumers of business higher-quality services, it also places a strong emphasis on process optimization. Project specifications frequently demand assets, asset components, and design and construction elements with lengthy design lives. Long-term durability must be studied, planned for, and managed [19–20] to prevent the systems, architectural parts, and modules from disintegrating over time.

Designers consider the flow-through effects of durability from the very start till the conclusion of a project. The cost of preventative interventions, the efficacy and price of corrective treatments, and the price of ongoing planned maintenance are all evaluated using this method. These need to be managed to keep the overall cost and return on investment to a minimum. In this quality management statement, the quality assurance (QA) process is linked to a company's quality management process, guaranteeing that the aims and objectives of an application or product are achieved. To ensure that a project is done right, the QA system does operational assessments, compares them to a standard, watches activities, and follows regulatory procedures.

6.7.5 Change Management

Change management is the term used in application design to describe the process of upgrading from one version of an application product to another. It monitors, controls, and encourages artefact alterations, including code updates, change requests, and document updates. The CCP (Change Control Process) examines, documents, and approves modifications to application software [21]. A high-quality software suite is created for every application by completing each stage of the Software Development Life Cycle (SDLC). Although it's not a part of the SDLC, change management is essential to the success of any software project.

Without the CIA, no system would be complete. To ensure the platform's security and privacy, however, appropriate security measures must be added. These security measures have a substantial influence on the platform's functionality. For effective security adoption, striking the correct balance between accessibility requirements and security restrictions is essential. Protecting software applications from exploitation requires the use of up-to-date encryption, appropriate authentication requirements, regular addressing of known vulnerabilities, and software quality assurance management practises. Even in a setting that appears to be incredibly secure, competent attackers could be able to gain access. This is why it's crucial to safeguard crucial software using a security durability strategy.

6.8 Security Durability Integrate with Development Process

6.8.1 Secure and Durable Serviceability

Security is a major worry, and if current trends continue, the situation could deteriorate significantly in the future. There are no established solutions available for ready reference for the software security challenge. It needs different solutions during secure software development because it is a long-term problem with many different parts.

Software companies are currently confronted with problems relating to software's secure service life. There is constant demand to lower the cost of secure software development and to improve the maintenance process to lessen the financial load. To design truly secure software, security attributes should be considered early on in the development process. Because durability is seen as a security feature, it should be improved to extend the service life of secure software. The term "serviceability" refers to the longevity of secure software. Because of this, long-lasting security software has become a serious concern in the world we live in today.

Many development models have been suggested and utilised in the past to calculate the likelihood of security failure. The value of secure software is primarily derived from its secure serviceability to boost productivity and efficiencies, as well as from its resilience to attack and capacity to always operate at needed levels throughout the service life of secure software. A notable concern in the field of software development is the secure serviceability of software. A significant issue that shortens the service duration is the dearth of secure software services. Service-oriented design is impacted significantly by serviceability and security. Service-oriented design is a top priority for the companies that make software so that it can be used for longer than expected.

A few techniques for evaluating safe software services include the subjective approach, the hybrid approach, and the objective approach. Measurements of key aspects of software security, such as coupling, cohesion, and abstraction, are the main focus of the objective method. The second method assesses the characteristics of secure services and measures design flaws. It may enable developers to examine alternate security properties, i.e., durability. The third strategy additionally incorporates the first and second strategies. It is critical to creating secure software with a longer lifespan and a lower likelihood of security failure. Finding new, obscure security elements is crucial since they might limit how long a piece of protected software can be used.

To achieve secure software for a longer duration, it is required that services are secured. Durability makes it easy to enhance the service time of secure software. Durability may be considered as the period within which software performs securely. With the help of durability consideration, developers may be able to enhance the duration of working or service life of secure software. This section discusses the durability as well as secure services of the software after its development. It is clear that durability is an essential attribute of secure software services, but it is hard to achieve while designing security during software development. The objective of this section is to discuss enhancing serviceability as well as security for improving the service life of software.

To come up with secure and durable software, there is a need to develop a trustworthy security design. It is required to identify and establish the relationship between durability and security attributes that should be improved to secure software services. Security durability is determined by other security attributes as well as serviceability properties. There is a need to develop a conceptual model of secure software services for a longer duration. To achieve durable security during software development,

Fig. 7 shows a strategic flowchart that would help to design durable security.

As a first step, all strategies of security design concerning durability are classified. Afterwards, categorization of different characteristics of security and durability, that affect each other, is required. In the next step, durability restrictions for secure software development are laid out. For the implementation of durable security attributes, significant tools or activities are identified. If available tools are not sufficient, then identification or development of new tools for enhancing the durable security of software is done. If any related strategy is missing, it needs to be looked at and changed. If there are no missing strategies, it is secure to say that development strategies for long-term security have been met.

A discussion with management has been arranged to shape up and implement a durable security strategy. The strategy is finalised if the

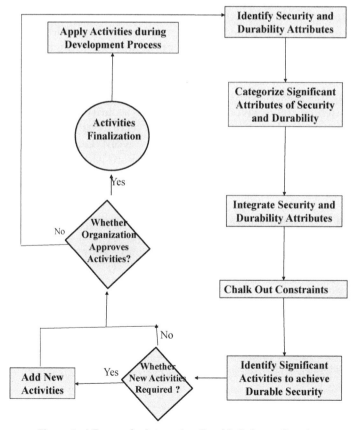

Figure 7: A Process for Integrating Durable Software Security.

organisation approves of the same. If disapproved, new tools are added, and working on those strategies continues till accepted by the organization. Organization approval is important for strategy implementation and designing security during software development. This flowchart would help the developers to figure out how to make more secure software in the long run.

6.8.2 *Service Oriented Design Properties: Durability Perspective*

One of the recognised paradigms for creating secure software is service-oriented design, which has been successfully used to create numerous secure software applications. The secure service was initially created by using a procedural approach to secure software. Services were secured using an object-oriented approach. A service-oriented design paradigm has replaced earlier paradigms in today's development. But, because the service-oriented design is the fundamental idea behind services, it differs greatly from object-oriented design. The ability to assess the security features of a service-oriented design may enable you to identify design issues earlier, saving your money and effort and extending the lifespan of your programme.

It is necessary to analyse the security features of the service-oriented design for this reason. Most design variables, whether object-oriented or service-oriented, have favourable effects on security properties. On the other hand, every design technique affects security attributes differently, both favourably and unfavourably. This work tackles the issue of longer-term security services. After the software is developed, it aids in extending the period of security. This will allow the developers to focus on delivering reliable and secure software services. Table 4 illustrates the

Table 4: Relationship between Service-Oriented Design and Durability Attributes.

	Coupling	Abstraction	Reusability	Discoverability	Cohesion
Scalability	X	-	-	-	X
Traceability	-	X	-	-	-
Accessibility	-	-	X	X	-
Efficiency	-	X	-	X	-
Extensibility	X	-	X	-	-
Effectiveness	-	X	-	-	-
Flexibility	-	-	X	X	-
Operational Control	-	-	X	X	-

connection between service-oriented characteristics and robust security characteristics [22].

Table 4 shows that durability factors affect different service-oriented design properties, such as scalability affects coupling and cohesion; traceability affects abstraction; accessibility affects reusability and discoverability; efficiency affects abstraction and discoverability; extensibility affects coupling and reusability; effectiveness affects abstraction; and finally, flexibility and operational controls affect reusability and discoverability. Other attributes of durability may affect different types of service-oriented properties, but for this research work, only these eight attributes have been considered. Our work would help the developers to work on security design based on software services.

6.8.3 Requirement Gathering

The use of the internet for every person has become vital in today's world. According to a study, approximately eighty-five percent of people are connected with each other via PCs, laptops, or mobile phones [23]. This extent of communication network and data sharing requires the security of information. Hence, organisations demand higher levels of security for software as well as systems. Security, which needs less maintenance, is in demand. Securing software is a never-ending process. Actually, organisations mainly focus on cost-effective security achievements for the long term, which may be achieved by integrating durable security during secure software development.

Enhancing security via durability is not only an easy process by enhancement, but also very complex. The outcome of this research can be used for developing secure software. If durability is an important security factor, then it may provide a new approach for developing secure software. The research discusses achieving durability while designing the security of software. Developing secure software will lead to quality software that the users can trust. Security is one of the most significant quality factors. If the security of software improves, the quality will also improve. For improved security, there is a need to identify new factors that affect the security of software. To make security that lasts and doesn't cost too much, it's important to look into the link between security and durability.

The durability of secure software will be improved by addressing security threats. Unfortunately, intrinsically vulnerable software design and coding methodologies are being used. When available logic modules are joined, their implementations are rolled out, which introduces vulnerabilities rather than removing them. Security vulnerabilities are one of the most serious concerns in the software development industry at present. Security flaws and the search for ways to "break" software's security are frequently overlooked. Even when they aren't forgotten, completing the breadth and depth of software security basics is a time-consuming process that needs to be kept up.

A security requirements specification (SRS) is a process for gathering security requirements from its users [24]. Security requirement elicitation is a complex process as it is done through interviews, walk-throughs, etc. The users might be confused about expressing their requirements. This complexity gives birth to an incomplete SRS document, which covers fewer or insufficient security details, leading to a confusing design of security. These types of difficulties are triggered when a new security attribute is applied in software design. Hence, these difficulties should be identified to apply durability efficiently.

Figure 8 describes the activities that are important for achieving durability of security during the early stages of software development. Firstly, all requirements for enhancing security and durability during software development should be gathered. In addition, two activities are involved, including identifying durable security strategies as well as identifying previously used activities for security design during software development. The next step consists of the development of the design (which is a secure and durable design).

Further, testing of durable security will ensure that it is properly achieved or not. If it is not achieved, one must start from the first activities onward. There is an evolution of durable security and management of durable security in the coming activities. In this way, durable security has evolved with proper management. In addition, review and revision of all activities are done, which depends on users' satisfaction and business continuity. During software development, security can be improved for a long time by doing these things.

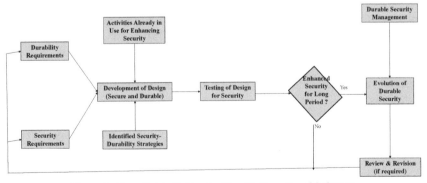

Figure 8: Essential Activities for Durable Security of Software.

6.8.4 Simplify Security Durability

With the help of durability, developers may enhance the duration of work or service life of the software. From the above discussion, it is clear that durability is an essential attribute of software security, but it is hard to achieve during software development [25]. Integration, durability, and security have become major concerns in today's era. The importance of software is derived not only from its security to increase productivity and efficiency, but also from its resilience to attack and the ability to always perform at the needed levels during the working life of the software. This section mainly discusses the basic concepts and facilitating factors at an early stage of the development process. The steps for the integration of these processes are depicted in Fig. 9.

According to Fig. 9, the first step is to integrate the industry scenario and security needs of the users. After this process, a list (or set) of the key security factors, as identified, is prepared. Alongside, a set of durability attributes are identified. The next step is to map the relationship between the identified and selected durability attributes and security attributes. Further, a data repository helps in gaining data from users as well as practitioners so that the value of security durability can be assessed. The next step is to apply soft computing techniques to find the weightages and ranks of different security durability attributes. Based on this prioritization, the guidelines are identified and selected for the developers. All these steps are contained and facilitated during software development. If a review or change is needed, the process will begin by gathering information about the security needs and industry scenarios.

6.9 Practices for Integrating Durability Concept

The three pillars of an effective end-to-end system for continuous development are integration, delivery, and deployment. To develop, run, and maintain software and durability integration capabilities within the work-product facilities, it is necessary to comprehend and support all the aspects of the software durability lifecycle, including planning, systems, requirements, design, builds, installations, integration, subcontractors, quality, and delivery. It's not always necessary to start from scratch when developing mission-critical business systems. Instead, a plan for systems integration could help make changes while keeping the number of operating structures as small as possible.

However, the success of the project hinges on the judgments made for the optimal integration of durability into systems. Ninety percent of the companies, according to a report, currently lack an application integration strategy for achieving the requisites of durability and security [24].

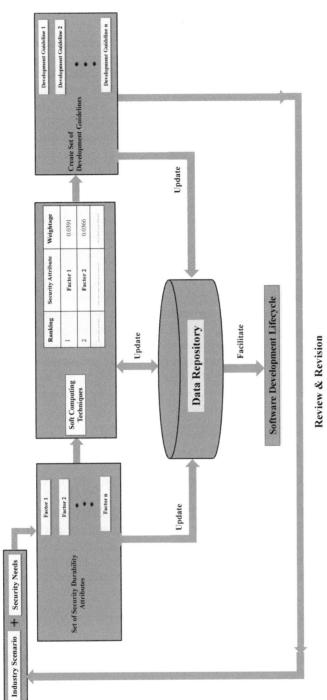

Figure 9: Significant Stages for Secure Software Development Selection Process.

However, if the right methods for integrating durability into the systems are applied, the result will be a seamless, sturdy end product that will last for a long time. Here, we examine our durability system integration procedures to ensure that the current software infrastructure is utilised to its fullest potential.

6.9.1 Quantum Security Technique

Security Durability Designs (SSDs) are used for the length of quantum computing and are defined by the software's expected life span. Over time, the effective use of software in quantum computing necessitates security enhancements because they can counteract new security threats that emerge [22]. Quantum computers have rendered cryptography-based balancing obsolete. The quantum enhanced strategy is a suspect method in which the quantum advancements made are unable to crack encryption calculations such as AES, DES, Rijndael, and others. Although the current cryptographic calculations are effective, improving security in the quantum period will necessitate more grounded techniques.

The key will receive the cryptography cycle information in this quantum enhanced situation. The quantum key appropriation is a novel, well-adjusted way to organise encryption in which the engineer employs the issue's vulnerability rule to ensure that information cannot be modified with the software. Quantum cryptography employs a variety of quantum dispersion keys, numerically centred techniques (for example, cross-section centred cryptography), hash-centered markings, and code-centered marks, all of which are beneficial to programming and software security. The techniques that follow ensure the product's toughness. Quantum cryptography will ensure the security of computer programmes as well as the long-term viability of the product.

(a) Quantum Key Distribution

The programme of information, known as an encryption key with the help of qubits, that has amazing conductivity to typical computer frameworks is known as quantum key distribution. Quantum key circulation required a separate fibre optic technology-based line for the in-line motion until recently. They can now be transferred merely by being in proximity to a fiber-optic-based line. This cuts down on the cost of correspondence. There is one additional piece of correspondence that is dependent on satellite communication. This correspondence method is known as "spooky action at a distance", and it is based on Einstein's theory [22].

(b) Lattice-Based Cryptography Algorithm

This proposed technique ensures that information is protected against quantum computing in the context of post quantum-based security procedures [22]. Hoffsten, Pipher, and Silverman combined lattice-based encryption, which is now reliable or unbreakable [22]. The lattice-based erections are an n-dimensional intermittent gap, in which the n-dimensional vector c1......cn∈R^n lattice-based generated set of vectors are shows in Equation (1).

$$\mathcal{L}(c1,.,.,.,cn) = \left\{ \sum_{i=1}^{n} x_i\, c_i : x_i \in \mathbb{Z} \right\}. \tag{1}$$

The vectors c1, c2, ..., cn are recognized as elementary lattices. Here, Z is the arbitrary session of lattice, R is the set of real numbers, and L is the dimension of lattice. The problems of lattice-centered security procedures are the short vector problem (SVP) and Lenstra–Lenstra–Lovasz (LLL) algorithm [22]. In SVP, participation lattice is indiscriminate, and its approximation is short. In 1982, the researcher gave the LLL algorithm. This algorithm has the approximation of , where n is the magnitude of lattice.

(c) Fully Homomorphic Algorithm

Without revealing the information, Fully Homomorphic Algorithm (FHA) encryption allows anyone to govern the information between two groups while preventing it from being uncovered [22]. In terms of a political decision-making technique, we can understand this concept. Three main partners or collecting individuals, as well as the pioneers for whom people vote, make up a political decision. In a political election, the election commission acts as an outsider, counting the number of votes expected for each candidate and revealing the results before the deadline. As a result of FHA, the knowledge is in an open area that has yet to be discovered by an outsider. The fact that FHA encryption cannot be broken in the post-quantum period is a huge advantage.

(d) Quantum Hash Function

A quantum hash function is a hash function that transfers a subjective line of information to a fixed-length result and has any computational power [22]. As a result, we must pack any piece of information into fixed-length esteems, such as names, federal retirement aide numbers, MP3 records, and so on. We need our hash capacity to work in a deterministic, public, and pseudorandom manner for everything to fall into place. We must understand that the hash of some random information 'x' will always be the same—that is, the hash is computationally controlled by its execution. A deterministic hash is useless unless it can be used by everybody. As a result, we need that the execution is open to all.

6.9.2 Usable-Security of Software

Currently, the notion of usable security has a large study basis, with hundreds of papers in dozens of peer-reviewed journals ranging from social interaction, computer security, and usability to technology, finance, psychology, and sociology [23]. The discipline has been successful in making the human factor aware of the need to achieve cybersecurity objectives. Human awareness and knowledge have been incorporated into business and the formation of new firms, as well as major government activities in the United States and Europe [24]. Security is frequently regarded as an annoyance by the end users. Security restrictions could have an impact on the end-functionality users and usability. However, if the software or application is to be safeguarded from being hacked, security is also essential. As a result, it's critical to strike the right balance between functionality, usability, and security [25]. This is depicted in the diagram below. The usability triangle is seen in Fig. 10.

In most organisations, security inspections are viewed as a cost. Typically, the adoption of sustainable security policies is a source of contention among many stakeholders inside the organisation. For example, the entire company would like to put functionality first. They are adamant about building the application feature exactly as defined in the project's requirements stage. While the end users expect all the features to function properly, they also expect it to be simple to use. The easier it is for a programme to please the end users, the better. Then there's the issue of security. Although most security checks may be made transparent to the end users, others, such as two-factor verification, may impose a burden on them. However, given the sensitive nature of the application data, such enhanced security features may be required. As a result, balancing function, usability, and security can be tough at times, as all

Functionality

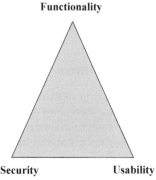

Security   **Usability**

Figure 10: The Usability Triangle.

three are vitally important. The selection of criteria is an important step in evaluating the usability and security of various institutional software programmes.

(a) Functionality

This is established by the goal that something is supposed to be achieved. For instance, when a malevolent person looks for a weak gap, increasing the number of functions in a piece of software increases the surface area that can be targeted.

(b) Security

This encompasses the measures taken to safeguard a system, software, or hardware, as well as guaranteeing that only those with permission to view them can do so. A really secure system, for example, would be housed in a solid box with no entry ports, controls, or interface and be capable of blocking all electromagnetic radiation. The user, on the other hand, would be rendered ineffectual because they wouldn't be able to access it or use it for what it was designed for. When it comes to security, developers must think about the user's perspective. Despite the customers claiming to be driven and security-conscious, many people did not intervene individually, according to an investigation by IT businesses and banking users. They equated job limits to security precautions. Furthermore, user behaviour was unaffected by criteria for expected security behaviour, such as awareness programmes. However, lowering security to improve functionality and usability exposes any system or device to attack, so a way to retain the ease of use and functionality without jeopardising security must be devised.

(c) Usability

It is the degree to which something is capable or suited for a specific purpose. There is a trade-off between security and usability in today's environment, which frequently leads to conflict between individuals and security managers.

6.9.3 Sustainable-Security of Software

System security management is a method for preventing malicious threats from various adversarial objectives and clients. As a result of the quick expansion of software systems, security is growing as a crucial component of a sustainable environment as a result. Mikhailov's objective of safeguarding systems is appropriate in this situation [4]. According to the study, making a safe and secure software system, making sure that the software system remains dependable, and training software systems engineers and end users on how to create a secure software system, are all components of making a stable software system.

It is now a business and social requirement to adapt to environmentally friendly building practises to create products and services that are viable and long-lasting. It is equally important in this league to understand that the security of software systems should prioritise sustainability while maintaining security. Many individuals also think that when it comes to technology, dependability and security cannot be compromised. Estimating and maintaining CIA in a safe environment while a software system is being developed is one of the most dependable methods for producing effective and stable software systems. Everyone must maintain security since sustainability is crucial in today's software systems. On the other hand, security monitoring requires a lot of expertise, which makes the solutions harder to scale, more complicated, and less likely to be used more than once.

Additionally, due to various methods of creation and implementation, sustainable software has a minor impact on culture, the economy, humanity, and the climate and has a positive effect on the environment when used. According to Sahu, K., and Srivastava, R. K., "Sustainable software development tries to serve the consumers' needs while maintaining natural systems and the environment" [21]. The relationship between security and long-term viability can be defined by considering the variables that affect both. A hierarchy of sustainable-security aspects is also shown in Fig. 11 [4].

Figure 11 shows how availability, integrity, confidentiality, and energy consumption, as well as perdurability and software-based resource optimization, affect the software system's long-term security. Collaboration between these traits has the potential to improve long-term security. As a result, the above characteristics will be considered when determining the long-term security of software systems. The definitions and interpretations of sustainable-security features are as follows:

Security (F1): Software systems' security is an important characteristic that protects associated systems from destructive attacks and various

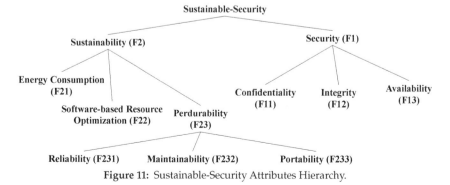

Figure 11: Sustainable-Security Attributes Hierarchy.

dangers created by hackers and malicious information, ensuring that the software continues to function successfully in the face of potential threats. To provide secrecy, authentication, and availability, security is also required. These features, on the other hand, must be linked with the concept of sustainability.

Sustainability (F2): Sustainability is defined as meeting the present customer expectations while not jeopardising the future generations' ability to meet their requirements. The security of sustainably developed software systems may contribute in achieving life's sustainability goals. In addition, security technologies have a growing influence on our daily life. As a result of combining security with sustainability, the world will have a secure and long-lasting software system.

Confidentiality (F11): In terms of security, confidentiality means ensuring that sensitive information can only be accessed by those who are authorised to do so, as well as confirming the data of the intended consumer. Furthermore, secrecy is a security trait that is linked to long-term security. As a result, it has a variety of effects on long-term security.

Integrity (F12): Integrity is all about maintaining the trustworthiness of information. Maintaining integrity improves long-term security. As a result, it is included as a well-informed quality of long-term security. Integrity is essential for achieving long-term security. The quantitative evaluation of long-term security will aid in assuring secure software systems' long-term sustainability.

Availability (F13): Availability confirms that in a sustainable ecosystem, knowledge is accessible to authorised consumers. If the hackers are not allowed to compromise on integrity and confidentiality, they can try to bring the server down and make the data unavailable for a brief time. This has a negative influence on the software systems' long-term viability and security. As a result, while assessing long-term security, availability must be taken into account.

Energy Consumption (F21) in Sustainable Security: Energy consumption in the context of Sustainable Security refers to the amount of energy required by a system to carry out its security functions and meet security standards. This is an important sustainability idea to consider while thinking about sustainable security.

Software-based Resource Optimization (F22): Software-based resource management is a collection of prototypes and strategies for aligning the existing resources, such as equipment, money, and people, with the organization's security standards to achieve well-known security and sustainability goals. If you can accomplish the results you desire in the time and money you have available while using the fewest resources feasible, it's called "resource optimization".

Perdurability (F23) is the concept of designing adaptable, recyclable, and long-lasting information security solutions, i.e., features that allow data to survive for a long period while keeping its quality-related functionality. Perdurability is a characteristic of sustainability, but it has security implications. As a result, it is a critical aspect in the context of long-term security systems.

Reliability (F231): Reliability is defined as the degree to which the sustainable security of software systems operates securely in a specified sustainable environment for a set period. Reliability is either 1 or 0 in any case. As a result, long-term viability is fully dependent on long-term security.

Maintainability (F232): Maintainability refers to the degree of efficacy and efficiency with which the intended authors can upgrade the software system to ensure its long-term viability. It refers to how well a system has been rectified or understood. Maintainability is a concept in software systems that can also be used to assess long-term security.

Portability (F233): The ease with which software systems and their security can be transferred from one software product to another is termed as portability. The efficacy of moving security applications from one site to another is measured as portability in sustainable-security. Computer security and sustainability developers must learn to work with shared-environment concepts. This is because security and long-term sustainability can coexist.

Even though various ways of combining the two have been devised, each procedure has its own set of limitations and benefits. Security sustainability must be incorporated into sustainable-security from the very start of the development process and be maintained before security services are implemented. Sustainability appears to be the source of all the uncertainties that exist between sustainability and security.

6.9.4 Security Tactics of Software

Software's overall security can be significantly impacted by the way it is designed. For architects, creating a secure software application design is a challenging undertaking [23]. The security of software programmes is impacted by several intricate problems. The amount of protection needed increases in direct proportion to the number of vulnerabilities. Security design solutions must be put into practise to meet these security standards. The methods for designing, identifying, and mitigating vulnerabilities and threats are known as security design strategies. As a result, one of the primary means by which the hackers discover new and perilous flaws in software is through errors in the deployment of the security methods or the weakening of security measures during programme maintenance.

Despite of the significant efforts to maintain the software's security, systems continue to be insecure even after normal maintenance. The software might occasionally suffer from a minor design modification [23–25]. Given the need for secure software, it was suggested that we concentrate on architectural security solutions in the design process. Security methods are a helpful tool for analysing and evaluating the many parts of secure software architecture. A design approach known as a "security strategy" addresses a security issue at the architectural design level. Three different security strategies are available. These techniques are focused on usability, testability, and accessibility. Tactical planning, despite being fine-grained, is not atomic. It is possible to alter the security techniques' hierarchical structure. Following an extensive review of the literature, this effort aimed to create a hierarchy of the security methods, as depicted in Fig. 12.

Figure 12 shows how the security tactics are classified into three categories: availability, testability, and usability. Availability is crucial when it comes to creating and maintaining a secure system. The capacity of software to deliver a service that meets its requirements is known as availability. Testability refers to a system's ability to be tested for unsafe attacks, which is necessary for maintaining security. Usability refers to a system's ability to learn quickly, which ensures user security. There are further sub-attributes for availability, testability, and usability. The sub-attributes of the sub-attributes, such as fault detection, controlling input and output, and encouraging user initiative, are found in the next level of the hierarchy. The following are the traits, or techniques, of availability, testability, and usability:

Fault Detection (T11): There are four security tactics in the availability tactics. One of them is fault detection. Failure detection has an impact on data availability. It is influenced by three factors: ping (T111), echo (T112), and exceptions (T113). Failure is found by using ping and echo, and the occurrence of exceptions helps find failure.

Recovery Preparation and Recovery (T12): When developing availability security techniques, fault recovery is a critical problem.

Voting (T121), active redundancy (T122), and passive redundancy (T123) are three additional aspects to consider when preparing for and recovering from a fault. The voting process for a component aids in the recovery of a fault. Through active and passive redundancy, information from parallel parts that aren't working is sent to another part.

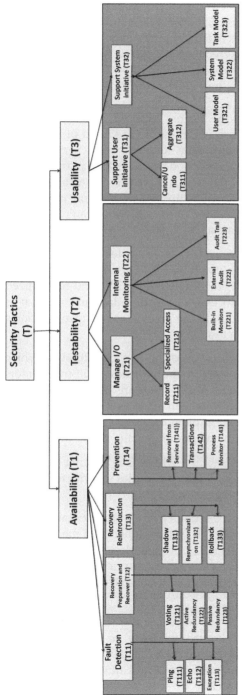

Figure 12: Hierarchical Structure of Security Tactics.

Fault recovery being reintroduced into security tactics is a key worry. It consists of three components: Shadow (T131), Resynchronization (T132), and Rollback (T133). When a deleted problem has previously been running in shadow mode, it is referred to as a shadow. Resynchronization is the process of improving a component's condition before it recovers. After the fault recovery is done, the part needs to be rolled back to the way it was before.

Fault prevention tactics include factors like removal from service (T141), transactions (T142), and process monitor (T143), all of which are responsible for preventing problems. The Removal from Service tactic removes a software module from the method that is used to perform some operations to avoid the predicted failures. A transaction is a collection of numerous sequential steps that can all be undone at the same time. Once a defect in the process has been found, a process monitor can remove the nonperforming process and recreate a new instance of it.

I/O Management (T21): While a system is being tested, this security approach is utilised to manage input and output. Two security techniques are included in the Managing I/O tactics: Record (T211) and Specialized Access (T212). "Record" is the process of collecting data and using it as input for a test. "Specialized access" is the process of capturing variable values for a component through a test.

Internal Monitoring (T22): Internal Monitoring is a condition in which a component can use its internal state to apply tactics. Built-in monitors (T221), external audits (T222), and audit trails are the three security approaches (T223). Built-in monitors assist in attaining the goal of internal monitoring and security technique implementation. The audit trail and external audit look at the logs of the work done by the inside monitors.

Maintain User Initiative (T31): Usability, which is consumer-driven, is concerned with maintaining user initiative. It includes security techniques such as Cancel/Undo (T311) and Aggregate (T312).

Support System Initiative (T32): This usability-based security tactic is nice to users, but it is designed to benefit the system rather than the user. As a result, techniques like User Model (T321), System Model (T322), and Task Model (T323) are included (T323). It is vital to keep a model in place to support system objectives. As a result, three user, system, and task-based tactic models have been created.

Security tactics are crucial for constructing a secure system. Additionally, its qualities and sub-attributes play an even bigger role in constructing this security with its methods. Testability strategies, for example, are split into two categories: input and output management and internal monitoring. Using architectural techniques, you can build more secure systems with things like records, specialised access, built-in monitors, external audit, and audit trial techniques.

6.10 Conclusion

A tailored security assessment method is required for well-organized, sustainable-security engineering and its effective execution in creating secure and durable software systems. This work concludes that cyber security challenges and breaches have been a significant challenge for researchers and security specialists over the past few years. Experts and researchers have used a wide variety of methods and techniques to build secure and durable systems. When designing secure software or web applications, it's important to be flexible and creative. Professionals in the field of information security are always thinking of new ways to improve software's utility. There is a growing urgency to prioritise design features or alternatives in response to the specific needs of software deployed in different industries in light of the increasing prevalence of cybercrime. For the most part, our research focuses on current practises for incorporating security into software development. Security for software and web applications is built into every step of the development process, from initial concept to final inspection. IT companies would have to recalibrate their priorities because the commercial viability of high-quality software is inextricably linked with sustainable security and durability.

Points to Remember

- Durability is a security attribute that refers to the software's ability to complete a task on time. Software security qualities, as well as longevity, have an impact on software security.
- Identification of security attributes enhances software development security. These characteristics prepare them for a crucial role in the field of security.
- For a full risk assessment, one needs to know everything about the economic effects, including the laws and regulations, as well as the software-supported business model.
- Confidentiality, access control, authentication, software integrity, and other security issues are now necessary for making software that is safe.
- Risk management, control, and security management all work together to make sure that software is made in a secure way. Throughout the software development process, risk management technology helps with risk reduction activities.

- The study says that making a stable software system means making a durable and secure software system, while ensuring that the software system stays reliable, and teaching software systems engineers how to design a secure software system.

Review Questions

Objective Type Questions

1. The simultaneous loss of confidentiality, integrity, and availability is referred to as a:
   a. Collective Loss
   b. Security Loss
   c. Durability Loss
   d. Loss or Theft

2. Which one of these is not a service-oriented design concept
   a. Coupling
   b. Abstraction
   c. Operational Control
   d. Reusability

3. The software is responsible for a public method that can read or change a private variable and is related to which security factor.
   a. Confidentiality
   b. Access Control
   c. Integrity
   d. Authentication

4. The Usability triangle doesn't contain which one of the given factors:
   a. Functionality
   b. Security
   c. Usability
   d. Durability

5. .... is the concept of designing adaptable, recyclable, and long-lasting information security solutions
   a. Reliability
   b. Perdurability
   c. Energy Consumption
   d. Sustainability

6. Attributes of security tactics do not include which one of these:
   a. Availability
   b. Testability
   c. Usability
   d. Durability

Short Answer Type Questions

1. Define perdurability for Sustainable security.
2. What are security tactics and their attributes?
3. How usability and durability are related to secure software.
4. Briefly explain the same.
5. Name security risk and its related security factors for security durability.
6. What is a Lattice based cryptography algorithm?

Descriptive Questions

1. Define the relation of security attributes and durability attributes in detail. How is security durability achieved through it?
2. Define the security durability blueprint in detail.

References

1. Kumar, R. 2018. Fuzzy Multi Criteria Decision Analysis for Security Durability Assessment, Doctoral Dissertation Submitted at Babasaheb Bhimrao Ambedkar University. Available at: https://shodhganga.inflibnet.ac.in/handle/10603/262367.
2. McGraw, G. 2006. Software security. Building security in.
3. Kaur, J., Alka, R. and Khan, A. 2018. Major software security risks at design phase. ICIC Express Lett Int J Res Surv.
4. Alfakeeh, A.S., Almalawi, A., Alsolami, F.J., Abushark, Y.B., Khan, A.I., Bahaddad, A.A.S. and Khan, R.A. 2022. Sustainable-security assessment through a multi perspective benchmarking framework. CMC-Computers Materials & Continua, 71(3): 6011–6037.
5. Kumar, R., Zarour, M., Alenezi, M., Agrawal, A. and Khan, R.A. 2019. Measuring security durability of software through fuzzy-based decision-making process. International Journal of Computational Intelligence Systems, 12(2): 627.
6. Attaallah, A., Algarni, A. and Khan, R.A. 2021. Managing security-risks for improving security-durability of institutional web-applications: design perspective. CMC-Computers Materials & Continua, 66(2): 1849–1865.
7. Kirvan, P. and Gillis, A.S. 03/06/2021. Governance, Risk Management and Compliance (GRC). Available at: https://www.techtarget.com/searchsecurity/definition/governance-risk-management-and-compliance-GRC?utm_campaign=searchSecurity&utm_content=image-n&utm_medium=syndication&utm_source=flipboard&utm_term=21–90.

8. Attaallah, A. and Khan, R.A. 2002. Estimating usable-security through hesitant fuzzy linguistic term sets based technique. Computers, Materials & Continua, 70(3): 5683–5705.

9. Alenezi, M., Agrawal, A., Kumar, R., and Khan, R.A. 2020. Evaluating performance of web application security through a fuzzy based hybrid multi-criteria decision-making approach: design tactics perspective. In IEEE Access, 8: 25543–25556, doi: 10.1109/ACCESS.2020.2970784.

10. Alfakeeh, S., Almalawi, A., Alsolami, F.J., Abushark, Y.B., Asif Irshad Khan, Adel Aboud S. Bahaddad, Alka Agrawal, Rajeev Kumar and Raees Ahmad Khan. 2022. Hesitant fuzzy-sets based decision-making model for security risk assessment. Computers, Materials & Continua, 70(2): 2297–2317.

11. Kumar, R., Khan, A.I., Abushark, Y.B., Alam, M.M., Agrawal, A. and Khan, R.A. 2020. A knowledge-based integrated system of hesitant fuzzy set, ahp and topsis for evaluating security-durability of web applications. IEEE Access, 8: 48870–48885.

12. Parker, D.B. 1992. Restating the foundation of information security. Proceedings of the Eighth International Conference on Information Security, Netherlands, pp. 139–151.

13. Kaur, J., Khan, A.I., Abushark, Y.B., Alam, M.M., Khan, S.A., Agrawal, A. and Khan, R.A. 2020. Security risk assessment of healthcare web application through adaptive neuro-fuzzy inference system: A design perspective. Risk Management and Healthcare Policy, 13: 355.

14. Kumar, R., Khan, S.A. and Khan, R.A. 2016. Durability challenges in software engineering. Crosstalk-The Journal of Defense Software Engineering, 29–31.

15. SaaS Industry Market Report. 2018. Key Global Trends & Growth Forecasts. Available at: https://financesonline.com/2018-saas-industry-market-report-key-global-trends-growth-forecasts/.

16. New Data. 2017. Software as a Service Industry Revenue up 23% This Year as Shift to the Cloud Continues. Available at: https://www.geekwire.com/2017/new-data-software-service-industry-revenue-23-year-shift-cloud-continues/.

17. CA Veracode Report. 2018. Available at: https://techbeacon.com/sorry-state-software-security-secure-development-key.

18. Is Your Security Up to Date? 2016. Available at: https://www.cisco.com/c/m/en_us/offers/sc04/2016-annual-security-report/index.html.

19. Ensmenger, N. 2014. When good software goes bad: the surprising durability of an ephemeral technology. In MICE (Mistakes, Ignorance, Contingency, and Error) Conference. Munich, pp. 1–16.

20. Ansari, M.T.J., Agrawal, A. and Khan, R.A. 2022. DURASec: Durable security blueprints for web-applications empowering digital india initiative. EAI Endorsed Transactions on Scalable Information Systems, e25–e25.

21. Sahu, K., Alzahrani, F.A., Srivastava, R.K. and Kumar, R. 2020. Hesitant fuzzy sets based symmetrical model of decision-making for estimating the durability of Web application. Symmetry, 12(11): 1770.

22. Alyami, H., Nadeem, M., Alharbi, A., Alosaimi, W., Ansari, M.T.J., Pandey, D. and Khan, R.A. 2021. The evaluation of software security through quantum computing techniques: a durability perspective. Applied Sciences, 11(24): 11784.

23. Alenezi, M., Agrawal, A., Kumar, R., and Khan, R.A. 2020. Evaluating performance of Web application security through a fuzzy based hybrid multi-criteria decision-making approach: Design tactics perspective. IEEE Access, 8: 25543–25556.

24. Durable Cost Savings in Government IT. 2016. Available at: https://fcw.com/articles/2016/04/22/cost-savings-oped.aspx.

25. Feenstra, R.C. and Knittel, C.R. 2009. Re-assessing the US quality adjustment to computer prices: the role of durability and changing software. In Price Index Concepts and Measurement, University of Chicago Press, pp. 129–160.

Useful Links

https://link.springer.com/chapter/10.1007/978-981-10-3433-6_13

https://www.durable-north-america.com/service/duraprint-software.html

https://www.linkedin.com/pulse/8-mandates-developing-durable-software-systems-matin-bajighar

https://www.service-architecture.com/articles/database/durability.html

https://kelty.org/or/papers/Kelty-Erickson-Durability-2015.pdf

CHAPTER 7

Integrating Human Trust with Software Durability

7.1 Objectives

Human trust is an important feature for developing software that is both reliable and durable at the same time. In fact, several sources have cited that human trust is the key component that inherits various security and key factors in the software's life cycle. Now, if we consider human trust as a core component in software development, it also includes some extra sub-factors that systematically affect human trust. This Chapter aims at understanding the integral role of human trust and its subfactors that can add to enhancing the durability of the software being developed. Furthermore, the Chapter also intends to explore the following Objectives:

- To define the principles and dimensions of human trust concerning software durability.

- To discuss the role and responsibilities of an organisation for enhancing the durability of software, including pre-development, account manager, business analytics, software architect, domain expert, and software developer.

- To propose significant elements of human trust management procedures concerning durability.

- To propose the importance of human trust during the development process of durable software.

7.2 Fundamental Principles

7.2.1 The Evolution of the Human Trust Concept

Durability management in the context of software services calls for human trust between the sender and the recipient [1]. Referring to the manifesto, people's dialogues and their desire to change are crucial in the process of software development. But is it even feasible? There must be a formal agreement if there is any assignment. Human trust is not the foundation of the contract. Interestingly, as a case in point, the one consulting firm provided various clients with two different outcomes when delivering the software, even when the manager and scrum master for both the software projects were the same. The beginning of the software projects and the human interface were the two aspects where the two software projects diverged most. The first project was a big success because it was built on people's trust. On the other hand, the other software project, which was going through a more traditional process, was judged to be just average. Hence, the significance of human trust in crafting the desired end product cannot be ignored.

The management must be responsive enough to ensure and sustain the element of trust between the person delivering and the person receiving [2]. As it is known, human trust is the most significant aspect of any kind of ecosystem. It is always the highest priority factor for every security or durability management plan. Therefore, it also contains various other sub-factors that affect human trust, especially in durable and long-life software. It is always recommended to make them trustworthy and to contain human trust factors most effectively. For instance, any kind of software system like air trafficking needs a human trust-enabled environment because if it is not a human trust-aware system, then the customers and the end users would always hesitate to use such a system [3]. The various entities, human trust relationships, and assumptions in this context are discussed as follows:

Entity 1: Organisations

Explanation: Organisation X, partner organisations, vendor organisations, sub-vendor organisations, public sector agents.

Entity 2: Persons

Explanation: People in the organisations above, users of the system Y, people in the Internet community, e.g., possible hackers and crackers.

Entity 3: Software Agents

Explanation: Software agents used and built during the development, software agents as communicating partners of Y, active and passive attackers.

Entity 4: Technological Artefacts

Explanation: The tools used in the development, the network in the development and use environments, the software and hardware components in Y.

Entity 5: Data Artefacts

Explanation: Information related to system building on the Internet, data resources in X, the information provided by the partner organisations or vendor organisations during the development, data input to Y, and data resources in Y.

Entity 6: Activities

Explanation: Development activities in X, in the partner and vendor organisations, and activities in the business process where Y is used.

Some entities and human trust relationships, as well as the assumptions about software durability, appear during a specific development phase, but there are also human trust relationships that persist throughout software development and use [4]. The analysis that follows and the tabular structure of the derived information is a representative sample of these entities' concerns and an indicative list of some human trust types that are formed. Most of the time, these trust relationships and types determine the quality requirements and how the quality features of the software are handled during development and in the final prototype or information product or service.

7.2.1.1 Human Trust during Durable Planning and Analysis

Planning and analysis refer to the initiation of a software development project and requirements analysis actions. In some forms, the plan includes the developer's contacts and requirement specifications. Several output documents are produced in this phase, including the calls for bids, requirements specifications, and contracts [5]. The parties involved in the process are essentially the client organization, managers and the development group in the client organization, end-users, consultants, and developing organisations. Planning consists of various human-to-human trust relationships. This form of human trust is essential for effective interpersonal and social functioning, which further assures durability. The next step is to analyse some of the possible human trust assumptions (also those related to quality features), mostly in person-to-person relationships during planning and analysis. Human trust relationships during planning and analysis are discussed as follows:

Relationship 1

Trustor: Managers

Trustee: Project members in the same organization

Types and Quality Features: Competent, give reliable information, not willing to cause harm.

Relationship 2

Trustor: Managers and members of the development group at the client organization

Trustee: Requirements' analyst

Types and Quality Features: Competent and effective in the analysis of requirements, gives reliable information.

Relationship 3

Trustor: Requirements' analyst

Trustee: End-users/domain experts

Types and Quality Features: Give reliable information.

Relationship 4

Trustor: End-users

Trustee: Requirements' analyst

Types and Quality Features: Analysts' correct clarification and expression of end-users needs; end-users trust analysts' skills and methods to reveal their genuine needs.

Relationship 5

Trustor: Managers

Trustee: Bids, requirements analysis report

Types and Quality Features: Correct information

Relationship 6

Trustor: Managers at the client organisation

Trustee: Potential and chosen vendors

Types and Quality Features: Competent, open, caring, reliable.

The first four entries describe interpersonal human trust relationships. First, the managers in any of the participating organisations may assume that people working on the project in the organisation are competent and give correct input and no malicious people willing to cause harm [6].

This kind of human trust assumption is significant in that greater human trust evolves from management that encourages less egoism or self-interest, and fosters greater concern for the employees. It was found that the degree of human trust in individual actors makes a difference: higher levels of human trust increase the likelihood that determinants of cooperation will result in favourable outcomes, while lower levels of human trust decrease the likelihood. The lack of human trust may, in the worst case, lead to extremely strained durability and thus hinder software performance. Mistrust can happen when employees feel like the tasks they do and the management control systems they have to learn don't match up.

Second, the managers and members of the development group at the client organisation assume that the requirements analyst is competent and effective in the analysis and gives reliable information [7]. This assumption highlights that human trust is a fundamental element in IT professionals' skills, especially because effective change management requires credibility; if managers do not trust IT professionals, they will not let themselves be influenced by their change agents' efforts for improved software durability performance. Since human trust changes and evolves as the organisations adapt to the constantly changing business targets in the course of engineering durable and secure software, these fluxes tend to create fear, instability, and distrust amongst the individuals. So, it is important for the IT professionals to be able to get their managers and team members to trust them.

The last two relationships introduce human trust interactions where the trustee is not directly an individual or a group. Instead, the trustees are either data artefacts or organizations. Considering data artefacts, for example, the managers assume that the bids and requirements analysis report includes correct information [8]. This kind of human trust may be derived from human trust in individuals as document authors or from human trust in earlier experiences with the organisation providing the documents. Similarly, human trust assumptions about an organisation are often related to the properties of the people in the organization. Human trust is especially important for software projects that are outsourced and involve at least two organizations. A balance between human trust and traditional project control structures improves the performance, and thus, the durability of the software.

7.2.1.2 Human Trust during Durable Design

During design, one could observe many human trust relationships among a plethora of entities [9]. These are not only person-to-person relationships; they might also be other entities involved as trustees while the trustor entity is a person. Design includes architecture, protocol, software, document type, metadata, interface, and audio/visual design and redesigns after feedback. The work processes and roles of people in them (process owners) in the client organisation may also need redesigning. During the design phase, the requirements' specifications are refined and turned into various forms of prototypes. During this phase, the prototypes are also tested and shown to the end-user community representatives.

Collaboration may be needed with the business partners of the client organization. For example, developing document or metadata standards for the client organisation may require collaboration with some other external organizations. The main deliverables (outputs) of the design phase are, normally, various design documents, prototypes, and agreements with partners to be involved in the designed solution for durability. This is particularly the case in the recently rising outsourcing of development projects. Human trust relationships during durable design are discussed as follows:

Relationship 1

Trustor: Durability Designer

Trustee: Requirement specifications

Types and Quality Features: Information is consistent, complete, without extra data, using familiar modelling methods and techniques for improving durability.

Relationship 2

Trustor: Manager and development group in the client organization

Trustee: Durability Designers

Types and Quality Features: Human trust in traditional project control structures; human trust in organizational control; human trust in managerial relationships.

Relationship 3

Trustor: Durability Designer

Trustee: Durability Designer

Types and Quality Features: Acting according to general group norms; similar knowledge of work.

Relationship 4

Trustor: Durability Designer

Trustee: Technical development environment

Types and Quality Features: Secure, durable, and reliable.

Relationship 5

Trustor: Manager

Trustee: Specifications

Types and Quality Features: Describe high quality, implementable, and with solutions based on durability requirements' specifications.

Relationship 6

Trustor: Durability Designer

Trustee: Organizations providing services in the future operational environment

Types and Quality Features: Organizations participating in the communication network have good credentials.

Relationship 7

Trustor: Durability Designer

Trustee: External software in the future operational environment

Types and Quality Features: Only Durable, reliable, and authenticated software used in the communication network.

Relationship 8

Trustor: Development group

Trustee: Another development group

Types and Quality Features: Knowledge based human trust, performance-based human trust, calculus-based human trust, identification-based human trust.

A variety of human trust assumptions have to be made during the design phase of durability [10–11]. This structures the information that is analysed in this section and presents a summarised knowledge of the human trust relationships that are formed during the design phase of the durable software development process. Assumptions are rarely stated clearly, and there may be some dangerous, hidden human trust assumptions, especially about how the new durability solution will be used and how it will work in the future. More so in the cases where the development is divided into several outsourcing components, the management of human trust may be extremely complicated. The durability designer or a group of durability designers are the main trustors here. They can trust other people or artefacts if they have certain quality and durability characteristics, whether personal or artefact-quality and durability features. The groups that any designer interacts with are usually the other designers and the development group in the client organization. Human trust manifests itself in each of these relationships.

Furthermore, a durability designer must trust organisations that provide services in the future operational environment, in which case she or he must verify that the organisations participating in the communication network have good credentials. A durability designer will also need to check the durability of the technical development environment, specifically its quality, security, and reliability. These quality and durability checks are done again to certify that external software in the future operational environment meets the quality standard directive which states that only trusted and authenticated software can be used in the communication network.

Yet another integral aspect to reckon with in this row is that most software durability designers assume that: (i) the initial requirements specification documents are clear, consistent, complete, and computable, and (ii) the modelling methods used to make the specifications are known.

Other entities-stakeholders that have a significant role as trustors in the design phase are the managers, who also participate in normally bonded human trust relationships [12]. The trustees can be humans or deliverables-artefacts. When, for instance, a manager trusts a specification document, the latter should possess high quality in terms of implementability and realisation of the practical needs, as those were identified and defined in the earlier durability requirements analysis phase. When a manager, the development group, and the clients work in tandem with the durability designers, the interface involves human trust in traditional project control structures, human trust in organisational control, and, apparently, human trust in managerial relationships.

7.2.1.3 Human Trust during Implementation

The design specifications are meant to guide the implementation phase towards a solution that can be fully durable, maintained, and tested [13]. The resultant software-based system is expected to be trustworthy and fulfil the needs and software durability properties expressed in the requirements' specification or discovered otherwise during the development work [2–3]. The, otherwise called, realisation phase normally includes the following artefacts and activities: implemented software, tailored legacy software, new software applications supplied for the durable system's purpose and scope, software testing and installation, installation of communication connections, data conversions, creation of new data resources (web pages, databases, etc.), end-user training, and new work practises [4–5]. Thus, implementation refers not only to the technical implementation and installation but also to the institutionalisation of the system. During this phase, the developer might deliver test materials, new hardware, installed software components, installed communication connections, new data resources, training materials, end-user guides, and agreements for updates and maintenance.

Again, in this phase, like in the design phase, the trustors are humans or groups of them, while the trustee can also be an entity that is not human. Regarding person-to-person human trust relationships, it is important to emphasise that close collaboration with business partners is needed. Interpersonal human trust, for instance, among managers (trustors) and programmers (trustees), refers to human trust developed in managerial relationships. That includes acting according to general group norms and the possession of similar knowledge of work [6–7]. Notably, though the trustor and the trustee can be the same entities in the human trust relationships occurring in the implementation phase, the durability features required in the type of human trust or the personal quality assumptions can be different. It is hereby referred to as just a chosen sample of new human trust relationships that were not met in the earlier phases of the lifecycle.

For a closer look at the different types of human trust that are described here, some important relationships and the durability and quality features that go along with their assumptions about human trust are then looked at. Human trust in teamwork, especially virtual teamwork, seems to be an important part of durability-quality management that has a big impact on the software process.

An important new human trust relationship that is formed during the implementation phase is between the programmer and the user. A programmer needs to trust the user's inputs and understand the users' needs to be absolutely correct [10–11]. Hence, correctness, like consistency and completeness, is a quality property that is used in many models. In the human trust relationships that are derived, it is usually related to the artefact entities rather than the people. In the realisation phase, a programmer and a tester normally assume that the design specifications and the initial requirements are consistent, correct, and complete. Furthermore, a tester expects that the end-user information (drawn from test cases and use cases) is clear, consistent, and complete. Since it is at the system's implementation phase, it is normal that programmers and testers would only trust design and specification documents if they also demonstrate computability, which is a clear indication of future implementability and durability [12–13]. Human trust relationships during implementation are discussed as follows:

Relationship 1

Trustor: Programmer

Trustee: Durability Design specifications

Types and Durability-Quality Features: Consistent, correct, complete, computable, and implementable.

Relationship 2

Trustor: Programmer

Trustee: Technical development environment

Types and Durability- Quality Features: Secure and reliable environment.

Relationship 3

Trustor: Manager

Trustee: Programmer

Types and Durability-Quality Features: Acting according to general group norms; similar knowledge of work; human trust in managerial relationships.

Relationship 4

Trustor: Programmer

Trustee: Programmer

Types and Durability-Quality Features: Acting according to general group norms; similar knowledge of work.

Relationship 5

Trustor: Programmer

Trustee: Technical staff in the client organization

Types and Durability- Quality Features: Similar knowledge of work.

Relationship 6

Trustor: Programmer

Trustee: User input in the future system

Types and Durability-Quality Features: Correct.

Relationship 7

Trustor: Project manager

Trustee: Client's representatives

Types and Durability-Quality Features: Human trust in people's team-work.

Relationship 8

Trustor: Tester

Trustee: Initial durability requirements

Types and Durability-Quality Features: Consistent, correct, and complete.

Relationship 9

Trustor: Manager in the client organization

Trustee: Technical staff in the client organization

Types and Durability-Quality Features: Human trust in team-work; human trust in persons.

Relationship 10

Trustor: Trainer

Trustee: End-users

Types and Durability-Quality Features: Learnability, usability.

Relationship 11

Trustor: Tester

Trustee: End-user information (drawn from test-cases and use-cases)

Types and Durability-Quality Features: Clear, consistent, complete.

Relationship 12

Trustor: People at the client organization

Trustee: Implemented system

Types and Durability-Quality Features: The software, hardware, operating systems, and networks are reliable; security issues have been taken care of in the solution; data is correct and accurate in the installation.

It is also of utmost importance that the people at the client organisation will have to trust the final stage artefact which is the implemented system itself. Starting from the data correctness and accuracy during installation and the durability of the software, hardware, operating systems, and networks, durability seems to be a basic quality requirement for software artefacts and system components. In addition, system security considerations come on board as human trust assumptions [13]. Several interpersonal human trust issues also start to rise after installation, considering the human trust relationship among the trainers and the end-users and regarding the information system's usability and learning function. The main things that the stakeholders care about and what they expect from other entities are shown by the types of human trust and quality features in stakeholder assumptions.

7.2.2 *Human Trust Analysis into Durability Concept*

Digital innovation has completely changed the way businesses operate today. The whole customer choice landscape, the company's environment, and performance have all changed as a result. Customers nowadays are more demanding, informed, and picky, and the methods by which they connect with brands today largely determine the fundamental components that mould business ties in the new digital era. How can consumers choose whether or not to believe a company? How long will the software operate and provide its services without the need for maintenance? To address this context, the authors have focussed on the factors that influence people's trust in the digital age we live in today and made some recommendations about how businesses may win over their customers' trust and loyalty. Human trust has long been at the core of crafting reputation and business relationships, but the concept is challenging to define and measure. Basically, there are four dimensions of human trust concerning software durability, which are as follows:

7.2.2.1 *Competence*

Competence in business refers to the management of a company's operations as well as technical and operational concerns related to the product's features or service durability and quality [9]. Digital interactions are distrusted for a variety of reasons, including poor usability, anaesthetic design, and lack of maintainability. On the other hand, convincing potential customers that developers value durability and original thought can greatly increase their likelihood of doing business with an organisation.

7.2.2.2 *Benevolence*

Consumers' perceptions of a developer's team and, more particularly, the soft skills that the organisation's employees exhibit as they interact with consumers are more strongly linked to generosity [11]. Customers now form an emotional connection with a brand, and the outcome is largely determined by whether they believe that the company values them as a customer and has their best interests at heart. The ability of the developers to maintain human trust in this dimension is dependent on their ability to value customers, give them a sense of importance, and express gratitude for doing business with them. It's also critical to keep in mind that, provided the customer has sufficiently earned confidence at this stage, developers will have the opportunity to hear any grievances they may have.

7.2.2.3 *Integrity*

Integrity refers to the values and principles that shape and direct a corporation [12]. It generally refers to an organisation's integrity and capacity to fulfil its commitments for durability, but it also alludes to the shared ideals that support a deeper and more fulfilling relationship with a customer. Doing business with a company that upholds durable beliefs such as sustainability and low maintenance, and makes a quality and durable product ideal. This kind of engagement makes the customers happy and lets them have a good relationship with the brand, which builds trust and encourages long-term loyalty.

7.2.2.4 Predictability

Based on the knowledge gathered and lessons learned, predictability may be seen in brand reputation and the customers' expectations of a brand. Scientific research has shown that confidence promotes optimism and results in more favourable impressions [13]. When businesses keep their commitments with the targets of durability and conduct themselves honestly, customers are more likely to share their positive experiences. It may be right to assume that the customers don't expect software to be flawless. However, how software withstands problems shows how durable the software is and whether or not the customers can rely on it.

7.2.3 Durability and Human Trust Characteristics

Details of this section are given in Chapter 2.

7.2.4 Systems, Software, Human Trust, and Durability

Certain characteristics of durable systems can be relied upon. The growing complexity of computer and communication systems drives the need for human trust and the ways of establishing it for durability [12]. One simply needs to read about the most recent data breach at a significant bank or store to see the scope and gravity of the issue. The security and dependability of national infrastructures and developing global data networks are now interchangeable terms. Despite being vital, this connection exposes significant portions of a user's daily life to risks that are continually evolving. Numerous incidents at the turn of the century demonstrated the necessity of creating dependable and trustworthy systems. Several thousand computers around the world were infected by dangerous viruses like Code Red and the SQL Slammer worm.

Millions of Americans lost electricity due to power outages. Since the terrorist attacks of September 11, 2001, there has been a call for increased security that balances individual liberties [13]. Today, the necessity of security and dependability is demonstrated repeatedly. By taking advantage of the connections between technology and areas like health care (pacemakers, for example), transportation (traffic lights, cars, aeroplanes), power grids (industrial control), telecommunications (spam and botnets), and financial systems, attackers can infiltrate every aspect of a society (for example, identity theft and credit card fraud). By assisting in the development of more trustworthy and durable systems and the detection of assaults, flaws, and availability threats, durability focuses on solving these fundamental societal challenges. Then, experts in these fields fix them by simulating these systems and looking at how secure and long-lasting they are.

7.3 Organizational Roles and Responsibilities

When a software development project begins, developers want to have a team of skilled, experienced professionals who are experts in their sector. However, hiring skilled professionals alone does not guarantee an expert team or an efficient and durable software development process. A competent offshore software development team does not just arise. And other factors besides competence also affect how effective they are. A business makes sure that the developers who work on an outsourced software development project understand and clearly define their roles and responsibilities.

Defining the duties and responsibilities of the durable software development team is crucial when outsourcing, especially when a project team consists of both internal personnel and the outsourced team supplied by a trusted organisation. A software development project's overall efficiency can be increased by outlining the roles and responsibilities explicitly to make it easier for the users to understand what they are paying for and why. This will enable them to stay clear of any extra or secret charges. Therefore, it's imperative to enlist each responsibility at the very outset of the process. Project managers are given tasks and responsibilities when the client and their provider decide on the project's scope.

Managers, in turn, define durability objectives and divide them into detailed tasks that are given to the qualified individuals under their supervision. This method makes planning easier, thus ensuring that the project is e finished on time and well within the stipulated budget. Everyone is conscious of their behaviour. People are fully aware of their responsibilities to achieve the project's common goals and objectives of durability. When everyone is clear about their responsibilities, there will be fewer misunderstandings, obstacles, and conflicts as they collaborate. It's simpler and more direct to communicate when there are fewer issues to address. So, as shown in Fig. 1 and discussed further down [6–10], the roles and responsibilities of team members in durable software development projects are:

7.3.1 Pre-Development

Before a developer writes the first line of code for a future product or durable service, there is still a lot of work and consideration that needs to go into that project. Before contracts are signed and the durability development really gets going, this part will acquaint them with the

Figure 1: Selected Roles and Responsibilities of an Organization.

important people they will encounter during the discovery phase of this durable software development project. From the first meetings with the vendor to the strategy and understanding of the results they are all seeking to achieve.

7.3.2 *Account Manager*

The role of account managers is crucial in any business-to-business relationship. Durable software development is not an exception. The account manager is the first person a user encounters when approaching a software development company with a project that has to be implemented. One of the responsibilities of the account manager is to establish and maintain a mutually cohesive and long-term relationship between the client and the outsourcing company they represent. After the organisation completes its portion of the project, it will serve as a client success manager, keeping an eye on the company's performance and the durable software product or service their business is helping to produce. When this first step is over, the account manager provides two important documents:

- A document with a cost estimate, project timelines, and terms and conditions outlining things like alternate payment methods and teamwork.
- A proposal document that outlines the technical and commercial strategy the organization has chosen for carrying out the project.

These documents will give an overview of the procedures the vendor is planning to set up for the durability project, the team of external software developers they are putting together, any potential dangers and underlying presumptions, and details of the expenditure as well as the overall budget.

7.3.3 Business Analyst

One can move on to development if the developer is satisfied. Making such a shift would require the developers to be confident in their ability to achieve their durability objectives with the plans they have made. And this would be accurate if all of the business studies, technical specifications, and other project information were available and ready to use right now. However, most clients don't immediately know what they want to build. The durable software development process's discovery phase is essential. Here, laying the groundwork for the success of a durable software solution becomes pivotal. This could take anything from a few hours to a few weeks, depending on whether it's a simple task or a big, complicated answer. One of the first people that the developers encounter is a business analyst. Unfortunately, although being one of the most crucial jobs in a software development team, it is occasionally ignored.

7.3.4 Software Architect

Many of the users don't know what technology they want to use. Software organisations must thus present them with someone knowledgeable about the technology that will best serve their commercial requirements. The technical brains behind the operation are those who are referred to as software architects. Proper software architecture is essential for high-quality durability projects. The main responsibility of a software architect is to choose the best architectural framework for the software model and goals of that project. They will focus on clarity while providing technical leadership and simplification of the project. High-level design choices for the project, including coding standards, environments, tools, platforms, and so on, are under their control. A software architect will give the developers a complete system durability design paper as part of the discovery phase. A plan for how the vendor will build the durability solution, including design and programming guidelines, content for each iteration, and an agreement on what the client wants from the technology and the environment as a whole.

7.3.5 Delivery Manager

A delivery manager has a thorough understanding of the customer's durability requirements, both technically and in terms of how the client plans to use it to advance their business. This becomes vital in a durable software development environment as the delivery manager is in charge of controlling the client's requests, managing expectations, and supervising the delivery process from discovery to deployment. A delivery manager is a person with substantial commercial and technical experience. The delivery managers determine the most effective procedures or delivery techniques and provide the customers with the information they need to make wise choices, and help them measure and assess the outcomes. They organise multiple team activities to overcome any challenging roadblocks, keep the project moving forward, and maximise value while working within these constraints.

7.3.6 Domain Expert

A business analyst might suggest hiring a domain expert, commonly referred to as a subject-matter expert, during the discovery phase. These people command in-depth knowledge and a wide range of abilities with proven expertise in a certain industry or field of commerce. In this case, a durability subject expert is needed for domain expertise. When it comes to defining durability needs, professional counsel can help to save a lot of time. Durability domain experts' opinions on the given project help the development team to produce a vision statement for a higher-durability software solution. Domain experts rarely possess any technical understanding, but this should be considered an advantage. They can focus completely on durability goals because they lack technical expertise, which helps the durability development team grasp the problem they are trying to solve. They might also help them make good wireframes and prototypes in the early stages of the project.

7.3.7 Software Developer

Software developers, also referred to as coders, are organizations' necessary and indispensable soldiers in any software development project, regardless of its complexity or size. Writing and implementing clean, effective code in accordance with the given technical standards is their only duty for the project. It's also important to note that the more effectively the management communicates the technical needs to the durability development team, the lesser is the possibility of technical debt.

While writing code and creating the durable software product from scratch, the durability software engineers will need to do the following:

- Calculate how long it will take to finish the specified assignment.
- When they attain a goal or report on the progress of their work, they must update their team lead or the project manager.

7.4 Significant Elements of Human Trust Management

7.4.1 *Human Computer Trust*

Human trust is crucial in interactions between people and computers. It erodes ambiguity and minimises the risk entailed in any endeavour. The subject of human-computer trust has received attention as a result of the quick development of computer and networking technology. The majority of human trust is a social phenomenon. It is a notion with several dimensions, disciplines, and facets [2]. Researchers have talked about trust among people in a lot of different ways, many of which reflect the assumptions of different academic fields.

In these definitions, the terms "confidence", "belief", and "expectation" about an entity's dependability, integrity, capacity, etc., are frequently used [3]. Human trust is a crucial element in many types of human contact, enabling people to act despite uncertainty and the possibility of unfavourable outcomes [5]. Human-Computer Interaction (HCI) and human factors experts have recently looked into how people behave online. The fact that design can affect a user's trust has had an effect on user interface design, website design, and interaction in general [8].

The focus of the current study is to understand how the user's trust is inextricably linked with both the efficacy of the product as well as the durability of the product. The aesthetics of an interface might hint at user confidence or convey durability [6]. On the other hand, Lee and Chung discovered that user happiness and human trust are also influenced by the quality and durability of the computer system and the information it provides [3]. According to the Theory of Reasoned Action (TRA), beliefs influence attitudes, which influence behavioural intentions, which influence actual behaviour. Numerous researchers have defined human trust as a behaviour that has been proven to be effective in social interaction and workplace collaboration [2]. Studies have shown that there is a strong link between what people plan to do and what they end up doing, especially when using software systems [5].

However, prior research did not examine or develop a comprehensive model of the interplay between human and computer trust. As a result, there isn't a set standard for boosting confidence in human-computer interactions. Notably, the focus of our research is not on human trust "through" computer systems, such as trust in a remote computer system user based on computer interactions. But our focus is on human-computer interaction for software durability.

7.4.2 *System Trust Solutions*

We can observe how different technologies can raise people's confidence in human-computer interaction: Human trust management for computer systems and computer communications includes designing the user interface, letting people know about information and showing it to them, and managing human trust. The goal of notification in a system trust solution is to quickly and effectively provide users' requests for essential information without interfering with their ongoing responsibilities. According to a body of research, giving someone confidence in information increases their trust in the system's durability.

7.4.3 *Managing Human Trust*

Human trust management research is essential for enhancing the user's confidence in computer systems and computer communications rather than identifying particular interface elements that are perceived as indicators of trustworthiness for further improving software durability [5]. Gathering the information required to decide on a human trust relationship, analysing the durability requirements for that relationship, monitoring and re-evaluating current human trust relationships, and automating the process are all parts of human trust management. Human trust management includes all security regulations, credentials, and human interactions.

In a digital world where traditional durability paradigms are ineffectual due to a lack of centralised control and imprecise environmental awareness, human trust management has lately gained popularity as a feasible option for promoting collaboration between organisations. Various human trust management strategies have been reported in the literature. Systems for managing human trust can be categorised into two categories. One is human trust management systems with increased durability, such as those built on trusted computing technology. This kind of solution makes use of durable measures to guarantee the dependability of a computer system.

The second choice is solutions based on human trust assessment, including reputation systems. In a technological way to define trustworthiness for digital processing, the factors affecting human trust will be assessed by a continuous or discrete real number, known as a "human trust value". For computing human trust, human trust relationships between entities are designed, evaluated, and set up using a human trust model. The human trust model could relate to numerous lines of research in various fields for various aims and could be linguistic, graphical, or mathematical. Future computer systems must have a human trust evaluation method to deliver human trust intelligence and further durability software with it.

Because of this, reputation-based human trust management (also known as a reputation system) is a unique approach to determining and maintaining human trust. Recently, a variety of methods for enabling durable communication and teamwork among computing nodes in a distributed system have been created. Additional technologies are also required to further develop effective human trust management. These include identity management, risk management, and privacy enhancement.

7.4.4 Human Computer Trust Model

The Human-Computer Trust Model will be significantly influenced by three essential factors: interaction intention, system human trust, and communication human trust (HCTI) [6, 9–13]. Various sub-constructs make up each root construct. The construct names are meant to be neutral for any specific theoretical perspective and to capture the core of the construct. Figure 2 shows the definitions of the three most important parts of a construction and measurement scale.

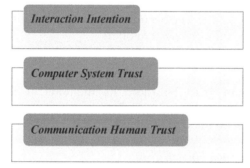

Figure 2: Constructing and Measuring Scales.

7.4.4.1 Interaction Intention

Interaction Intention is the extent to which a person wants or is likely to talk to a computer system. It would incorporate the following:

- A Person's Personality: The unique combination of a person's feelings, thoughts, and behaviours make up their personality.
- Social Factors: The individual's internalisation of the subjective culture of the reference group and the particular interpersonal agreements they have formed with others in particular social contexts.
- Personal Motivation: Personal motivation is the idea that using a computer will lead to things you want that have nothing to do with the activity itself, like more productivity, benefits, or money.
- Perceived Usefulness: A person's perception of the usefulness of a particular computer system is a measurement of how much they believe doing so will increase their ability to earn money.

- Reputation: The notion that the goals of HCI are influenced by what people think of a computer system and its designer.
- Perceived Ease of Use: A person's perception of how simple they believe a system will be to use.
- Relative Advantage: The degree to which a computer system is thought to be superior to another system that performs similarly or to its predecessor.
- Recommendation: Information is given with a recommendation for a plan of action.

7.4.4.2 Computer System Trust

The level of human confidence in a system's software.

- System Quality: Quality is crucial to how well the system can do several critical tasks.
- Information Quality: The accuracy and dependability of the data or content that a computer system offers.
- UI Quality: The ease of use, the sense of usage, and the sense of interaction.
- System Human Trust Solution: Its methods or technologies for enhancing its trustworthiness, such as security, privacy, dependability, and usability, and making the users trust it.

7.4.4.3 Communication Human Trust

The degree of trustworthiness in communications via a computer system.

- Perceived Privacy: The extent to which a person believes that when they use a computer system, their personal information won't be compromised.
- Perceived Identity: A person's conviction that a computer system will accurately identify the communications entities.
- Communication Context: Any data that can be used to assess the state of computer-based communications.

7.4.5 The Importance of Human Trust

The quality and durability of an object, a person, or a piece of information are not properties that are inherent in the object [12–13]. On the other hand, credibility and quality are perceived traits. When looking for high-quality, durable software development, engineers look for things that are (1) easy to find in a way that lets them judge their quality and (2) thought to be of high durability and quality. The first stage is necessary because the individual engineer must actively establish the quality of the information since the information's quality does not dwell on it as a label that can be read.

How much human faith one is ready to place in a source or piece of information ultimately determines its perceived quality [10–12] claims that the real glue holding a firm together is human trust, not technical ability, competence, or management. Last but not least, to be able to rely on anything that a person has placed their trust in, they must have faith in their ability to understand the transmitted message correctly. Depending on a variety of factors, people's levels of human trust in one another vary. Based on the data that backs them up [11], describes four different categories of human trust:

- First-hand experience (e.g., interacting with people over time and understanding their needs, the organisations assess their own expertise and trustworthiness).
- Referring to the vendor's reputation and what others have said about them (e.g., asking someone for advice based on having been recommended by a colleague).
- Basic analysis of surface properties (e.g., assessing people by the way they dress or the language they use).
- Generalizations and stereotypes at different levels are necessary for each of the four types of trust.

As a result, having first-hand knowledge of an information source or knowing someone who has first-hand knowledge of the source helps the consumers to assess the source's credibility. According to this [12] result, human trust is founded on the community of practise, and other studies have shown that people's inclination to trust one another depends on developing the software's durability for its longevity.

7.5 Conclusion

Human trust assumes significant importance in designing and delivering durable software. As established, human trust is the most critical aspect of software's durability and security. Using human trust-enabled apps rather than untrusted software is always beneficial and long-lasting. This Chapter presented a perspective on this important topic and provided useful information about the human trust element in software development and its many factors. The chapter also talked about the many facets that go into making good software for assuring durability, as well as how each one can help make software last longer and be more trustworthy.

Points to Remember

- Human trust is the most significant aspect of any kind of ecosystem; more so in the context of delivering software solutions to the intended clients. The developers, as well as the organisations' management, must ensure that trust underpins all interactions between them and the end users.

- It's difficult to add human trust to software in a simple way to make it more durable and reliable. Designing an application in such a way that it can manage both trust and durability on the same plate is the most important job for any designer.

- It was found that the degree of human trust in individual actors makes a difference: higher levels of human trust increase the likelihood that determinants of cooperation will result in favourable outcomes, while lower levels of human trust decrease the likelihood. The lack of human trust may, in the worst case, lead to extremely strained durability and thus hinder software performance.

- A durability designer will have to trust organisations that provide services in the future operational environment, in which case she/he will have to check if the organisations participating in the communication network have good credentials. A durability designer, moreover, will have to check the durability of the technical development environment and, in particular, check its quality, security, and reliability.

Review Questions

Objective Type Questions

1. Human Trust ensures .... in any software.
   a. Durability
   b. Predictability
   c. Scalability
   d. None of the above
2. Account Manager provides the...............
   a. SRS
   b. Proposal Document
   c. Data Flow Models
   d. None

3. .... is the co-attribute of human trust.
   a. Reliability
   b. Security
   c. Predictability
   d. All of the above
4. Human trust affects the market value of software product
   a. True
   b. False
5. Project Members from the same organization need to be trusted by...............
   a. Manager
   b. Client
   c. Chief Executive Officer
   d. None

Short Answer Type Questions

1. What do you mean by Human Trust?
2. Describe an organization as an entity for human trust.
3. What are software agents?
4. What is the role of a Software Architect?
5. Who is Business Analyst?

Descriptive Questions

1. Describe the evolution of Human Trust.
2. How can you maintain trust during design and implementation?
3. What do you mean by human computer trust?
4. What is Trust Management?
5. Describe various roles of human trust in software development.

References

1. Patnaik, P. 2022. Human-machine interactions: a synthesis of threats and opportunities. In Advances in Deep Learning Applications for Smart Cities (pp. 101–122). IGI Global.
2. Digital Marketing Software Market Size. 2022. Share and Global Market Forecast to 2022 | COVID-19 Impact Analysis | MarketsandMarkets. https://www.marketsandmarkets.com/Market-Reports/digital-marketing-software-market-52158190.html.

3. Data Breach Investigations Report. 2020. Executive Summary. https://enterprise.verizon.com/resources/executivebriefs/2020-dbir-executive-brief.pdf.

4. Staff, C.U. 05/06/2021. The biggest software failures in recent history. Computerworld https://www.computerworld.com/article/3412197/top-software-failures-in-recent-history.html.

5. Monika Sharma. September 02, 2019. Software Characteristics. https://www.includehelp.com/basics/software-characteristics.aspx.

6. Andrew, M. 2021. Software Development Roles and Responsibilities in Outsourcing. Available at: https://qarea.com/blog/software-development-roles-and-responsibilities-in-outsourcing.

7. Yan, Z., Kantola, R. and Zhang, P. 2011, November. A research model for human-computer trust interaction. In 2011 IEEE 10th International Conference on Trust, Security and Privacy in Computing and Communications (pp. 274–281). IEEE.

8. Lewis, J. 2018. 4 Dimensions of Customer Trust: How To Get The Most of it, Available at: https://www.providesupport.com/blog/4-dimensions-of-customer-trust-how-to-get-the-most-of-it/.

9. Hertzum, M. 2002. The importance of trust in software engineers' assessment and choice of information sources. Information and Organization, 12(1): 1–18.

10. Yan, Z., Kantola, R. and Zhang, P. 2011. A research model for human-computer trust interaction. 2011 IEEE 10th International Conference on Trust, Security and Privacy in Computing and Communications, pp. 274–281, doi: 10.1109/TrustCom.2011.37.

11. Yan, Z. 2014. User Trust and Human-Computer Trust Interaction. IGI Global. https://doi.org/10.4018/978-1-4666-4765-7.ch007.

12. Madsen, M. and Gregor, S. 2021. Measuring Human-Computer Trust. Available at: https://citeseerx.ist.psu.edu/viewdoc/download?doi=10.1.1.93.3874&rep=rep1&type=pdf.

13. Petrén, M.G. 2012. Trust–the Key for Successful Delivery Using Agile Methods. Project Management Institute. Available at: https://www.pmi.org/learning/library/trust-successful-delivery-agile-methods-6419.

Useful Links

https://tateeda.com/blog/fundamental-principles-of-good-software-design
https://www.entrepreneur.com/article/276046
https://moam.info/
https://blog.hubspot.com/customers/3-ways-to-delight-your-customers-to-earn-their-trust
https://vwo.com/blog/trust-in-ecommerce/
https://www.jstor.org/stable/23015482

CHAPTER 8

Software Durability Assessment Methodology

8.1 Objectives

Identifying features of durability is a difficult process because specialists have different opinions about the importance of aspects that influence the software's durability quotient. According to the best practises in this area, it would be judicious to note that many experts believe that quality is the most significant aspect in determining durability. Hence, our investigative study will essentially focus on the assessment based on attributes that define and establish the quality. With that as the key premise, this chapter employs multi-criteria decision-based strategies to handle the multi-criteria choice availability for appropriate technique selection. Additionally, it has been discovered that a mathematical assessment of software durability might have an impact on the software's service life and low-cost management. The following are the key objectives of this chapter:

- To implement the fuzzy sets-based AHP procedure and the fuzzy sets-based SAM procedures for assessing software durability for quality improvement.
- To achieve the software durability of online applications by using the procedure of fuzzy set-based AHP-SAM.
- To enlist empirical data about how formal and well-proven durability parameters are implemented throughout the software development life cycle.
- Forthcoming benefits of durability assessment are discussed in the various domains, including source code durability, documentation, user interface, and durability; security and privacy; durable performance; business logic; architecture durability; data durability; interoperability.

8.2 Software Durability Assessment

Durability ensures that the software is available when it is needed and that it meets the user's expectations. The durability must be evaluated to ensure that it meets a set of basic quality and durability standards, both of which are critical for effectively adopting software engineering concepts [3]. The software's durability is determined by examining the methodologies, tools, and procedures used to design and test it. The purpose of the durability evaluation is to identify areas for improvement and to propose a strategy for doing so. The key areas of attention for the durability evaluation are described below:

- Getting advice on how to extend the life of software services
- Getting an objective and unbiased assessment of the durability
- Obtaining a baseline for enhancing the quality and productivity of the software life cycle (defined as a set of previously examined and accepted software components and documentation that serve as the foundation for future development).

Software durability testing determines whether the software's lifespan is effective and efficient in achieving its objectives. The capability of selected software durability attributes determines this. A durability characteristic's capacity decides whether or not a durability attribute with some variations may match the user's needs [4]. It also assesses how well the software fits the user's requirements in terms of longevity. The organisation benefits from durability assessments because it aids in the improvement of existing procedures. It also identifies the strengths, weaknesses, and dangers associated with sustaining the software's expected life duration.

The durability assessment leads to the estimation of life-span capability and the enhancement of durability. The analysis of the software life span for a particular period with a consistent maintenance method is known as durability capacity determination [5]. Furthermore, determining durability capability identifies the capabilities of a durability feature as well as the hazards associated with it. The software development life cycle's adjustments to be made are identified by the durability assessment and enhancement.

Furthermore, software durability evaluation and enhancement are a set of criteria that are used to guide goals and essential operations, as well as grade the organisation based on its level of software service life estimation and improvement. It also uses the assessment results to determine the capabilities of a durability attribute during software development.

8.3 Measurement Categories

The estimated parameters, location of the measured parameter, and whether the measuring system is permanently or portable fixed in the structure are the measurement categories for software durability assessment [4–5]. The following are the direct and indirect parameters determined for durability assessment:

8.3.1 Indirect Parameters

These parameters provide no direct information on the durability state of the software; however, the risk of failure and the rate of failure can be estimated.

8.3.2 Direct Parameters

Direct parameters like the durability rate of the reinforcement provide direct information on the durability state of the software.

8.4 Multi Criteria Decision Analysis

The evaluation of software durability appears to include a variety of factors. To analyse software security, for example, qualities such as confidentiality, integrity, availability, and authentication must be evaluated [2, 5]. Software durability has several characteristics, many of which have been thoroughly explained in earlier chapters. As a result, determining software durability is a multi-criteria challenge. In this study, multi criterion decision making techniques will be employed to examine software longevity and its contributing factors. One of the most important approaches for assessing several criteria with many levels is Multiple Criteria Decision Making (MCDM) or Multiple Criteria Decision Analysis (MCDA).

The MCDA methodology aids in the decision-making process when there are several competing factors. MCDA approaches can be used to handle multiple-criteria problems in everyday life, such as selecting one criterion from a set of criteria. MCDA-based research has only been around for a few years. Furthermore, the widespread use of the internet in everyday life has resulted in a slew of issues across a variety of dimensions. A decision matrix is commonly used to describe an MCDA situation. Suppose there are s alternatives to be assessed based on t attributes, a decision matrix is a s × t matrix with each element Y_{ij} being the j-th attribute value of the i-th alternative.

MCDA methods have been used in the field of information technology for a variety of objectives, including information security, reliability, and quality, but no work has been done in the context of using decision models to analyse software durability. Although, many different decision-making models are available, deciding on a single approach or a combination of ways is a difficult undertaking as this is mostly dependent on the type of the problem. The authors have employed a multiple-criteria decision-making process in this study to select the appropriate durability attributes and assess software durability. The authors conducted an exhaustive literature review on the available models, as stated in the ensuing part, to understand the efficacy of MCDM techniques.

8.5 Pertinent Work on Decision Making Analysis

The MCDM approaches are the most effective techniques for resolving the uncertainty associated with attribute selection to improve software durability. In the literature, the fuzzy in hybrid with multi-criteria approach has been applied several times. The following are some of the relevant works on MCDA:

Kanza Gulzar et al., 2017 [6]
In terms of experimental evaluation, the authors suggested a fuzzy technique for prioritising usability requirement conflicts. The research introduced a novel paradigm for translating usability objectives to linguistic assessment by the users with the aid of fuzzy logic. Furthermore, the suggested framework prioritises usability needs and traits that are in conflict. The MATLAB fuzzy logic toolbox was utilised to implement the report. By automating the entire process of finding and resolving usability requirement conflicts, the suggested framework aims to assist the requirement analyst in making better judgments.

Afrin A. et al., 2017 [7]
The authors discussed a study in which they selected requirements of the software using fuzzy based AHP and TOPSIS methodologies. There are two categories of software requirements, according to his research: functional and non-functional. These needs are influenced by a number of things. In this example, a group requirements elicitation technique is used to determine the developer's useful requirements. Fuzzy based AHP and TOPSIS methodologies are used to eliminate ambiguity and choose the optimal option for developers. The findings of combining MCDM approaches yielded better outcomes than using simply one methodology.

Edmundas Kazimieras Zavadskas et al., 2016 [8]
This paper organised sustainability challenges into three domains based on economic, environmental, and social elements in the suggested

approach of hybrid MCDM methodologies to evaluate the sustainability of companies and organisations. The authors also discovered that the most common MCDM methods in constructing hybrid approaches include well-known methods with strong mathematical backgrounds and desirable attributes, such as AHP, ANP, DANP, TOPSIS, and VIKOR. In the end, this study showed that hybrid approaches, rather than a single MCDM method, are recommended for better results.

Chong C. Y. et al., 2014 [9]
The authors used the software development guidelines and fuzzy AHP to address the issue of prioritising and completing quality characteristics for virtual lab development. It's vital to make sure that all the qualities included in the Service Level Agreement (SLA) are in the order of priority. Prioritizing performance parameters is necessary to concentrate on the capabilities that are of the greatest significance while ensuring that the basic minimum standard is satisfied for the other features. This study prioritised the quality criteria using a prominent MCDM technique for FAHP. After the prioritisation of quality attributes, a set of rules for achieving the quality attributes in a virtual lab environment was produced. The use of fuzzy AHP in the study revealed that participants prioritised usability, efficiency, reliability, maintainability, portability, and security in decreasing order of importance, allowing for the formulation of a set of non-conflicting, suitable software development rules as well as regulations.

Davoud Goli, 2013 [10]
The author described a way of using the Fuzzy TOPSIS methodology to choose the best computer security software from a list of seven options. The study cites that there are several antivirus software options in the market, but their selection is based on aspects like power, the convenience of use, cost, and so on. The most popular antivirus software has been shortlisted and evaluated in this study to see how it performs against the set of criteria. As a result, this problem is classified as an MCDM problem and is assessed by using the Fuzzy TOPSIS methodology, followed by a sensitivity analysis that considers three aspects as being sensitive to the outcomes.

Irfan Syamsuddin, 2013 [11]
The study proposed decision analysis based on the Ternary Analytic Hierarchy Process (T-AHP) as a unique framework to assist the managers in conducting strategic evaluations connected with the challenges in information security. To test the consistency of the final estimation, sensitivity analysis was used to broaden this analysis by considering multiple "what-if" scenarios.

S. K. Dubey et al., 2013 [12]

Using a fuzzy multi-criterion weighted average technique, the authors suggested a way of assessing software usability ratings. The usability of software is a key criterion for its quality. The practicality of this strategy was then tested using MS Word 2003 in a case study. The evaluation attributes were extracted from ISO 9126-1. To evaluate the usability of a case study, a hierarchy of attributes was created. The final usability of Ms. Word 2003 is calculated by using the ratings of the attributes in this study. Other developers can use this methodology to assess the usability of any software.

Li Shi et al., 2012 [13]

The authors presented a fresh weighted TOPSIS approach combined with improved TOPSIS methodologies for evaluating software trustworthiness. The entropy weighting approach was utilised to determine the objective weights in this study. Thereafter, the priorities of the attributes of trustworthiness using the combination weighting method were calculated. Furthermore, this information was used in the TOPSIS approach to assess the dependability of PLM software, with an aircraft equipment company in China as a case study. To validate the results, a sensitivity analysis was executed on the results.

Nadir Omer Fadl Elssied, 2011 [14]

The author asserts that fuzzy set theory is particularly effective for evaluating the security of e-government. The study reviews the use of fuzzy algorithms in the realm of e-government security and offers a comparison of five Fuzzy-based techniques. The study concludes that for achieving good performance in the artificial intelligence sector, new evaluation methodologies are required, especially for evaluating effectiveness and efficiency. It also says that, while the existing approaches generate good results, fully secure software is still out of reach, meaning that there is still a lot of work to be done in this area.

Aşkın Özdağoğlu et al., 2007 [15]

The authors examined and contrasted the methodologies of AHP and Fuzzy-AHP with the help of a case study. Employee selection for the shop floor of a manufacturing platform in the food sector was the subject of the case study used here. To handle the hierarchical fuzzy issues, the fuzzy extension of AHP, fuzzy AHP, was created to eliminate performance hazards. Fuzzy AHP is most suited for decision-making in applications where data must be retrieved in linguistic values, according to the study. The Fuzzy logic method is ideally suited for applications in the software sector since it can handle ambiguity in linguistic data. AHP evaluates priorities using linguistic values and a weighing mechanism within the present choices utilising pair-wise comparisons.

Liming Zhu et al., 2005 [16]

The authors discussed their study on sensitivity analysis and the tradeoff in the evaluation of the software architecture using an analytical hierarchy process. Different architectural design alternatives are evaluated against many quality-attributes in software architecture evaluation. To reach a final design decision, these features generally have inherent conflicts and must be examined simultaneously. The authors presented many in-depth analysis methodologies that can be applied to AHP to uncover crucial tradeoffs and sensitive spots in the decision-making process in this paper. They also applied their method to a real-world distributed architecture. The findings were encouraging in that they clarified major choice implications in terms of key design compromises and the architecture's ability to manage future quality characteristic modifications.

Van Laarhoven et al., 1983 [17]

The authors were the first to implement the Fuzzy AHP, which involved comparing Triangular Fuzzy Numbers (TFNs) based on their membership functions. The Fuzzy AHP approach has been applied for decision-making in a range of study domains, including selecting, prioritising, and assessing, among others. The approach was used on two levels by the researchers. The first stage involved determining fuzzy weights for the decision criteria, and the second involved determining fuzzy weights for each of the decision criteria's alternatives. After that, fuzzy scores for the options were obtained by combining these results in the right way. Decision-makers can utilise these fuzzy ratings to choose one of the alternatives, according to this study.

As is evident from the perusal of the above Literature, MCDA is a widely used method for assessing the difficulties in the process of software development. Furthermore, as proven by the literature, it is not only a helpful technique for analysing software durability, but the outcomes of this procedure are also useful in real-world circumstances.

8.6 Durability Assessment through Decision Making Technique

Software development is a time-consuming and expensive process that must adhere to strict deadlines. As a result, software engineers face the problem of creating software that is both user-centric and long-lasting. For more than a decade, software's lifetime has been an important setting for all developers. An effective way to produce durable software is to evaluate and monitor software durability variables such as reliability during the development phases [1, 4–5]. Software durability is not something that can be achieved overnight; rather, it is a development strategy that focuses on creating long-lasting software. More than 73 percent of the firms seek to enhance their technology until 2025, according to a technical analysis produced by Software-as-a-Service (SaaS), an operations and management company [2].

In fact, the topic of maintenance was also covered in Cisco's Global Cloud Index from 2013–2018. It has been estimated that by the end of 2025, 59 percent of the cloud workflows will be delivered via SaaS. Organizations devote a significant amount of time and money to extending the life of software [2–3]. These studies demonstrate the need for long-lasting software in today's world. Experts Kelty C. and Erickson S. advocated the development of a new notion of software durability in 2015 [5]. According to them, software durability is defined as extending the life of software for a set period to provide services that meet the needs of the user. Practitioners also understand that the market value of software is determined by its durability [4]. This property of software deteriorates over time, and its ability to work for a long time deteriorates. As a result, the software services are reliant on software availability.

Agrawal A. et al., developed a novel concept of software engineering durability for analysing and enhancing software durability [2]. The authors claim that software durability is determined by four primary factors: trustworthiness, reliability, human trust, security, and usefulness. Furthermore, the combination of software and durability aids in the provision of long-term software services. Moreover, software durability can be estimated by using the durability and quality attributes [6]. Additionally, assessment is a judgement that is influenced by a variety of factors. As a result, estimating software durability is classified as an MCDM challenge. For evaluating a decision with numerous criteria, MCDM approaches are becoming increasingly popular [7].

There are a variety of MCDM strategies for resolving such construction issues [7]. However, determining the durability of a product is critical. The authors employed a fuzzy-based hybrid method in this study [8–11]. This hybrid method employs a series of pair-wise comparisons to determine the weights of the criteria and rank the options in order of preference. We have also attempted to evaluate software durability using a hybrid technique for a more conclusive examination of the same.

8.7 Durability Assessment Mechanism

Durability is one of the most significant software quality features for both the end users and developers [11]. Estimating software durability is important for enhancing the quality of software and its life span [12–13]. Durability testing is necessary to extend the life of software and may be beneficial for meeting the software development policies, goals, and user satisfaction. Software service life cannot be durable if the durability is not measured. The measurement of software durability in this case consists of two steps: mechanism selection and description, as well as implementation.

8.7.1 Mechanism Selection and Description

Some of the studies done in this context cite that including durability in and as part of the design process can help to improve the potential of other quality attributes [6–8]. A software product is durable if its function performs well enough for the user to be satisfied for the predicted amount of time. Furthermore, it is critical to build a link between the software development process and durability concept. The identification and classification of durability attributes aid in the assessment and improvement of software durability. The relationship between durability characteristics (at various levels) was identified in the previous chapter to design durable software. Many direct and indirect factors influence the expected life span or durability. Dependability, trustworthiness, usability, security, and human trust are direct elements, whereas indirect factors include reliability, consumer integrity, and so on. Paying close attention to these characteristics throughout the early stages of software development may improve the software's long-term viability. Furthermore, to ensure the desired level of durability, a durability assessment is required. The evaluation procedure must include not only the assessment of the attributes that contribute to durability, but must also determine which ones are the most important [12–13]. In a nutshell, the procedures of discovering, prioritising, and evaluating the components are crucial.

The problem of durability assessment is a decision-making problem since there are many criteria in the form of durability attributes after an evaluation. Durability assessment is thus related to multiple-criteria decision-making problems in technical terms. The problem of decision making can be resolved by using a variety of ways and methodologies [14–15]. In addition, the MCDA approach is a discipline aimed at assisting specialists when confronted with several conflicting items for evaluation [9–10]. When dealing with two or more competing situations at the same time, the MCDA method is ideal. AHP and Fuzzy AHP, for example, are two MCDA approaches [2, 11]. The preceding methodologies differ in terms of whether their decisions are objective or subjective. The Fuzzy AHP is used to test the durability in this study. Furthermore, the findings aid in the formulation of development strategies for achieving the desired software durability. This could aid software engineers in creating long-lasting software.

8.7.2 Implementation Procedure

The authors have proposed a unified technique, known as the Fuzzy AHP technique [2], to overcome the underlying issue of durability assessment. Although AHP is effective for analysing a group choice, several practitioners have discovered that unified AHP is better for taking more specific decisions with their weights as well [3–6]. To deal with the ambiguity and uncertainty of practitioners, the authors used a unified form of AHP (also known as "fuzzy AHP"), which combines fuzzy set theory with the AHP technique [11] to assess the software's durability. Figure 1 depicts the flow chart of the adopted methodology. The flow chart depicts the method of determining durability. Fuzzy operations, fuzzification, defuzzification, planning, and analysis, confirmation, and estimation are among the five phases or steps.

The recognition of problems, the selection of solutions for the problems, and the definition of the scope and boundaries of the AHP are all part of the planning phase. The fuzzification phase deals with the procedure's initial steps, such as describing the membership function on a scale. The Fuzzy operations segment is concerned with the execution of pair-wise comparison matrices using expert views and TFNs. The transition of fuzzified weights into defuzzified values is dealt with in the defuzzification step, whereas weights, ratings, and assessment are dealt with in the final phase. Furthermore, the last phase addresses performance (improvement), sensitivity analysis, and statistical analysis to validate the results. The process is broken down into phases and described in sub-parts as follows:

8.7.2.1 Planning Phase

With a hierarchical structure comprising numerous criteria, AHP is utilised as a decision-making technique for predicting the priority numbers for various alternatives [8–11]. According to the findings, AHP is better for selecting the best options from a vast number of possibilities, whereas fuzzy is best for dealing with linguistic factors. As a result, Fuzzy AHP is employed in this study to achieve superior results.

8.7.2.2 Fuzzification Phase

The authors have provided a brief introduction to both methodologies as well as a unified tactic of them to better comprehend the Fuzzy AHP methodology. The AHP is a decision process defined by Saaty as "a decision method that decomposes a complex multi-criteria decision problem into a hierarchy" [18]. AHP's main advantage is the relative ease

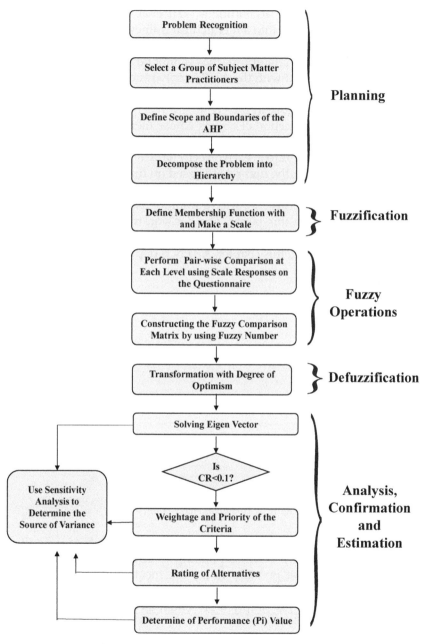

Figure 1: Flow Chart of the Fuzzy AHP Technique.

with which it handles several conditions. AHP enables the experts to break down a complex problem into a hierarchical framework that includes the goal, sub-objectives, objectives, and alternatives. When there is uncertainty in the data, traditional AHP approaches cannot be applied. The fuzzy set theory was incorporated with the AHP to solve such uncertainty. To deal with the uncertainty produced by imprecision and ambiguity, Zadeh created the fuzzy set theory in 1965 [19].

A fuzzy set is a collection of objects whose membership is rated on a scale of one to ten. A membership function, which assigns a membership grade between one and zero to each object, characterises such a set. From a reasonable perspective, the fuzzy AHP based on fuzzy interval arithmetic using TFNs has been presented to simplify the fuzzy AHP approach. Fuzzy AHP was used to prioritise security-durability aspects in the context of the topic addressed in this paper. The decision maker can make easier decisions with the help of a TFN [2]. As a result, TFNs are employed as a membership function in this chapter. A TFN is depicted in Fig. 2.

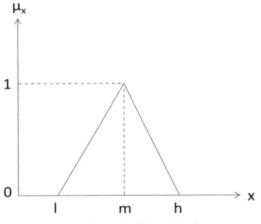

Figure 2: Triangular Fuzzy Number.

In Fig. 2, μ_x is signified as a membership function where μ signifies membership importance of corresponding x. The parameters, h, l, and m represent the largest possible value, the most promising value and the smallest possible value, respectively that designates a fuzzy event. In addition, a TFN (μ_{ij}) is simply represented as (l, m, h). The TFN μ_{ij} is signified in Eq. (1).

$$\mu_{ij} = (l_{ij}, m_{ij}, h_{ij}) \tag{1}$$

$$where \; l_{ij} \leq m_{ij} \leq h_{ij}$$

and

$$l_{ij}, m_{ij}, h_{ij} \in [1/9, 9]$$

$$l_{ij} = min(B_{ijk}),$$

$$m_{ij} = (B_{ij1} \cdot B_{ij2} \ldots \ldots \ldots \ldots B_{ijk})1/k$$

$$and \; h_{ij} = max(B_{ijk})$$

where B_{ijk} denotes the decision of the practitioners k for the significance of two criteria, i.e., C_i and C_j. Fuzzy numbers perform best to combine the scattered views of the practitioners because each number in the pairwise comparison matrix denotes the subjective judgement of practitioners and is an ambiguous idea [2, 11]. To build the fuzzy judgement matrix used in the AHP procedure [18] and indicated in Eq. (2), Saaty proposed the pair-wise comparisons.

$$A = [a_{ij}] = \begin{array}{c} \\ \\ \\ \\ \\ \\ \end{array} \begin{array}{c} C_1 \\ C_2 \\ \vdots \\ \\ C_n \end{array} \begin{array}{ccc} C_1 & C_2 \ldots\ldots & C_n \\ \begin{bmatrix} 1 & a_{11}\ldots\ldots & a_{1n} \\ 1/a_{21} & 1\ldots.. & a_{2n} \\ . & . & . \\ . & . & . \\ 1/a_{n1} & 1/a_{n2}\ldots\ldots & 1 \end{bmatrix} \end{array} \qquad (2)$$

where i = 1,2,3.........n and j = 1,2,3..............n and a_{ij}= 1: when i=j; and a_{ij}=1/a_{ij}; when i≠j

where $[a_{ij}]$ signifies a TFN for the relative significance of two criteria C_i and C_j. Corresponding linguistic scale for membership functions (1 to 9) is specified in Table 1.

Table 1 displays the conversion of linguistic amounts to numeric amounts and numeric amounts to TFN amounts. TFN amounts can be used to make a pair-wise comparison matrix of relative criteria, where aij signifies the relative significance of criteria I in the scale compared to criteria j. Identify the relative importance of each group of qualities. Furthermore, many experts' decisions on durability are summarised as fuzzy pair-wise comparison matrixes. It's also employed to describe the pair-wise fuzzy judgement matrix that's employed in the AHP method. The linguistic rating scale is presented in Table 2 for determining the alternative importance.

Table 2 depicts the 1 to 0 rating scale, with 0.1 denoting "Very Low" (VL), 0.3 denoting "Low" (L), and so on. Every piece of data acquired from an expert for a certain option is given the accompanying fuzzy

Table 1: Linguistic Scale.

S. No.	Linguistic Values	Numeric Values	Fuzzified Numbers (TFNs) $[a_{ij}]$	$1/[a_{ij}]$
1	Equal Important (Eq)	1	(1,1,1)	(1,1,1)
2	Intermediate Value between Equal and Weakly (E & W)	2	(1,2,3)	(1/3,1/2,1)
3	Weakly Important (WI)	3	(2,3,4)	(1/4,1/3,1/2)
4	Intermediate Value between Weakly and Essential (W & E)	4	(3,4,5)	(1/5,1/4,1/3)
5	Essential Important (EI)	5	(4,5,6)	(1/6,1/5,1/4)
6	Intermediate Value between Essential and Very Strongly (E & VS)	6	(5,6,7)	(1/7,1/6,1/5)
7	Very Strongly Important (VS)	7	(6,7,8)	(1/8,1/7,1/6)
8	Intermediate Value between Very Strongly and Extremely (VS & ES)	8	(7,8,9)	(1/9,1/8,1/7)
9	Extremely Important (ES)	9	(7,9,9)	(1/9,1/9,1/7)

Table 2: Rating Scale.

S. No.	Linguistic Value	Numeric Value of Ratings	Fuzzified Ratings (TFNs)
1	Very Low (VL)	0.1	(0.0, 0.1, 0.3)
2	Low (L)	0.3	(0.1, 0.3, 0.5)
3	Medium (M)	0.7	(0.5, 0.7, 0.9)
4	High (H)	0.9	(0.7, 0.9, 1.0)
5	Very High (VH)	1.0	(0.9, 1.0, 1.0)

values. Collecting data as given by different experts is the first step in the assessment process. Questionnaires, checklists, and other methods can be used to collect data. The information gathered from the practitioners is compared pair by pair to determine the relative significance of each criterion for which one element is preferred over another in relation to each criterion. However, for a complicated topic, human perceptions and judgments are expressed by linguistic and ambiguous terminology [18–19].

8.7.2.3 *Fuzzy Operations*

In the next step of the assessment, various linguistic data sets are transformed into quantitative data sets, which are then turned into TFN values. Alternatives such as TFNs are employed to limit the ambiguity of the parameters with which they are associated [8–10]. Fuzzy procedures are required to combine all of the data into a single form. If, two TFNs $M_1 = (l1, m1, h1)$ and $M_2 = (l2, m2, h2)$ are given. Then, the operation's rules on them are specified below in Eq. (3)–(5).

$$(l_1, m_1, h_1) + (l_2, m_2, h_2) = (l_1 + l_2, m_1 + m_2, h_1 + h_2) \quad (3)$$

$$(l_1, m_1, h_1) \times (l_2, m_2, h_2) = (l_1 \times l_2, m_1 \times m_2, h_1 \times h_2) \quad (4)$$

$$(l_1, m_1, h_1)^{-1} = (\frac{1}{h_1}, \frac{1}{m_1}, \frac{1}{l_1}) \quad (5)$$

These fuzzy operations are employed in a variety of sectors for decision making, including rating, weights, decision making, and so on [11–12]. The imprecision and ambiguities that arise due to conflicting opinions can be converted into specific results by applying the logic of fuzzy sets.

8.7.2.4 *Defuzzification*

Defuzzification procedure is employed after the comparison matrix is constructed to produce a quantifiable amount based on the calculated TFN amounts. The defuzzification method employed in this book was developed from [13–15], which is often referred to as the *alpha cut technique;* enlisted here from Eq. (6)–(9).

$$\tilde{A} = [\tilde{a}_{ij}] = \begin{array}{c} \\ C_1 \\ C_2 \\ \vdots \\ C_n \end{array} \begin{matrix} C_1 & C_2 \;\ldots\ldots & C_n \\ \begin{bmatrix} 1 & \tilde{a}_{11} \ldots\ldots & \tilde{a}_{1i} \\ 1/\tilde{a}_{21} & 1\ldots.. & \tilde{a}_{2i} \\ . & . & . \\ . & . & . \\ 1/\tilde{a}_{jl} & 1/\tilde{a}_{j2} \ldots\ldots & 1 \end{bmatrix} \end{matrix} \quad (6)$$

Matrix $\tilde{A}$ is defined as the defuzzified AHP. Where $[\tilde{a}_{ij}]$ signifies a TFN and displays the relative significance between two criteria Ci and Cj. Several defuzzification techniques have been presented in the literature such as center of sums, alpha cut, and centroid, etc. [16–17]. The authors have employed the *alpha cut technique* for defuzzification procedure. Alpha cut facilitates one to define a fuzzy set as a composition of crisp sets. Crisp sets simply define whether an element is either a member of the set or not. To defuzzify fuzzy matrix (Ã) into a crisp matrix, $(\rho_{\alpha,\beta})$ is presented in Eq. (7)–(9) (alpha cut method).

$$\rho_{\alpha,\beta}(\tilde{a}_{ij}) = [\beta.\eta_\alpha(l_{ij}) + (1-\beta).\eta_\alpha(h_{ij})] \tag{7}$$

where $0 \leq \alpha \leq 1$ *and* $0 \leq \beta \leq 1$
such that,

$$\eta_\alpha(l_{ij}) = (m_{ij} - l_{ij}).\alpha + l_{ij} \tag{8}$$

$$\eta_\alpha(h_{ij}) = h_{ij} - (h_{ij} - m_{ij}).\alpha \tag{9}$$

In Eq. (7)–(9), η_α (l_{ij}) signifies the left-end boundary amount of alpha cut for $\tilde{a}_{ij}$ and η_α (l_{ij}) signifies the right-end boundary amount of alpha cut for $\tilde{a}_{ij}$. Further, α and β carry the meaning of preferences and risk tolerance of participants. Mostly, α and β can be stable or in a fluctuating condition. These two amounts range between 0 and 1, in such a way that a lesser amount indicates greater uncertainty in decision making. Meanwhile, the amount of α comes to a stable state when it is increasing particularly. Furthermore, α and β can be any number between 0 and 1, and investigation is normally set as the following 10 numbers, 0.1, 0.2, up to 0.9 for uncertainty emulation. Since risk tolerance and preferences are not the focus of this study, an amount of 0.5 for α and β is employed to signify a balanced amount. This indicates that attributes are neither extremely optimistic nor pessimistic about their comparison. Variation due to value of α and β is discussed in sensitivity analysis portion. Although, the single pair wise comparison matrix is shown in Eq. (10).

$$\rho_{\alpha,\beta}(\tilde{A}) = \rho_{\alpha,\beta}[\tilde{a}_{ij}] = \begin{array}{c} C_1 \\ C_2 \\ \vdots \\ C_n \end{array} \begin{bmatrix} 1 & \rho_{\alpha,\beta}(\tilde{a}_{11})\dots\dots & \rho_{\alpha,\beta}(\tilde{a}_{1i}) \\ 1/\rho_{\alpha,\beta}(\tilde{a}_{21}) & 1\dots.. & \rho_{\alpha,\beta}(\tilde{a}_{2i}) \\ . & . & . \\ . & . & . \\ 1/\rho_{\alpha,\beta}(\tilde{a}_{j1}) & 1/\rho_{\alpha,\beta}(\tilde{a}_{j2})\dots\dots & 1 \end{bmatrix} \tag{10}$$

The next part of the section is about defuzzification and validating the matrix's consistency.

8.7.2.5 *Analysis, Confirmation and Estimation*

The next step is to determine the eigenvalue and eigenvector of the fuzzy pair wise comparison matrix (Eq. (11)). The purpose of calculating the eigenvector is to determine the aggregated weightage of a particular criteria. Assume that W denotes the eigenvector, I denotes unitary matrix while λ denotes the eigenvalue of fuzzy pair-wise comparison matrix $\tilde{A}$ or $[\tilde{a}_{ij}]$.

$$[(\rho_{\alpha,\beta} \times \tilde{A}) - \lambda \times I]. \, W = 0 \tag{11}$$

where $\tilde{A}$ η_{ij} is a fuzzy matrix containing fuzzy numbers of the $\rho_{\alpha,\beta}$ $(\tilde{A})$ $\rho_{\alpha,\beta} \times \tilde{A}$. Equation (11) is based on the linear transformation of vectors. By employing Eq. (1)–(11), the weightage of a particular criteria with respect to all other possible criteria can be acquired. The eigenvectors of associated characteristics were then estimated using Eq. (11) as presented in Eq. (12).

$$[(\rho_{\alpha,\beta} \times \tilde{A}) - \lambda \times I].W = \begin{bmatrix} 1 & \rho_{\alpha,\beta}(\tilde{a}_{11})\ldots\ldots & \rho_{\alpha,\beta}(\tilde{a}_{1i}) \\ 1/\rho_{\alpha,\beta}(\tilde{a}_{21}) & 1\ldots.. & \rho_{\alpha,\beta}(\tilde{a}_{2i}) \\ . & . & . \\ . & . & . \\ . & . & . \\ 1/\rho_{\alpha,\beta}(\tilde{a}_{j1}) & 1/\rho_{\alpha,\beta}(\tilde{a}_{j2})\ldots\ldots & 1 \end{bmatrix} \tag{12}$$

Multiplying eigenvalue λ with unitary matrix I produces an identity matrix that cancels out each other. Thus, the notation λI is discarded in this case. Employing Eq. (11)–(12) outcomes are presented in Eq. (13).

$$\begin{bmatrix} 1 & \rho_{\alpha,\beta}(\tilde{a}_{11})\ldots\ldots & \rho_{\alpha,\beta}(\tilde{a}_{1i}) \\ 1/\rho_{\alpha,\beta}(\tilde{a}_{21}) & 1\ldots.. & \rho_{\alpha,\beta}(\tilde{a}_{2i}) \\ . & . & . \\ . & . & . \\ . & . & . \\ 1/\rho_{\alpha,\beta}(\tilde{a}_{j1}) & 1/\rho_{\alpha,\beta}(\tilde{a}_{j2})\ldots\ldots & 1 \end{bmatrix} X \begin{bmatrix} W1 \\ W2 \\ . \\ . \\ . \\ . \\ Wn \end{bmatrix} = \begin{bmatrix} 0 \\ 0 \\ . \\ . \\ . \\ . \\ 0 \end{bmatrix} \tag{13}$$

Equation (13) shows the totaled results in terms of weights. Eq. (14) is employed to determine the Consistency Ratio (CR) for each matrix in the hierarchal configuration to control the technique's results.

$$CR = \frac{CI}{RI} \tag{14}$$

CI denotes the Consistency Index and RI denotes the Random Index [2]. Further, CI is estimated from Eq. (15).

$$CI = \frac{\lambda}{(n-1)} \tag{15}$$

Table 3: Random Index.

N	1	2	3	4	5	6	7	8	9
Random Index (RI)	0.00	0.00	0.58	0.90	1.12	1.24	1.35	1.41	1.49

Where, n signifies the number of total responses and RI is given by Saaty [18]; the rank of matrix has been presented in Table 3.

With the help of Eq. (14)–(15) and Table 3, CR is intended. If CR < 0.1, the approximation is accepted and the outcomes are estimated after this with the help of Eq. 13; otherwise, a new comparison matrix is solicited.

This work evaluates the dependent weights and ranks them by using the hierarchical structure. The outcomes of the obtainable weights give some suggestions for practitioners to enhance the life span of software. The design of version 2 is updated according to the researcher's suggestions. Through the hierarchy, the authors estimate the independent (that are given in linguistic forms by the designers) and dependent ratings [14–16] of durability characteristics (for version 1 and version 2, respectively) with the help of Eq. (1)–(9). Then, the authors estimated the durability of the alternative. Overall durability is evaluated by Eq. (16) [17–19].

$$\text{Software Durability} = R_1 \times W_1 + R_2 \times W_2 + \ldots\ldots R_n \times W_n = \Sigma\, R_i \times W_i \quad (16)$$

Or

$$[R_1\, R_2\, R_3 \ldots R_i] * \begin{bmatrix} W_1 \\ W_2 \\ W_i \end{bmatrix} = \Sigma\, R_i \times W_i$$

where R stands for the rating amounts, W for the corresponding attribute's weight, and I for the number of attributes that determine durability. The findings clearly demonstrate the impact of the researcher's recommendations and this research project.

8.8 Benefits of Durability Assessment

Investing in a new software product is always a significant choice. Once spending such a large sum of money on a new tool or technique that will most likely be widely used within an updated software product, it is critical to thoroughly evaluate the implications before updating software to ensure that it will meet user's requirements and provide a positive return on the customer's investment with long-term services. Developers can evaluate both the software's objective aspects, such as its ability to link with existing systems, and more subjective factors, such as environment, practitioners find the interface comfortable to use with constant upkeep, when determining its longevity. Practitioners will be able to create a better educated decision about the mechanism after finishing the durability assessment. Here are some things to think about when analysing software durability. Moreover, each attribute might help the development organisations to keep the user happy with their end product. Following are the benefits of software durability assessment:

8.8.1 Source Code Durability

The software will be secure, reliable, trustworthy, and long-lasting if it has good source code. While code durability is a personal preference, good source code follows a consistent style, has been documented, can be tested, and is simple to understand. Update statistical analysis methods and construct automatic tools to analyse the software's durability, or likelihood of running without failure for an estimated period, to determine whether it is high enough for the user's needs. Practitioners should also make sure that the code is simple to test and integrate with other applications under the perspective of constant maintenance. Keep a look out for a high number of defect reports or a long time to identify a flaw, as these indicate less durable source code.

8.8.2 Documentation, User Interface, and Durability

A long-lasting software programme is simple to learn and use daily, saving time and worry for end users. Although this is a highly subjective approach that differs from person to person, there are some crucial characteristics to consider when assessing the durability or longevity of software, such as the documentation and user interface. Because these parts are clearly identified, practitioners will logically go toward the proper buttons and sections to execute tasks if an interface is intuitive. If practitioners require assistance, excellent documentation can swiftly resolve difficulties with durability, allowing practitioners to finish their tasks rather than waste time looking for solutions.

8.8.3 Security and Privacy

Security and privacy are critical components of any programme because all the firms deal with sensitive information from customers and employees. Software durability testing from the perspective of security and privacy helps the practitioners to protect the information and avoid a costly data breach.

8.8.4 Durable Performance

An extraordinary software programme has minimal unplanned downtime and can handle large amounts of data without putting the system under strain. Practitioners may find it challenging to accomplish their work on time if the updated software is slow to load or completely unavailable. Due to its durability, reliability, and durability in managing enormous amounts of data, high-performing software overcomes this problem.

8.8.5 Business Logic

The characteristic of a software programme that governs how data can be created, modified, and stored is known as business logic. For example, when a consumer adds an article to their online shopping cart, enters their payment and shipping information, then finalizes the purchase, business logic defines the sequence of activities. Consistency is ensured by complete business logic, and organizations can restrict how much information the practitioners/users may edit and view. This can be a useful logistical tool that also aids in the maintenance of organization-wide standard practices.

8.8.6 Architecture Durability

The fundamental structure of the software is its architecture. It is made up of different long-lasting software parts, their relationships, and the attributes associated with them that improve the software's service life. For example, if an organization requires speedy and long-lasting software, the programme will be developed to meet the organization's requirements. During the software development process, practitioners will be able to perform all the necessary activities within a specific time frame and modify the software to fit additional needs with constant maintenance.

8.8.7 Data Durability

If data accurately represents the real-world information and can be used to make informed decisions, it is deemed to be of high durability. Data that is durable should also be consistent, especially when dealing with vast amounts of data. To be called high durability, the data within software should follow comparable principles. To ensure that the software meets the user's needs, think about how it stores, collects, organises, and analyses data.

8.8.8 Interoperability

Assessing the durable software's interoperability or its ability to work across several devices or with different software systems confirms the software's durability for a long time. This allows the practitioners to use the software with the organizations' existing infrastructure rather than purchasing new equipment. As a result, both money and time are saved because the practitioners can start using the durable software as soon as possible to meet the envisioned objectives.

8.9 Conclusion

Since the field of durability is still in its infancy, software developers have relatively few references and proven durability estimation approaches to draw upon. Against this backdrop, the evaluation and prioritization of durability qualities would be an accurate reference for software developers. Our mechanism will assist the developers in focusing on the higher-priority features for engineering an end product with longer durability. Not only would this minimise the time involved and reduce the expenditure on maintenance costs, but also strengthen both the durability as well as the security of the product. The proposed work lays a solid theoretical foundation for Fuzzy AHP durability quantification in this field. It may also aid the researchers in determining the components that influence durability.

Points to Remember

- A multi-criteria decision-based technique is adopted to address the availability of multi-vector alternatives for the right selection of approaches.
- The evaluation and prioritisation of durability qualities will help the software developers to focus on the higher-priority features, and thus, save on maintenance costs and time.
- A notable way to achieve durable software is to evaluate and monitor the software durability criteria such as dependability during the development phases.
- Trustworthiness, dependability, human trust, security, and usability are five important aspects that affect software durability. Furthermore, the combination of software and durability aids in the provision of long-term software services.

Review Questions

Objective Type Questions

1. MCDA is called as
   a. Multi Criteria Decision Analysis
   b. Multi Criteria Descriptive Analysis
   c. Multi Criteria Decision Assessment
   d. Multiple Criteria Detail Analysis
2. The idea of fuzzy logic was proposed by
   a. Von-Neumann
   b. Lotfi A. Zadeh
   c. Alexey Ivakhnenko
   d. Alexey Ivakhnenko
3. Which of these is not a membership function:
   a. Triangular membership function
   b. Trapezoidal membership function
   c. s-shape membership function
   d. z-shape membership function
4. Consistency ratio is calculated by dividing the............... for the set of judgments by the Index for the corresponding random matrix
   a. Consistency index
   b. Random index
   c. Comparison matrices
   d. Random walk index
5. Concept of software durability was proposed by C., Kelty in:
   a. 2018
   b. 2015
   c. 2020
   d. 2008

Short Answer Type Questions

1. Name any three types of membership functions.
2. Define fuzzy logic.
3. Define direct and indirect parameters. Name three direct parameters.
4. Define the fuzzy AHP SAM method in brief.
5. What are the measurement categories for durability assessment?

Descriptive Questions

1. Describe the durability assessment mechanism in brief.
2. List five benefits of software durability assessment in detail.
3. Draw and explain the flow chart for the Implementation through the Fuzzy AHP Method.

References

1. Ensmenger, N. 2014. When good software goes bad: the surprising durability of an ephemeral technology. In MICE (Mistakes, Ignorance, Contingency, and Error) Conference. Munich, pp. 1–16.
2. Agrawal, A., Zarour, M., Alenezi, M., Kumar, R. and Khan, R.A. 2019. Security durability assessment through fuzzy analytic hierarchy process. PeerJ Computer Science, 5: e215.
3. Tekinerdogan, B., Sozer, H. and Aksit, M. 2008. Software architecture reliability analysis using failure scenarios. Journal of Systems and Software, 81(4): 558–575.
4. Subashini, S. and Kavitha, V. 2011. A survey on security issues in service delivery models of cloud computing. Journal of Network and Computer Applications, 34(1): 1–11.
5. Kelty, C. and Erickson, S. 2015. The Durability of Software, Meson Press, Germany, 1(5): 1–13.
6. Gulzar, K., Sang, J., Ramzan, M. and Kashif, M. 2017. Fuzzy approach to prioritize usability requirements conflicts: an experimental evaluation. IEEE Access, 5: 13570–13577.
7. Afrin, A. and Sadiq, M. 2017. An integrated approach for the selection of software requirements using fuzzy AHP and Fuzzy TOPSIS Method. In Intelligent Computing, Instrumentation and control technologies, IEEE Press, pp. 1094–1100.
8. Zavadskas, E.K., Govindan, K., Antucheviciene, J. and Turskis, Z. 2016. Hybrid multiple criteria decision-making methods: a review of applications for sustainability issues. Economic Research-EkonomskaIstraživanja, 29(1): 857–887.
9. Chong, C.Y., Lee, S.P. and Ling, T.C. 2014. Prioritizing and fulfilling quality attributes for virtual lab development through application of fuzzy analytic hierarchy process and software development guidelines. Malaysian Journal of Computer Science, 27(1): 1–19.
10. Goli, D. 2013. Group fuzzy TOPSIS methodology in computer security software selection. International Journal of Fuzzy Logic Systems, 3(2): 29–47.
11. Syamsuddin, I. 2013. Multi criteria evaluation and sensitivity analysis on information security. International Journal of Computer Applications, 69(24): 22–25.
12. Dubey, S.K. and Singh, A. 2013. Evaluation of usability using soft computing technique. International Journal of Science Engineering and Research, 4(12): 162–166.
13. Shi, L., Yang, S., Li, K. and Yu, B.G. 2012. Developing an evaluation approach for software trustworthiness using combination weights and TOPSIS. Journal of Software, 7(3): 532–543.
14. FadlElssied, N.O. and Ibrahim, O. 2011. A review of fuzzy mechanisms for e-government security. International Journal of Computer Applications, 34(7): 16–22.
15. Özdağoğlu, A. and Özdağoğlu, G. 2007. Comparison of AHP and Fuzzy AHP for the multi-criteria decision-making processes with linguistic evaluations. İstanbul Ticaret Üniversitesi Fen Bilimleri Dergisi, 6(11): 65–85.
16. Zhu, L., Aurum, A., Gorton, I. and Jeffery, R. 2005. Trade-off and sensitivity analysis in software architecture evaluation using analytic hierarchy process. Software Quality Journal, 13: 357–375.

17. Van Laarhoven, P.J.M. and Pedrycz, W. 1983. A fuzzy extension of Saaty's Priority theory. Fuzzy Sets and Systems, 11(3): 229–241.
18. Saaty, T.L. 1995. Transport planning with multiple criteria: the analytic hierarchy process applications and progress review. Journal of Advanced Transportation, 29(1): 81–126.
19. Zadeh, L.A. 1965. Fuzzy sets. Information and Control, 8(3): 338–353.

Useful Links

https://www.nwea.org/blog/2013/five-characteristics-quality-educational-assessments-part-one/

http://www.informatik.uni-bremen.de/uniform/gdpa/vmodel/d-asspro.htm

https://www.software.ac.uk/resources/guides-everything/software-evaluation-guide

https://www.softwareadvice.com/resources/how-to-evaluate-new-software/

https://www.tutorialspoint.com/software_quality_management/software_quality_management_process_assessment.htm

https://teachics.org/software-engineering-2/process-assessment-and-improvement/

https://www.imperial.ac.uk/staff/educational-development/teaching-toolkit/assessment-and-feedback/good-assessment/

https://nursekey.com/qualities-of-effective-assessment-procedures-validity-reliability-and-usability/

https://ecomputernotes.com/software-engineering/software-process-assessment

CHAPTER 9

A Case Study on Software Durability Assessment

9.1 Objectives

The durability of the software can best be explained as the function of the quality of software across its service life. The predicted software durability or software life-span is influenced by a variety of indirect or direct characteristics. Usability, dependability, security, human trust, and trustworthiness are direct characteristics, whereas indirect characteristics include consumer integrity, reliability, and so on. Durability is essentially influenced by five characteristics: dependability, usability, security, trustworthiness, and human trust. Moreover, a durability assessment is required for the software's durability assurance. However, assessing software durability by using these five attributes is a complex process, and hence, in this book, we are only considering three attributes for software durability assessment. Since the assessment approach entails not only quantifying but also selecting the most important characteristics of durability, the objectives that have been set forth in this chapter are as follows:

- Identifying, prioritizing, and evaluating the attributes of software durability.
- To use a real-time example of Babasaheb Bhimrao Ambedkar University, Lucknow (BBAU Software) to assess the durability through objective and subjective estimation.
- Employing the Fuzzy AHP approach to estimate the local or independent weights of durability characteristics and then placing the independent weights in a hierarchy
- Gauge the feasibility of such a methodology for conducting a durability assessment.

9.2 Evaluating the Weights of Characteristics

Integrating durability into the design may boost the potential of other quality characteristics, according to the preceding debate and literature studies [1]. Further, it's critical to first establish a link between durability and its relevance. A software product is long-lasting if it performs well for the user over a long period. Identifying and classifying durability characteristics during the process of software development aids in improving the service life of the software. The relationship between durability characteristics has been determined at various levels in Chapter 2, to design durable software. These characteristics, at various levels, are segregated into a unified hierarchical structure by using the Fuzzy AHP approach, as presented in Fig. 1.

The characteristics hierarchy of software durability, which is categorised into three tiers, is depicted in Fig. 1. The relationship between software durability characteristics is presented at various levels of the hierarchy. In addition, a characteristic at level 1 has an effect on one or more characteristics at the higher level, but not all of them are affected in the same way. It may be different. Reliability, for example, has an impact on trustworthiness, human trust, and dependability [3–4], but the impact values are different at both levels. Furthermore, the hierarchy of the characteristics helps in distinguishing between the influence of the same property and the impact of another characteristic at a higher level. Only a few characteristics, such as availability, have a direct impact on durability, such as reliability, human trust, and dependability. Characteristics at level 1 are designated as C1, C2, and C3 to estimate durability. C11, C12, C13, C14, and C15 for C1 and C21, C22,..C25 for C2 and C31, C32,..C35 for C3 are the level 2 characteristics. Level 3 characteristics are denoted as C111..........C115 for C11, and so on, as presented in Fig. 1.

9.2.1 Construction of Pair-Wise Comparison Matrices

The linkage of numerous qualitative criteria frequently causes assessment of various characteristics to fail. Fuzzy AHP is an appropriate estimation technique for dealing with problems with unclear inputs. Fuzzy AHP can handle ambiguous judgmental inputs from a large number of experts, as well as surveys gathered from expert judgments. It can also turn qualitative inputs into quantitative outcomes such as performance, weighting, and ranking. To determine the weights of the durability characteristics, pair-wise comparison matrixes in the form of questionnaires were created for each set of characteristics, and data was collected by sending questionnaires to 50 industry and academic professionals of diverse affiliations. The relevance of durability characteristics was measured by using twenty valid responses in this study.

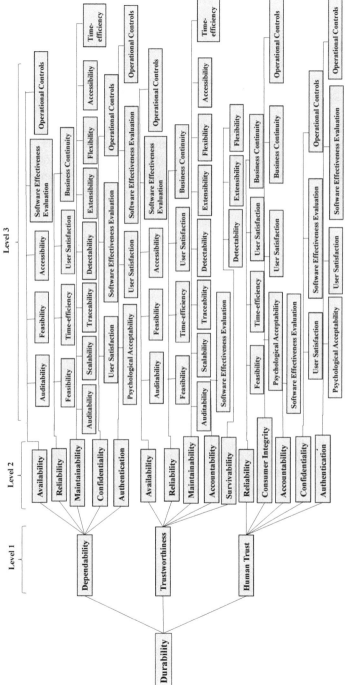

Figure 1: Hierarchy Modeling of Durability Characteristics.

The information gathered through experts' opinions was organised in the form of decision matrices. Opinions of the expert's opinions were gathered by using the Eigenvector approach. A "data just once" strategy was also employed to eliminate duplicate data and redundancy. These repetitions were employed into account throughout the calculation since each characteristic has a varied impact on durability at various levels of the hierarchy. Table 1 displays the scale employed to create the pair-wise comparison matrices in Chapter 8. This is a nine-point scale spanning from 1 to 9, with a higher score indicating greater importance. This scale also assisted in the conversion of numerical values into TFNs. TFNs can be computed from the pair-wise judgement matrix to compute the fuzzified values of the linguistic phrases. TFN also makes it easier for a person to make decisions. Further, TFN is employed in this study as the membership function.

Table 1: Fuzzy based Aggregated Pair-Wise Comparison Matrix at Level 1.

	C1	C2	C3
Dependability (C1)	1.00000, 1.00000, 1.00000	1.34790, 1.81800, 2.38590	1.41310, 1.96510, 2.48200
Trustworthiness (C2)	-	1.00000, 1.00000, 1.00000	0.85400, 1.10870, 1.45320
Human Trust (C3)	-	-	1.00000, 1.00000, 1.00000

9.2.2 Aggregation of Pair-Wise Comparison Matrices

Researchers transformed numerical results into TFN and aggregated these values using Table 1 and Eq. (1)–(5) from Chapter 8. From Table 1 to Table 11, aggregated pair-wise comparison matrices are given for all sets of characteristics in the hierarchy.

Due to repeated characteristics at level 2, some sets of characteristics at level 3 are repeated when the set of characteristics is considered independently. Hence, fuzzy based aggregated pair-wise comparison matrixes of characteristics at level 3 for C21, C22, and C23 (related to trustworthiness) are the same as for C11, C12, and C13, respectively. According to the hierarchy, accountability (C24) depends only on software effectiveness estimation (C241) concerning durability. Therefore, there is no need to fuzzify the pair-wise comparison matrix. Further, the fuzzy based aggregated pair-wise comparison matrix for the C25 of characteristics at level 3 is presented in Table 10.

Again, fuzzy based aggregated pair-wise comparison matrixes of characteristics at level 3 for C31, C34, and C35 (related to human trust)

Table 2: Fuzzy based Aggregated Pair-Wise Comparison Matrix at Level 2 for C1.

	C11	C12	C13	C14	C15
Availability (C11)	1.00000, 1.00000, 1.00000	0.31270, 0.43950, 0.62520	0.87330, 0.90120, 0.94650	0.22610, 0.29280, 0.41660	0.25800, 0.33860, 0.50550
Reliability (C12)	-	1.00000, 1.00000, 1.00000	2.04510, 3.16990, 4.23300	0.26650, 0.36570, 0.59110	0.69060, 1.00590, 1.51170
Maintainability (C13)	-	-	1.00000, 1.00000, 1.00000	0.36670, 0.52510, 0.96590	0.36040, 0.52200, 0.80740
Confidentiality (C14)	-	-	-	1.00000, 1.00000, 1.00000	0.89600, 1.14860, 1.39030
Authentication (C15)	-	-	-	-	1.00000, 1.00000, 1.00000

Table 3: Fuzzy based Aggregated Pair-Wise Comparison Matrix at Level 2 for C2.

	C21	C22	C23	C24	C25
Availability (C21)	1.00000, 1.00000, 1.00000	0.55980, 0.89940, 1.37050	0.79120, 0.88310, 1.02040	0.49560, 0.70290, 0.93300	0.40670, 0.54970, 0.78760
Reliability (C22)	-	1.00000, 1.00000, 1.00000	0.80010, 1.23760, 1.78120	0.38360, 0.54830, 0.83440	0.48760, 0.67100, 0.89000
Maintainability (C23)	-	-	1.00000, 1.00000, 1.00000	0.59660, 0.70930, 0.90950	0.27700, 0.38540, 0.63400
Accountability (C24)	-	-	-	1.00000, 1.00000, 1.00000	0.55060, 0.58810, 0.66470
Survivability (C25)	-	-	-	-	1.00000, 1.00000, 1.00000

are the same as for C12, C14, and C15, respectively. Further, accountability (C33) depends only on software effectiveness estimation (C331) concerning durability. So, there is no need to fuzzify the pair-wise comparison matrix. In the next portion, after the aggregation of fuzzified pair-wise comparison matrixes, the defuzzification procedure is implemented.

Table 4: Fuzzy based Aggregated Pair-Wise Comparison Matrix at Level 2 for C3.

	C31	C32	C33	C34	C35
Reliability (C31)	1.00000, 1.00000, 1.00000	0.97100, 1.24750, 1.60940	1.05920, 1.58490, 2.22060	0.77330, 1.01180, 1.28810	0.76120, 0.91200, 1.09650
Consumer Integrity (C32)	-	1.00000, 1.00000, 1.00000	0.63520, 0.91430, 1.34300	0.42730, 0.63350, 0.96600	0.34760, 0.49000, 0.87340
Accountability (C33)	-	-	1.00000, 1.00000, 1.00000	0.51460, 0.65750, 0.78460	0.52130, 0.65970, 0.91910
Confidentiality (C34)	-	-	-	1.00000, 1.00000, 1.00000	0.55620, 0.64480, 0.81220
Authentication (C35)	-	-	-	-	1.00000, 1.00000, 1.00000

Table 5: Fuzzy based Aggregated Pair-Wise Comparison Matrix at Level 3 for C11.

	C111	C112	C113	C114	C115
Auditability (C111)	1.00000, 1.00000, 1.00000	1.87220, 2.57100, 3.20350	1.46400, 1.68420, 1.97430	1.44610, 2.43850, 3.38650	0.46770, 0.57240, 0.78450
Feasibility (C112)	-	1.00000, 1.00000, 1.00000	0.60830, 0.77540, 1.02650	0.77080, 0.95040, 1.23610	0.16300, 0.19530, 0.24970
Accessibility (C113)	-	-	1.00000, 1.00000, 1.00000	0.76940, 1.05020, 1.35530	0.20860, 0.24620, 0.31170
Software Effectiveness Estimation (C114)	-	-	-	1.00000, 1.00000, 1.00000	0.19560, 0.22830, 0.29030
Operational Controls (C115)	-	-	-	-	1.00000, 1.00000, 1.00000

9.2.3 Defuzzification Procedure and Independent Weights

For receiving the linguistic amounts from the aggregated TFN amounts, the *alpha cut* method is employed for the defuzzification procedure [1]. The alpha cut method is formulated in Eq. (6)–(9) in Chapter VIII. For instance, if n_{12}'s $TFN = (l_{12}, m_{12}, h_{12}) = (1.34790, 1.81800, 2.38590)$

Table 6: Fuzzy based Aggregated Pair-Wise Comparison Matrix at Level 3 for C12.

	C121	C122	C123	C124
Feasibility (C121)	1.00000, 1.00000, 1.00000	1.75610, 2.34980, 3.03350	1.48300, 1.95750, 2.52930	1.12840, 1.55430, 1.98840
Time-efficiency (C122)	-	1.00000, 1.00000, 1.00000	0.5695, 0.7860, 1.1555	0.56980, 0.71950, 0.96990
User Satisfaction (C123)	-	-	1.00000, 1.00000, 1.00000	0.62700, 0.81230, 1.07180
Business Continuity (C124)	-	-	-	1.00000, 1.00000, 1.00000

Then,

$$\eta_{0.5}(l_{12}) = (m_{12} - l_{12}).0.5 + l_{12}$$

$$\eta_{0.5}(l_{12}) = (1.8180 - 1.3479) \times 0.5 + 1.3479 = 1.5830$$

$$\eta_{0.5}(h_{12}) = h_{12} - (h_{12} - m_{12}).\,0.5$$

$$\eta_{0.5}(h_{12}) = 2.3859 - (2.3859 - 1.8180) \times 0.5 = 2.1019$$

$$\eta_{0.5,\,0.5}(\eta_{12}) = [0.5\,\eta_{0.5}(l_{12}) + (1 - 0.5)\,\eta_{0.5}(h_{12})]$$

$$\eta_{0.5,\,0.5}(\eta_{12}) = [0.5 \times 1.5830 + (1 - 0.5) \times 2.10190] = 0.7915 + 1.0510 = 1.8425$$

$$\eta_{0.5,\,0.5}(\eta_{21}) = 1/\,1.8425 = 0.5427$$

Similarly, all aggregated TFN values of the defuzzified numbers are presented in Table 12 to Table 22. In this book, α and β are employed to be equal to 0.5. Where α and β carry the meaning of participants' preferences and risk tolerance. The values of $\alpha = 0.5$ and $\beta = 0.5$ specified that characteristics are *neither extremely optimistic nor pessimistic* about their judgment. Further, fluctuations in results due to the value of α and β are discussed in the sensitivity analysis, as given in the next section of this chapter. After the defuzzification procedure of the pair-wise matrix, the consistency ratio (CR) is measured with the support of Eq. (10)–(15) and Table 3. To continue the Fuzzy AHP analysis, CR must be acceptable. If CR is less than 0.1, then weights are measured, otherwise, refined pair-wise matrixes are prepared and the procedure is repeated. The independent weights of durability characteristics are measured by y applying Eq. (12) to the CR value,

Table 7: Fuzzy based Aggregated Pair-Wise Comparison Matrix at Level 3 for C13.

	C131	C132	C133	C134	C135	C136	C137	C138
Auditability (131)	1.00000, 1.00000, 1.00000	1.00000, 1.51570, 1.93310	0.48960, 0.63720, 1.00000	0.41520, 0.57430, 1.00000	0.22150, 0.28710, 0.41520	0.31460, 0.46100, 0.87050	0.65750, 1.16530, 1.68830	0.24440, 0.32380, 0.48010
Scalability (132)	-	1.00000, 1.00000, 1.00000	0.57430, 0.66570, 0.80220	0.30390, 0.39360, 0.56610	0.26790, 0.35210, 0.51760	0.16630, 0.19690, 0.25310	0.39300, 0.57430, 1.05640	0.16920, 0.20760, 0.27590
Traceability (133)	-	-	1.00000, 1.00000, 1.00000	1.00000, 1.31950, 1.55180	0.30090, 0.43520, 0.80270	0.80270, 0.87050, 1.00000	1.26190, 1.82500, 2.43340	0.17280, 0.20910, 0.26480
Detectability (134)	-	-	-	1.00000, 1.00000, 1.00000	0.53860, 0.91430, 1.58360	0.60830, 1.05920, 1.68290	0.75030, 1.34650, 1.96110	0.67900, 0.74890, 0.87050
Extensibility (135)	-	-	-	-	1.00000, 1.00000, 1.00000	0.41520, 0.63720, 1.17910	0.94650, 1.10950, 1.24570	0.25000, 0.33000, 0.50000
Flexibility (136)	-	-	-	-	-	1.00000, 1.00000, 1.00000	1.88810, 2.55080, 3.16970	0.80270, 1.03520, 1.31600
Accessibility (137)	-	-	-	-	-	-	1.00000, 1.00000, 1.00000	0.21360, 0.25750, 0.31950
Time-efficiency (138)	-	-	-	-	-	-	-	1.00000, 1.00000, 1.00000

Table 8: Fuzzy based Aggregated Pair-Wise Comparison Matrix at Level 3 for C14.

	C141	C142	C143
User Satisfaction (C141)	1.00000, 1.00000, 1.00000	0.68980, 0.88600, 1.10020	0.22550, 0.27620, 0.35740
Software Effectiveness Estimation (C142)	-	1.00000, 1.00000, 1.00000	0.30510, 0.38920, 0.56090
Operational Controls (C143)	-	-	1.00000, 1.00000, 1.00000

Table 9: Fuzzy based Aggregated Pair-Wise Comparison Matrix at Level 3 for C15.

	C151	C152	C153	C154
Psychological Acceptability (C151)	1.00000, 1.00000, 1.00000	1.00000, 1.37410, 1.71180	0.56100, 0.83600, 1.07810	0.30400, 0.37660, 0.47230
User Satisfaction (C152)	-	1.00000, 1.00000, 1.00000	0.30300, 0.42080, 0.60520	0.19160, 0.23030, 0.30010
Software Effectiveness Estimation (C153)	-	-	1.00000, 1.00000, 1.00000	0.51380, 0.79590, 1.20320
Operational Controls (C154)	-	-	-	1.00000, 1.00000, 1.00000

Table 10: Fuzzy based Aggregated Pair-Wise Comparison Matrix at Level 3 for C25.

	C251	C252	C253
Detectability (C251)	1.00000, 1.00000, 1.00000	0.69500, 0.95020, 1.34570	1.14860, 1.43850, 1.69620
Extensibility (C252)	-	1.00000, 1.00000, 1.00000	1.19280, 1.58260, 2.14970
Flexibility (C253)	-	-	1.00000, 1.00000, 1.00000

Table 11: Fuzzy based Aggregated Pair-Wise Comparison Matrix at Level 3 for C32.

	C321	C322	C323	C324
Psychological Acceptability (C321)	1.00000, 1.00000, 1.00000	1.07810, 1.5990, 2.1130	0.82060, 1.11180, 1.61500	0.56700, 0.71320, 0.87390
User Satisfaction (C322)	-	1.00000, 1.00000, 1.00000	0.32300, 0.44800, 0.60510	0.25840, 0.31720, 0.41680
Business Continuity (C323)	-	-	1.00000, 1.00000, 1.00000	0.66610, 1.05640, 1.54270
Operational Controls (C324)	-	-	-	1.00000, 1.00000, 1.00000

Table 12: Independent Weight of Durability Characteristics at Level 1.

	C1	C2	C3	Weights
Dependability (C1)	1.00000	1.84250	1.95640	0.48670
Trustworthiness (C2)	0.54270	1.00000	1.13120	0.26980
Human Trust (C3)	0.51110	0.88400	1.00000	0.24350
				CR = 0.0003800

For example:

$$[\rho_{\alpha,\beta}(\eta_{ij}) - \lambda I] = \begin{bmatrix} 1 & 1.8425 & 1.9564 \\ 0.5427 & 1 & 1.1312 \\ 0.5111 & 0.8840 & 1 \end{bmatrix}$$

$$\begin{bmatrix} 1 & 1.8425 & 1.9564 \\ 0.5427 & 1 & 1.1312 \\ 0.5111 & 0.8840 & 1 \end{bmatrix} \begin{bmatrix} \rho_{\text{Dependability}} \\ \rho_{\text{Trustworthiness}} \\ \rho_{\text{Human Trust}} \end{bmatrix} = \begin{bmatrix} 0 \\ 0 \\ 0 \end{bmatrix}$$

$$\begin{bmatrix} \rho_{\text{Dependability}} \\ \rho_{\text{Trustworthiness}} \\ \rho_{\text{Human Trust}} \end{bmatrix} = \begin{bmatrix} 0.4867 \\ 0.2698 \\ 0.2435 \end{bmatrix}$$

Similarly, the procedure is repeated to check the CR and obtain the independent weights. The independent weights and CR values for each pair-wise comparison matrix are presented in Table 12 to Table 22, respectively.

Table 12 displays the independent weights of durability characteristics at level 1 through the hierarchy. The consistency ratio (CR) is 0.0003800, which is less than 0.1. This CR value is acceptable to continue Fuzzy AHP analysis. This set of characteristics has three characteristics, including dependability (0.48670), trustworthiness (0.26980), and human trust (0.24350), and dependability is the highest weighted characteristic among them.

Table 13: Independent Weight of Durability Characteristics at Level 2 for C1.

	C11	C12	C13	C14	C15	Weights
Availability (C11)	1.00000	0.45420	0.90560	0.30710	0.36020	0.09460
Reliability (C12)	2.20170	1.00000	3.15450	0.39730	1.05360	0.22920
Maintainability (C13)	1.10420	0.31701	1.00000	0.59570	0.55300	0.11920
Confidentiality (C14)	3.25630	2.51700	1.67870	1.00000	1.14590	0.32330
Authentication (C15)	2.77620	0.94910	1.80830	0.87270	1.00000	0.23370
						C.R. = 0.041100

The independent weights for C1 of the second level characteristics are presented in Table 13. CR is 0.041100, which is less than 0.1. This CR value is acceptable to continue Fuzzy AHP analysis. This set of characteristics has five characteristics, including availability (0.09460), reliability (0.22920), maintainability (0.11920), confidentiality (0.32330), and authentication (0.23370), and confidentiality is the highest weighted characteristic among them.

Table 14: Independent Weight of Durability Characteristics at Level 2 for C2.

	C21	C22	C23	C24	C25	Weights
Availability (C21)	1.00000	0.93230	0.89450	0.70860	0.57340	0.15410
Reliability (C22)	1.07260	1.00000	1.26420	0.57870	0.66470	0.16920
Maintainability (C23)	1.11790	0.79100	1.00000	0.73040	0.42050	0.14760
Accountability (C24)	1.41120	1.72800	1.36910	1.00000	0.59790	0.22140
Survivability (C25)	1.74400	1.50440	2.37810	1.67250	1.00000	0.30770
					C.R. = 0.010100	

The independent weights for C2 of the second level characteristics are presented in Table 14. CR is 0.010100, which is less than 0.1. This CR value is acceptable to continue Fuzzy AHP analysis. This set of characteristics has five characteristics, including availability (0.15410), reliability (0.16920), maintainability (0.14760), accountability (0.22140), and survivability (0.30770), and survivability is the highest weighted characteristic among them.

Table 15: Independent Weight of Durability Characteristics at Level 2 for C3.

	C31	C32	C33	C34	C35	Weights
Reliability (C31)	1.00000	1.26890	1.61240	1.02130	0.92040	0.22160
Consumer Integrity (C32)	0.78810	1.00000	1.26930	0.66510	0.55030	0.15960
Accountability (C33)	0.62020	0.78780	1.00000	0.65360	0.69000	0.14460
Confidentiality (C34)	0.97910	1.50350	1.53000	1.00000	0.66450	0.21150
Authentication (C35)	1.08650	1.81720	1.44930	1.50490	1.00000	0.26270
					C.R. = 0.006900	

Table 15 displays the independent weights for C3 of second level characteristics. The consistency ratio (CR) is 0.006900, which is less than 0.1. This CR value is acceptable to continue Fuzzy AHP analysis. This set of characteristics has five characteristics, including reliability (0.22160), consumer integrity (0.15960), accountability (0.14460), confidentiality (0.21150), authentication (0.26270), and authentication is the highest weighted characteristic among them.

Table 16: Independent Weight of Durability Characteristics at Level 3 for C11.

	C111	C112	C113	C114	C115	Weights
Auditability (C111)	1.00000	2.55440	1.70170	2.42740	0.59930	0.24000
Feasibility (C112)	0.39150	1.00000	0.79640	0.97690	0.20730	0.09520
Accessibility (C113)	0.58760	1.25560	1.00000	1.05630	0.25320	0.12000
Software Effectiveness Estimation (C114)	0.41200	1.02360	0.94670	1.00000	0.23570	0.10320
Operational Controls (C115)	1.66860	4.82390	3.94950	4.24270	1.00000	0.44160
						C.R. = 0.002500

The independent weights for C11 of the third level characteristics are presented in Table 16. CR is 0.002500, which is less than 0.1. This CR value is acceptable to continue Fuzzy AHP analysis. This set of characteristics has five characteristics, including auditability (0.24000), feasibility (0.09520), accessibility (0.12000), software effectiveness estimation (0.10320), and operational controls (0.44160), and operational controls is the highest weighted characteristic among them.

Table 17: Independent Weight of Durability Characteristics at Level 3 for C12.

	C121	C122	C123	C124	Weights
Feasibility (C121)	1.00000	2.37230	1.98190	1.55640	0.39050
Time-efficiency (C122)	0.42150	1.00000	0.82430	0.74470	0.16940
User Satisfaction (C123)	0.50460	1.21320	1.00000	0.83090	0.20040
Business Continuity (C124)	0.64250	1.34280	1.20350	1.00000	0.23970
					C.R. = 0.000600

The independent weights for C12 of the Third Level characteristics are presented in Table 17. CR is 0.000600, which is less than 0.1. This CR value is acceptable to continue Fuzzy AHP analysis. This set of characteristics has four characteristics, including feasibility (0.39050), time-efficiency (0.16940), user satisfaction (0.20040), and business continuity (0.23970), and feasibility is the highest weighted characteristic among them.

Table 18 displays the independent weights for C13 of the third level characteristics. The consistency ratio (CR) is 0.033300, which is less than 0.1. This CR value is acceptable to continue Fuzzy AHP analysis. This set of characteristics have eight characteristics including auditability (0.07330), scalability (0.04970), traceability (0.10310), detectability (0.12710), extensibility (0.14140), flexibility (0.17290), accessibility (0.07600), time-efficiency (0.25650) and time-efficiency is highest weighted characteristic among them.

Table 18: Independent Weight of Durability Characteristics at Level 3 for C13.

	C131	C132	C133	C134	C135	C136	C137	C138	Weights
Auditability (131)	1.00000	1.49120	0.69100	0.64100	0.30270	0.52680	1.16910	0.34300	0.07330
Scalability (132)	0.67060	1.00000	0.67700	0.41430	0.37240	0.20330	0.64950	0.21510	0.04970
Traceability (133)	1.44700	1.47710	1.00000	1.29770	0.49350	0.85200	1.83640	0.21400	0.10310
Detectability (134)	1.56000	2.41370	0.77060	1.00000	0.96360	1.10240	1.35110	0.73190	0.12710
Extensibility (135)	3.30360	2.68530	2.02630	1.03780	1.00000	0.71720	1.10280	0.43500	0.14140
Flexibility (136)	1.89820	4.91880	1.17370	0.90710	1.39430	1.00000	2.38520	1.04730	0.17290
Accessibility (137)	0.85540	1.53970	0.54450	0.74010	0.90679	0.41925	1.00000	0.26210	0.07600
Time-efficiency (138)	2.91540	4.64900	4.67290	1.36631	2.29890	0.95484	3.81530	1.00000	0.25650
								C.R. =	0.033300

Table 19: Independent Weight of Durability Characteristics at Level 3 for C14.

	C141	C142	C143	Weights
User Satisfaction (C141)	1.00000	0.89050	0.28390	0.18320
Software Effectiveness Estimation (C142)	1.12300	1.00000	0.41110	0.22390
Operational Controls (C143)	3.52240	2.43250	1.00000	0.59290
			C.R. =	0.006200

The independent weights for C14 of the third level characteristics are presented in Table 19. CR is 0.006200, which is less than 0.1. This CR value is acceptable to continue Fuzzy AHP analysis. This set of characteristics has three characteristics; including user satisfaction (0.18320), software effectiveness estimation (0.22390), and operational controls (0.59290), and operational controls is the highest weighted characteristic among them.

Table 20: Independent Weight of Durability Characteristics at Level 3 for C15.

	C151	C152	C153	C154	Weights
Psychological Acceptability (C151)	1.00000	1.36510	0.82780	0.38240	0.18110
User Satisfaction (C152)	0.73250	1.00000	0.43750	0.23810	0.11670
Software Effectiveness Estimation (C153)	1.20800	2.28570	1.00000	0.82720	0.27570
Operational Controls (C154)	2.61510	4.19990	1.2089	1.00000	0.42650
				C.R. =	0.015100

The independent weights for C15 of the third level characteristics are presented in Table 20. CR is 0.015100, which is less than 0.1. This CR value is acceptable to continue Fuzzy AHP analysis. This set of characteristics has four characteristics; including psychological acceptability (0.18110), user satisfaction (0.11670), software effectiveness estimation (0.27570), operational controls (0.42650), and operational controls is the highest weighted characteristic among them. Due to repeated characteristics in the second level, some sets of third level characteristics are repeated when the set of characteristics is considered independently. Hence, the independent weights of third level characteristics for C21, C22, and C23 are the same as for C11, C12, and C13, respectively.

Table 21: Independent Weight of Durability Characteristics at Level 3 for C25.

	C251	C252	C253	Weights
Detectability (C251)	1.00000	0.98530	1.35780	0.36110
Extensibility (C252)	1.01490	1.00000	1.62690	0.38730
Flexibility (C253)	0.73650	0.61470	1.00000	0.25160
				C.R. = 0.002600

The independent weights for C25 of the third level characteristics are presented in Table 21. CR is 0.002600, which is less than 0.1. This CR value is acceptable to continue Fuzzy AHP analysis. This set of characteristics has three characteristics, including detectability (0.36110), extensibility (0.38730), and flexibility (0.25160), and extensibility is the highest weighted characteristic among them.

Table 22: Independent Weight of Durability Characteristics at Level 3 for C32.

	C321	C322	C323	C324	Weights
Psychological Acceptability (C321)	1.00000	1.59730	1.16480	0.71680	0.25430
User Satisfaction (C322)	0.62610	1.00000	0.45610	0.32740	0.13020
Business Continuity (C323)	0.85850	2.19250	1.00000	1.08040	0.28290
Operational Controls (C324)	1.39510	3.05440	0.92560	1.00000	0.33260
					C.R. = 0.018700

The independent weights for C11 of the third level characteristics are presented in Table 22. CR is 0.018700, which is less than 0.1. This CR value is acceptable to continue Fuzzy AHP analysis. This set of characteristics has four characteristics, including psychological acceptability (0.25430), user satisfaction (0.13020), business continuity (0.28290), operational controls (0.33260), and operational controls is the highest weighted characteristic among them. Again, independent weights of third level characteristics for C31, C34, and C35 are the same as for C12, C14, and C15, respectively.

An independent weight represents the level-wise impact of these characteristics and is also called an independent weight. To estimate the weights of the durability characteristics throughout the hierarchy, global or dependent weights are measured in the next portion.

9.2.4 Dependent Weights of Each Characteristic

Throughout the hierarchy, global or dependent weights are also known as the dependent weights. Table 23 represents the dependent weights of each characteristic of durability as they go through the hierarchy.

The hierarchical structure associated with durability characteristics is a corroborative reference for the developers who can use the proposed framework for designing durable software. There are three stages of de-construction of durability characteristics including level 1, level 2, and level 3. The rank of each characteristic is based on the results at levels 1, 2, and 3.

An estimation of the ranks of each characteristic for improving the life span of the software is demonstrated by using the dependent weights. Fig. 2 and Fig. 3 demonstrate the dependent priorities of durability characteristics at level 2 and level 3, when repeated level 2 and level 3 characteristics are deleted.

After deleting the repeated characteristics, the dependent priority of durability characteristics at level 2 and level 3 are presented in Fig. 2 and Fig. 3. These priorities will aid in the formulation of development proposals and guidance.

9.3 Procedure for Improving Durability of Software

The aim of this Book is not limited to addressing and measuring the durability of software but to produce suggestions based on assessment. The advice gained from quantification will surely assist practitioners in enhancing the durability of software during development. It is critical to examine the qualities of design while developing any design guidelines for practitioners. The equivalent metrics for object-oriented design attributes are employed to measure them [3, 5]. Furthermore, if the object-oriented measurements are not translated into durability parameters, they are meaningless. There are numerous metric suites available to predict the durability of software, namely Requirements Statistics (SRs) [3], Critical Class Coupling (CCC) [4], Classified Instance Data Accessibility (CIDA) [5], Vulnerable Association of an Object Oriented Design (VA_OOD) [6], Critical Super Class Propagation (CSP) [7], Number of Design Stage Errors (NDSE) [8], Classified Attributes Inheritance (CAI) [9], Critical Class Extensibility (CCE) [10], Classified MethodsInheritance (CMI) [11],

Table 23: The Global Weights of Each Characteristic through Hierarchy.

The first level	The weight of first level	The second level	The independent weight of second level	The dependent weight of the second level	The third level	The independent weight of the third level	The (Global) dependent weight of the third level
C1	0.48670	C11	0.09460	0.04600	C111	0.24000	0.01100
					C112	0.09520	0.00400
					C113	0.12000	0.00600
					C114	0.10320	0.00500
					C115	0.44160	0.02000
		C12	0.22920	0.11200	C121	0.39050	0.04400
					C122	0.16940	0.01900
					C123	0.20040	0.02200
					C124	0.23970	0.02700
		C13	0.11920	0.05800	C131	0.07330	0.00400
					C132	0.04970	0.00300
					C133	0.10310	0.00600
					C134	0.12710	0.00700
					C135	0.14140	0.00800
					C136	0.17290	0.01000
					C137	0.07600	0.00400
					C138	0.25650	0.01500
		C14	0.32330	0.15700	C141	0.18320	0.02900
					C142	0.22390	0.03500
					C143	0.59290	0.09300
		C15	0.23370	0.11400	C151	0.18110	0.02100
					C152	0.11670	0.01300
					C153	0.27570	0.03100
					C154	0.42650	0.04900

C2							
C2	0.26980	C21	0.15410	0.04200	C211	0.24000	0.01000
					C212	0.09520	0.00400
					C213	0.12000	0.00500
					C214	0.10320	0.00400
					C215	0.44160	0.01800
		C22	0.16920	0.04600	C221	0.39050	0.01800
					C222	0.16940	0.00800
					C223	0.20040	0.00900
					C224	0.23970	0.01100
		C23	0.14760	0.04000	C231	0.07330	0.00300
					C232	0.04970	0.00200
					C233	0.10310	0.00400
					C234	0.12710	0.00500
					C235	0.14140	0.00600
					C236	0.17290	0.00700
					C237	0.07600	0.00300
					C238	0.25650	0.01000
		C24	0.22140	0.06000	C241	-	0.06000
		C25	0.30770	0.08300	C251	0.36110	0.03000
					C252	0.38730	0.03200
					C253	0.25160	0.02100

Table 23 contd. ...

...*Table 23 contd.*

The first level	The weight of first level	The second level	The independent weight of second level	The dependent weight of the second level	The third level	The independent weight of the third level	The (Global) dependent weight of the third level
C3	0.24350	C31	0.22160	0.05400	C311	0.39050	0.02100
					C312	0.16940	0.00900
					C313	0.20040	0.01100
					C314	0.23970	0.01300
		C32	0.15960	0.03900	C321	0.25430	0.01000
					C322	0.13020	0.00500
					C323	0.28290	0.01100
					C324	0.33260	0.01300
		C33	0.14460	0.03500	C331	-	0.03500
		C34	0.21150	0.05200	C341	0.18320	0.00900
					C342	0.22390	0.01200
					C343	0.59290	0.03100
		C35	0.26270	0.06400	C351	0.18110	0.01200
					C352	0.11670	0.00700
					C353	0.27570	0.01800
					C354	0.42650	0.02700

Second Level Characteristics	The final weight of the second level	Final Ranks of the Second Level
Availability	0.046	10
Reliability	0.112	3
Maintainability	0.058	7
Confidentiality	0.157	1
Authentication	0.114	2
Availability	0.042	12
Reliability	0.046	11
Maintainability	0.040	13
Accountability	0.060	6
Survivability	0.083	4
Reliability	0.054	8
Consumer Integrity	0.039	14
Accountability	0.035	15
Confidentiality	0.052	9
Authentication	0.064	5

Set of Attributes without Repetition

Priority	Characteristics of Level 2
1	Confidentiality
2	Authentication
3	Reliability
4	Survivability
5	Accountability
6	Maintainability
7	Availability
8	Consumer Integrity

Figure 2: Characteristics without Repetition at Level 2.

Third Level Characteristics	The Final Weight of the Third Level	Final Ranks of the Third Level
Auditability	0.011	29
Feasibility	0.004	52
Accessibility	0.006	45
Software Effective Evaluation	0.005	48
Operational Controls	0.020	18
Feasibility	0.044	4
Time-Efficiency	0.019	19
User Satisfaction	0.022	14
Business Continuity	0.027	12
Auditability	0.004	53
Scalability	0.003	58
Traceability	0.006	46
Detectability	0.007	42
Extensibility	0.008	40
Flexibility	0.010	33
Accessibility	0.004	54
Time-Efficiency	0.015	23
User Satisfaction	0.029	11
Software Effective Evaluation	0.035	5
Operational Controls	0.093	1
Psychological Acceptability	0.021	15
User Satisfaction	0.013	24
Software Effective Evaluation	0.031	8
Operational Controls	0.049	3
Auditability	0.010	34
Feasibility	0.004	55
Accessibility	0.005	49
Software Effective Evaluation	0.004	56
Operational Controls	0.018	20
Feasibility	0.018	21
Time-Efficiency	0.008	41
User Satisfaction	0.009	37
Business Continuity	0.011	30
Auditability	0.003	59
Scalability	0.002	61
Traceability	0.004	57
Detectability	0.005	50
Extensibility	0.006	47
Flexibility	0.007	43
Accessibility	0.003	60
Time-Efficiency	0.010	35
Software Effective Evaluation	0.060	2
Detectability	0.030	10
Extensibility	0.032	7
Flexibility	0.021	16
Feasibility	0.021	17
Time-Efficiency	0.009	38
User Satisfaction	0.011	31
Business Continuity	0.013	25
Psychological Acceptability	0.010	36
User Satisfaction	0.005	51
Business Continuity	0.011	32
Operational Controls	0.013	26
Software Effective Evaluation	0.035	6
User Satisfaction	0.009	39
Software Effective Evaluation	0.012	27
Operational Controls	0.031	9
Psychological Acceptability	0.012	28
User Satisfaction	0.007	44
Software Effective Evaluation	0.018	22
Operational Controls	0.027	13

Set of Attributes without Repetition

Priority	Characteristics of Level 3
1	Operational Controls
2	Software Effectiveness Evaluation
3	Feasibility
4	User Satisfaction
5	Time-efficiency
6	Auditability
7	Psychological Acceptability
8	Business Continuity
9	Accessibility
10	Extensibility
11	Flexibility
12	Detectability
13	Scalability
14	Traceability

Figure 3: Characteristics without Repetition at Level 3.

Critical Design Propagation (CDP) [12], Classified Methods Weight (CMW) [13], and many more. The measurements mentioned above are for the design phase. These measurements are used to assess the influence of the attributes. Most practitioners, for example, use Critical Class Coupling (CCC) to measure the coupling of classes [14].

The majority of design properties, such as service-oriented design and object-oriented design, have beneficial effects on the characteristics [15]. On the other hand, each design method has its benefits and drawbacks in terms of software services. In this work, the authors suggest only eight metrics for the practitioners' reference. These are the metrics that may be supportive for measuring and achieving the priorities of third-level characteristics, including the Classified Method Inheritance (CMI), Critical Class Extensibility (CCE), Critical Class Coupling (CCC), Critical Super Class Propagation (CSP), Critical Design Propagation (CDP), Classified Characteristics Inheritance (CAI), Classified Method Weight (CMW), and Classified Instance Data Accessibility (CIDA). Second, first, and overall durability are measured and accomplished because of the influence of priority at level 3. Many design characteristics are influenced by durability characteristics (at the third level), and the impact of these characteristics can be measured by using proposed metrics such as:

- Reusability, discoverability, design by contract, and design size are all affected by auditability. Affected design aspects of auditability can be measured and enhanced using CMI and CAI metrics. Furthermore, CMI calculates the ratio of classified methods to total classified methods, while CAI calculates the ratio of classified characteristics to the total classified characteristics.

- Design characteristics like coupling and reusability are affected by scalability. Affected design aspects of scalability may be measured and enhanced by using CCC and CMI metrics. Furthermore, CCC aids in calculating the ratio of all classes associated with the categorised characteristics.

- Design characteristics like reusability and discoverability are influenced by feasibility. Affected design properties of feasibility can be measured and improved using CAI and CMI metrics.

- Design characteristics including coupling, abstraction, and discoverability are influenced by traceability. The affected design aspects of traceability can be measured and enhanced by using CCC and CSP metrics. CSP also aids in the measurement of the ratio of critical super classes to total critical classes in an inheritance hierarchy, as well as the implementation of abstraction.

- Autonomy, discoverability, and cohesion are all affected by detectability. Affected design properties of detectability can be measured and improved by using the CCE metric. CCE also aids in determining the ratio between the number of non-finalized courses and the critical classes in a design.

- Design properties such as complexity and design size are influenced by accessibility. The affected design aspects of accessibility can be measured and improved by using CDP and CIDA metrics. CDP also assesses the relationship between the number of critical classes and the total number of classes in a design, as well as the impact of design size. CIDA is useful for calculating the ratio of classified instances with public characteristics to the total number of classified characteristics in a class, as well as determining the influence of design size.

- Design aspects such as design size and reusability are influenced by time efficiency. The affected design characteristics of time-efficiency can be measured and improved by using CMI and CAI metrics.

- Extensibility has an impact on the design characteristics like complexity and reusability. Affected design aspects of extensibility can be measured and enhanced by using CMI and CAI metrics.

- Design properties such as abstraction, design by contract, and cohesion are influenced by psychological acceptability. The affected design aspects of psychological acceptability can be measured and improved using the CSP metric.

- Design characteristics like abstraction and autonomy are influenced by user satisfaction. The affected design aspects of user satisfaction can be quantified and enhanced using CSP and CCE metrics.

- Estimation of software effectiveness has an impact on design properties like abstraction and coupling. The affected design properties of software effectiveness estimation can be quantified and improved using CCE, CMI, CAI, and CSP metrics.

- Design properties such as coupling and cohesion are affected by business continuity. The affected design properties of business continuity can be measured and enhanced by using CCC and CMW metrics.

- Design properties like coupling and statelessness are influenced by flexibility. The affected design characteristics of flexibility can be measured and enhanced by using CMW, CDP, and CCC metrics. CMW also aids in calculating the ratio between the number of categorised tactics and the total number of methods in a class. CDP assesses the relationship between the number of critical classes and the total number of classes, as well as the impact of a design's size.

- Design properties like coupling and statelessness are also affected by operational controls. The affected design characteristics of operational controls can be measured and improved using CMW, CDP, and CCC metrics.

The impact of second-level characteristics on durability can be determined by measuring third-level characteristics. The following are recommendations for measuring and improving the impact of durability characteristics at level 2:

- Level three characteristics, including user satisfaction, software effectiveness estimation, and operational controls, have an impact on confidentiality. The impact of confidentiality may be measured and improved with the use of design property measurements for these characteristics.

- Level three characteristics, including psychological acceptability, user satisfaction, software effectiveness estimation, and operational controls, have an impact on authentication. The impact of authentication can be measured and improved with the use of design property measurements for these characteristics.

- Characteristics at level three, including feasibility, time-efficiency, user satisfaction, and business continuity, have an impact on reliability. The impact of reliability may be quantified and enhanced with the use of design property measurements for these aspects.

- Characteristics at level three, including detectability, extensibility, and flexibility, have an impact on survivability. The impact of survivability can be measured and improved with the use of design characteristic metrics for these characteristics.

Through the measurement of second-level characteristics, the impact of first-level characteristics of durability may be measured. Further, to measure and improve the impact of first-level characteristics, the following are the referrals:

- Second-level characteristics such as availability, reliability, maintainability, confidentiality, and authentication have an impact on dependability. The influence of these second-level characteristics can be measured and improved using the impact of these second-level characteristics.

- Second-level characteristics like as availability, reliability, maintainability, accountability, and survivability have an impact on trustworthiness. The influence of these second-level characteristics can be measured and enhanced with the support of these second-level characteristics.

- Second-level characteristics such as reliability, consumer integrity, accountability, confidentiality, and authentication have an impact on human trust. The influence of these second-level characteristics can be measured and enhanced with the support of these second-level characteristics.

Practitioners should concentrate on improving the highly prioritised characteristics using the specified dependent priorities at level 1, level 2, and level 3, respectively, as well as the above discussion. To improve the impact of these properties on the overall longevity of software services, measurement using metrics is required. The technique for creating proposals or guidelines is described in Chapter 2. Below are some tips for better implementation and enhancement.

- To build a comprehensive durability idea in the organisational environment during the use of software services, and improve durability awareness among practitioners with proper education and training.

- In the recent information era, the economic component of life span should be fully understood and treated as one of the most essential considerations for organisations.

- Review the performance of durability policy implementations regularly by using the MCDM methods, which were developed in academia and the software industry to reflect real-world experiences.

- The development guidelines that have a positive impact on the most significant durability characteristic, in this case, dependability, have been compiled.

- A measure for dependability is constructed and measured based on the assessment.

- The crucial characteristics for the durability of software services are dependability, human trust, and trustworthiness.

- Table 12, Fig. 2, and Fig. 3 highlight the relevance of level 1, level 2, and level 3 characteristics, which must be followed by practitioners.

- If a dataset lacks these high-priority characteristics, practitioners must provide them via metrics to ensure the life span of software.

- Dependability, trustworthiness, and human trust are crucial characteristics at the first level.

- Confidentiality, authentication, and reliability, among all other durability properties mentioned in Fig. 2, are more desired and significant at level 2.

- Among all the other durability characteristics listed in Fig. 3, operational controls, software effectiveness estimation, and feasibility are more essential and required characteristics at level 3.

- There are no overlapping, duplicating, or conflicting relationships in this assessment; in case there are any, the practitioners should prioritise the most significant ones.

The authors examined the performance of durability from both subjective and objective perspectives to analyse the influence of given priorities, ideas, and recommendations. In addition, in the previous section of this chapter, subjective estimation was performed. This study uses two versions of the BBAU software, V1 and V2, to estimate the objective assessment. The procedure is detailed in the next section.

9.4 Ratings of the Characteristics

A rating is the estimation of something in terms of quantity, quality, or some combination of both. According to the Oxford Dictionary, *"a rating is a classification of something based on a comparative assessment of its quality, standard, or performance"* [16]. To estimate the objective weights, the authors have employed the ratings of durability characteristics taken from the software development team of Babasaheb Bhimrao Ambedkar, Central Government University in Lucknow, Uttar Pradesh, India [3]. The old design of the software is called V1, and the modified design of the software is called V2. Due to the sensitivity of the software, the development team did not give the design structure to the researchers, but two teams of the development organisations facilitated the experiments, which are called team 1 and team 2. Team 1 facilitated our work by reforming the old design into a modified design, and team 2 gave the ratings of durability characteristics.

Furthermore, according to the given priorities and recommendations, the suggested metrics will be supportive for team 1 to modify the design. The suggested metrics may be useful for team 1 in achieving the prioritised goals and reforming the software design. To measure the impact of durability characteristics for V1 and V2, team 2 collected the ratings. The researchers took the ratings and converted the linguistic values into numerical values with the support of the rating scale Table 2 (Chapter 8) and the fuzzy aggregation method is employed to estimate the ratings (also called objective weights) of durability characteristics for V1 and V2. Further, the fuzzy aggregation method was employed in various research areas for decision making, rating, and so on [1–3]. To fuzzify and aggregate the ratings, the next portion discusses the mechanism and implementation.

9.4.1 Fuzzified Average Ratings

Ratings of durability characteristics are collected at level 1, level 2, and level 3, respectively. With the support of the rating scale Table 2 (Chapter 8), linguistic values are converted into numerical values and numerical values into Triangular Fuzzy Numbers (TFNs). To confine the vagueness of the parameters which are related to alternatives, including TFN, is employed [3]. With the support of Eq. (1) and Eq. (3)–(5), fuzzified average ratings are measured. Table 24 represents the fuzzified average ratings of durability characteristics for V1 and V2.

Table 24 represents the fuzzy based average ratings of durability characteristics (characteristics at level 1, level 2, and level 3, respectively) for V1 and V2. Independent ratings of characteristics for V1 and V2 are measured in the next sub-section.

9.4.2 Defuzzification and Independent Ratings

With the support of Eq. (7)–(9) (discussed in Chapter VIII), independent ratings of characteristics are measured. These independent ratings are also called "local ratings". Further, Table 25 represents the independent ratings for V1 and V2.

Table 25 represents the independent ratings of durability characteristics at level 1, level 2, and level 3, respectively. Ratings for the set of characteristics at level 1 have three characteristics including dependability (0.6080, 0.7800), trustworthiness (0.6190, 0.8200) and human trust (0.5950, 0.8100) for V1 and V2 and trustworthiness is highest rated characteristic among them for V1 and V2 respectively. Ratings for the set of characteristics at level 2 have eight characteristics including reliability (0.7090, 0.7900), availability (0.6240, 0.8000), authentication (0.5480, 0.8300), maintainability (0.6260, 0.8200), confidentiality (0.7090, 0.6900), accountability (0.6100, 0.8100), consumer integrity (0.6280, 0.8800), survivability (0.6710, 0.8500) for V1 and V2 respectively. Reliability and confidentiality are equally highest rated characteristics among all for V1. Consumer integrity is the highest rated characteristic among all for V2.

Ratings for the set of characteristics at level 3 have fourteen characteristics, including software effectiveness estimation (0.6260, 0.7600), user satisfaction (0.7990, 0.6600), feasibility (0.6160, 0.6800), operational controls (0.7690, 0.7900), time-efficiency (0.5400, 0.8400), auditability (0.6590, 0.6100), psychological acceptability (0.6230, 0.7500), business continuity (0.6160, 0.6400), accessibility (0.6260, 0.6400), extensibility (0.6330, 0.6000), flexibility (0.6650, 0.5800), detectability (0.6150, 0.6300), scalability (0.6490, 0.6700), and traceability (0.5960, 0.6200). User satisfaction

Table 24: Average Ratings in Fuzzified Form.

S. No.	Characteristics of Level 1	Old Version (Version 1)	Modified Version (Version 2)
		Fuzzified Average Rating	
1	Dependability	0.44500, 0.61500, 0.75500	0.59000, 0.79000, 0.95000
2	Trustworthiness	0.45500, 0.64000, 0.74000	0.64000, 0.84000, 0.97000
3	Human Trust	0.44000, 0.60000, 0.74000	0.62000, 0.82000, 0.96000
S. No.	**Characteristics of Level 2**	**Fuzzified Average Rating**	
1	Reliability	0.53000, 0.72000, 0.865000	0.62000, 0.81000, 0.94000
2	Availability	0.46000, 0.63000, 0.77500	0.63000, 0.82000, 0.94000
3	Authentication	0.38000, 0.55000, 0.71000	0.67000, 0.85000, 0.95000
4	Maintainability	0.44500, 0.63500, 0.79000	0.65000, 0.84000, 0.95000
5	Confidentiality	0.56000, 0.72000, 0.83500	0.51000, 0.70000, 0.86000
6	Accountability	0.44500, 0.61500, 0.76500	0.64000, 0.83000, 0.95000
7	Consumer Integrity	0.46000, 0.63500, 0.78000	0.73000, 0.90000, 0.99000
8	Survivability	0.49500, 0.68000, 0.83000	0.69000, 0.87000, 0.98000
S. No.	**Characteristics of Level 3**	**Fuzzified Average Rating**	
1	Software Effectiveness Estimation	0.66000, 0.60000, 0.87500	0.61000, 0.75000, 0.93000
2	User Satisfaction	0.64000, 0.81000, 0.93500	0.52000, 0.64000, 0.84000
3	Feasibility	0.49000, 0.57000, 0.83500	0.53000, 0.65000, 0.89000
4	Operational Controls	0.75000, 0.67000, 0.98500	0.66000, 0.78000, 0.97000
5	Time-efficiency	0.35000, 0.52000, 0.77000	0.69000, 0.85000, 0.99000
6	Auditability	0.56000, 0.60000, 0.87500	0.47000, 0.58000, 0.83000
7	Psychological Acceptability	0.43000, 0.58000, 0.90000	0.61000, 0.72000, 0.96000
8	Business Continuity	0.42000, 0.57000, 0.90500	0.52000, 0.57000, 0.90000
9	Accessibility	0.49000, 0.61000, 0.79500	0.50000, 0.61000, 0.84000
10	Extensibility	0.44000, 0.60000, 0.89000	0.46000, 0.56000, 0.82000
11	Flexibility	0.50000, 0.66000, 0.84000	0.43000, 0.54000, 0.79000
12	Detectability	0.51000, 0.56000, 0.83000	0.49000, 0.59000, 0.85000
13	Scalability	0.46000, 0.62000, 0.89500	0.51000, 0.66000, 0.85000
14	Traceability	0.40000, 0.57000, 0.84500	0.49000, 0.57000, 0.87000

Table 25: Independent Rating of the Characteristics at Level 1, 2, and 3.

S. No.	Characteristics of Level 1	Old Version (Version 1)	Modified Version (Version 2)
		Defuzzified Independent Rating	
1	Dependability	0.60800	0.78000
2	Trustworthiness	0.61900	0.82000
3	Human Trust	0.59500	0.81000
S. No.	Characteristics of Level 2	Defuzzified Independent Rating	
1	Reliability	0.70900	0.79000
2	Availability	0.62400	0.80000
3	Authentication	0.54800	0.83000
4	Maintainability	0.62600	0.82000
5	Confidentiality	0.70900	0.69000
6	Accountability	0.61000	0.81000
7	Consumer Integrity	0.62800	0.88000
8	Survivability	0.67100	0.85000
S. No.	Characteristics of Level 3	Defuzzified Independent Rating	
1	Software Effectiveness Estimation	0.62600	0.76000
2	User Satisfaction	0.79900	0.66000
3	Feasibility	0.61600	0.68000
4	Operational Controls	0.76900	0.79000
5	Time-efficiency	0.54000	0.84000
6	Auditability	0.65900	0.61000
7	Psychological Acceptability	0.62300	0.75000
8	Business Continuity	0.61600	0.64000
9	Accessibility	0.62600	0.64000
10	Extensibility	0.63300	0.60000
11	Flexibility	0.66500	0.58000
12	Detectability	0.61500	0.63000
13	Scalability	0.64900	0.67000
14	Traceability	0.59600	0.62000

is the highest rated characteristic among all for V1. Time-efficiency is the highest-rated characteristic of all for V2. In this row, independent ratings display the level-wise impact of these characteristics for V1 and V2 and are also called independent ratings. To estimate the impact of the durability characteristics throughout the hierarchy, dependent ratings are measured in the next sub-section.

9.4.3 Dependent Rating of Each Characteristic

Table 25 above represents the independent ratings of every characteristic at levels 1, 2, and 3. The next step in this row is to calculate the dependent ratings of characteristics according to their place in the hierarchy. For calculating the dependent ratings, the lower level ratings are multiplied by the higher-level ratings. Table 26 represents the dependent ratings of each characteristic.

Many characteristics at levels 2 and 3 are similar, but their impact on higher-level characteristics varies. Dependent ratings are measured by using the hierarchy, but various characteristics have various implications. In the next section, the software's durability is measured by using dependent ratings and weights for V1 and V2.

9.5 Assessment of Software Durability

From Eq. (16), durability is measured for two alternatives, i.e., V1 and V2, with the support of dependent ratings (R_i) and weights (W_i) of characteristics. The calculation of the assessment is as follows:

Where values of the dependent weights are presented in the row and values of dependent ratings are presented in the columns. This work is done for the two alternatives, i.e., V1 and V2. Hence, dependent ratings are presented in the two columns. Overall software durability is presented in Table 27.

The values of the durability of BBAU software are presented in Table 27. The value of durability for the old version (V1) is 0.28520 and the value of durability for the modified version (V2) is 0.47000. Again, with the support of dependent weights and dependent ratings of both versions and Eq. (16), the impact of durability at the first level is measured, which is presented in Table 28 and Fig. 4.

The values of durability on first-level characteristics are presented in Table 28. The values for dependability are 0.13910 and 0.21870 for V1 and V2, respectively. The contributions of durability to trustworthiness are 0.07820 and 0.12460 for V1 and V2, respectively. For V1 and V2, the contributions of durability to human trust are 0.06790 and 0.12670, respectively. Again, with the support of dependent weights and dependent

[0.0104 0.0040 0.0052 0.0045 0.0199 0.0418 0.0179 0.0218 0.0262 0.0037 0.0026 0.0056 0.0069 0.0076 0.0097 0.0041 0.0146 0.0293 0.0356 0.0984 0.0209 0.0132 0.0316 0.0501 0.0095 0.0037 0.0048 0.0041 0.0182 0.0175 0.0075 0.0091 0.0110 0.0026 0.0018 0.0040 0.0049 0.0054 0.0069 0.0029 0.0104 0.0602 0.0308 0.0329 0.0211 0.0209 0.0089 0.0109 0.0131 0.0089 0.0045 0.0101 0.0119 0.0374 0.0093 0.0113 0.0312 0.0120 0.0076 0.0182 0.0288] ×

$$
\begin{bmatrix}
0.231 & 0.486 \\
0.219 & 0.415 \\
0.234 & 0.421 \\
0.288 & 0.505 \\
0.257 & 0.551 \\
0.250 & 0.410 \\
0.228 & 0.371 \\
0.356 & 0.461 \\
0.250 & 0.365 \\
0.231 & 0.498 \\
0.238 & 0.405 \\
0.219 & 0.372 \\
0.215 & 0.358 \\
0.231 & 0.392 \\
0.254 & 0.438 \\
0.234 & 0.431 \\
0.200 & 0.385 \\
0.356 & 0.398 \\
0.329 & 0.431 \\
0.294 & 0.470 \\
0.195 & 0.383 \\
0.272 & 0.483 \\
0.252 & 0.524 \\
0.225 & 0.571 \\
0.242 & 0.517 \\
0.230 & 0.441 \\
0.246 & 0.448 \\
0.302 & 0.537 \\
0.270 & 0.585 \\
0.263 & 0.435 \\
0.240 & 0.395 \\
0.373 & 0.490 \\
0.263 & 0.388 \\
0.242 & 0.529 \\
0.250 & 0.430 \\
0.230 & 0.395 \\
0.226 & 0.381 \\
0.242 & 0.416 \\
0.266 & 0.466 \\
0.246 & 0.459 \\
0.210 & 0.409 \\
0.360 & 0.511 \\
0.244 & 0.395 \\
0.261 & 0.431 \\
0.287 & 0.482 \\
0.246 & 0.425 \\
0.225 & 0.385 \\
0.350 & 0.478 \\
0.246 & 0.379 \\
0.219 & 0.421 \\
0.306 & 0.531 \\
0.215 & 0.421 \\
0.253 & 0.627 \\
0.275 & 0.531 \\
0.267 & 0.413 \\
0.248 & 0.448 \\
0.221 & 0.488 \\
0.212 & 0.397 \\
0.296 & 0.502 \\
0.275 & 0.544 \\
0.245 & 0.592
\end{bmatrix}
= \begin{matrix} \text{Version 1} \\ \text{Version 2} \end{matrix} = \begin{bmatrix} 0.2682 \\ 0.4650 \end{bmatrix}
$$

ratings of both versions and Eq. (16), the impact of durability at the second level is measured, which is presented in Table 29 and Fig. 5.

The values of durability on second-level characteristics are presented in Table 29. The coefficients of durability to reliability are 0.05840 and 0.09030 for V1 and V2, respectively. The contributions of durability to

Table 26: Global Ratings of Each Characteristic through Hierarchy.

The first level	The Ratings of the first level		The second level	Independent Ratings of second level		The Dependent Ratings of the second level		The level of the third level	The Independent Ratings of the third level		The Dependent Ratings of the third level	
	Version 1	Version 2		Version 1	Version 2	Version 1	Version 2		Version 1	Version 2	Version 1	Version 2
C1	0.60800	0.78000	C11	0.62400	0.80000	0.37900	0.62400	C111	0.65900	0.76000	0.25000	0.47400
								C112	0.61600	0.66000	0.23400	0.41200
								C113	0.62600	0.68000	0.23700	0.42400
								C114	0.78100	0.79000	0.29600	0.49300
								C115	0.76900	0.84000	0.29200	0.52400
			C12	0.70900	0.79000	0.43100	0.61600	C121	0.61600	0.66000	0.26600	0.40700
								C122	0.54000	0.61000	0.23300	0.37600
								C123	0.79900	0.75000	0.34400	0.46200
								C124	0.61600	0.64000	0.26600	0.39400
			C13	0.62600	0.82000	0.38100	0.64000	C131	0.65900	0.76000	0.25100	0.48600
								C132	0.64900	0.64000	0.24700	0.40900
								C133	0.59600	0.60000	0.22700	0.38400
								C134	0.61500	0.580	0.23400	0.37100
								C135	0.63300	0.63000	0.24100	0.40300
								C136	0.66500	0.67000	0.25300	0.42900
								C137	0.62600	0.68000	0.23800	0.43500
								C138	0.54000	0.61000	0.20600	0.39000
			C14	0.70900	0.69000	0.43100	0.53800	C141	0.79900	0.75000	0.34400	0.40400
								C142	0.78100	0.79000	0.33700	0.42500
								C143	0.76900	0.87000	0.33100	0.46800
			C15	0.57800	0.83000	0.35100	0.64700	C151	0.62300	0.62000	0.21900	0.40100
								C152	0.79900	0.75000	0.28100	0.48600
								C153	0.78100	0.79000	0.27400	0.51100
								C154	0.76900	0.84000	0.27000	0.54400

C2								Sub				
C2	0.61900	0.82000	C21	0.62400	0.80000	0.38600	0.65600	C211	0.65900	0.760	0.25400	0.49900
								C212	0.61600	0.66000	0.23800	0.43300
								C213	0.62600	0.68000	0.24200	0.44600
								C214	0.78100	0.79000	0.30200	0.51800
								C215	0.76900	0.84000	0.29700	0.55100
			C22	0.70900	0.79000	0.43900	0.64800	C221	0.61600	0.66000	0.27000	0.42800
								C222	0.54000	0.61000	0.23700	0.39500
								C223	0.79900	0.75000	0.35100	0.48600
								C224	0.61600	0.64000	0.27000	0.41500
			C23	0.62600	0.82000	0.38700	0.67200	C231	0.65900	0.76000	0.25500	0.51100
								C232	0.64900	0.64000	0.25100	0.43000
								C233	0.59600	0.60000	0.23100	0.40300
								C234	0.61500	0.58000	0.23800	0.39000
								C235	0.63300	0.63000	0.24500	0.42400
								C236	0.66500	0.67000	0.25800	0.45100
								C237	0.62600	0.68000	0.24300	0.45700
								C238	0.54000	0.61000	0.20900	0.41000
			C24	0.61000	0.81000	0.48300	0.64800	C241	0.78100	0.790	0.37800	0.51200
			C25	0.67100	0.85000	0.41500	0.69700	C251	0.61500	0.58000	0.25500	0.40400
								C252	0.63300	0.63000	0.26300	0.43900
								C253	0.66500	0.67000	0.27600	0.46700

Table 26 contd. ....

...Table 26 contd.

The first level	The Ratings of the first level		The second level	Independent Ratings of second level		The Dependent Ratings of the second level		The level of the third level	The Independent Ratings of the third level		The Dependent Ratings of the third level	
	Version 1	Version 2		Version 1	Version 2	Version 1	Version 2		Version 1	Version 2	Version 1	Version 2
C3	0.59500	0.87000	C31	0.70900	0.79000	0.42200	0.68700	C311	0.61600	0.66000	0.26000	0.45400
								C312	0.54000	0.61000	0.22800	0.41900
								C313	0.79900	0.75000	0.33700	0.51500
								C314	0.61600	0.64000	0.26000	0.44000
			C32	0.62800	0.88000	0.37400	0.76600	C321	0.62300	0.62000	0.23300	0.47500
								C322	0.79900	0.75000	0.29900	0.57400
								C323	0.78100	0.64000	0.29200	0.49000
								C324	0.76900	0.84000	0.28700	0.64300
			C33	0.61000	0.81000	0.36300	0.70500	C331	0.78100	0.79000	0.28300	0.55700
			C34	0.70900	0.69000	0.42200	0.60000	C341	0.79900	0.75000	0.33700	0.45000
								C342	0.78100	0.79000	0.32900	0.47400
								C343	0.76900	0.84000	0.32400	0.50400
			C35	0.54800	0.83000	0.32600	0.72200	C351	0.62300	0.62000	0.20300	0.44800
								C352	0.79900	0.750	0.26100	0.54200
								C353	0.78100	0.79000	0.25500	0.57000
								C354	0.76900	0.84000	0.25100	0.60700

Table 27: Overall Software Durability.

	Version 1	Version 2
Software Durability	0.28520	0.47000

availability are 0.02370 and 0.04330 for V1 and V2, respectively. The levels of durability for authentication are 0.04560 and 0.09310 for V1 and V2, respectively. Durability contributes 0.02270 and 0.04030 to maintainability in V1 and V2, respectively. For V1 and V2, the contributions of durability to confidentiality are 0.06960 and 0.09550, respectively. For V1 and V2, the contributions of durability to accountability are 0.03260 and 0.05020,

Table 28: Durability Impact at Level 1.

S. No.	Characteristics of Level 1	Version 1	Version 2
1	Dependability	0.13910	0.21870
2	Trustworthiness	0.07820	0.12460
3	Human Trust	0.06790	0.12670

respectively. For V1 and V2, the contributions of durability to consumer integrity are 0.01080 and 0.02140, respectively. Durability contributes 0.02190 and 0.03600 to survivability in V1 and V2, respectively. Again, with the support of dependent weights and dependent ratings of both versions and Eq. (16), the impact of durability at the third level is measured, as presented in Table 30 and Fig. 6.

Table 30 displays the values of durability characteristics at level 2. The contributions of durability for software effectiveness estimation

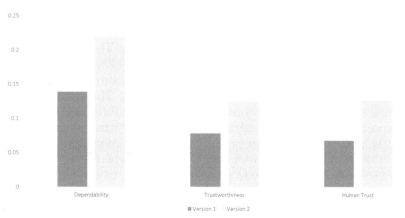

Figure 4: Graphical Representation at Level 1.

Table 29: Durability Impact at Level 2.

S. No.	Characteristics of Level 2	Version 1	Version 2
1	Reliability	0.05840	0.09030
2	Availability	0.02370	0.04330
3	Authentication	0.04560	0.09310
4	Maintainability	0.02270	0.04030
5	Confidentiality	0.06960	0.09550
6	Accountability	0.03260	0.05020
7	Consumer Integrity	0.01080	0.02140
8	Survivability	0.02190	0.03600

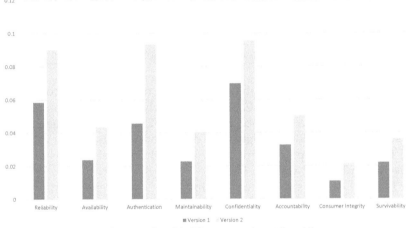

Figure 5: Graphical Representation at Level 2.

are 0.06410 and 0.10140 for V1 and V2, respectively. The contributions of durability for garnering user satisfaction are 0.03440 and 0.04900 for V1 and V2, respectively. The contributions of durability for feasibility are 0.02390 and 0.03850 for V1 and V2, respectively. The contributions to durability for operational controls are 0.07580 and 0.13100 for V1 and V2, respectively. Durability contributions for time-efficiency are 0.01360 and 0.02400 for V1 and V2, respectively. Durability contributes 0.00710 and 0.01370 to auditability in V1 and V2, respectively. For V1 and V2, the contributions of durability to psychological acceptability are 0.00940 and 0.01850, respectively. The levels of durability for business continuity are 0.01670 and 0.02630 for V1 and V2, respectively. For V1 and V2, the contributions of durability to accessibility are 0.00430 and 0.00790, respectively. Durability contributes 0.01180 and 0.01980 to extensibility

Table 30: Durability Impact at Level 3.

S. No.	Characteristics of Level 3	Version 1	Version 2
1	Software Effectiveness Estimation	0.06410	0.10140
2	User Satisfaction	0.03440	0.04900
3	Feasibility	0.02390	0.03850
4	Operational Controls	0.07580	0.13100
5	Time-efficiency	0.01360	0.02400
6	Auditability	0.00710	0.01370
7	Psychological Acceptability	0.00940	0.01850
8	Business Continuity	0.01670	0.02630
9	Accessibility	0.00430	0.00790
10	Extensibility	0.01180	0.01980
11	Flexibility	0.01010	0.01730
12	Detectability	0.01050	0.01670
13	Scalability	0.00120	0.00210
14	Traceability	0.00230	0.00390

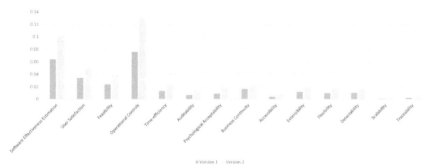

Figure 6: Graphical Representation at Level 3.

in V1 and V2, respectively. The durability contributions to flexibility are 0.01010 and 0.01730 for V1 and V2, respectively. The contributions of durability to detectability are 0.01050 and 0.01670 for V1 and V2, respectively. The durability contributions to scalability are 0.00120 and 0.00210 for V1 and V2, respectively. For V1 and V2, the contributions of durability to traceability are 0.00230 and 0.00390, respectively.

9.6 Sensitivity Analysis

The technique employed to determine how the independent variable values will affect a particular dependent variable under a given set of assumptions is defined as *sensitivity analysis* [16–17]. Sensitivity analysis focuses on measuring the effects of changes in the key values of the project and is reliant upon one or more input variables within the specific boundaries. In this chapter, the authors have employed the values of alpha and beta as 0.5 and 0.5, respectively, during the defuzzification procedure. The range of these two values falls *between 0 and 1* wherein the lower value indicates greater uncertainty in decision-making due to the preferences and risk tolerance of the participants. A 0.5 value for alpha and beta is employed to represent a balanced environment because the values of alpha and beta are dependent on the environmental uncertainties. This indicates that participants are neither extremely optimistic nor pessimistic about their judgments. These values will directly affect the weights of individual criteria, priority ranking, and the overall assessment.

If the participants involved in the priority assessment have strong background knowledge of software durability, the values of alpha and beta can be readjusted to indicate confident judgments. Furthermore, the sets of alpha and beta values are 81 (9x9), including (0.1, 0.1), (0.1, 0.2), (0.2, 0.1), (0.1, 0.3), (0.3, 0.1), etc. The accuracy of Fuzzy AHP can be further improved by investigating the impact of alpha and beta values on the dependent outcomes. An analysis is needed to determine the values accurately and emphatically. That's why, to check the fluctuations in the outcomes, the researchers employed ten combinations of alpha and beta values for V1 and V2, including E1 (0.1, 0.1), E2 (0.5, 0.1), E3 (0.5, 0.3), E4 (0.5, 0.7), E5 (0.5, 0.9), E6 (0.1, 0.5), E7 (0.3, 0.5), E8 (0.7, 0.5), E9 (0.9, 0.5), E10 (0.9, 0.9, 0.5) and E0 (0.5, 0.5). Furthermore, the value of alpha is constant for E2, E3, E4, and E5, while the value of beta is variable. While the value of beta is constant for E6, E7, E8, and E9, the value of alpha is variable. The outcomes are presented in Table 31 and Fig. 7.

Table 31 displays the fluctuation in outcomes due to alpha and beta values. For alpha and beta values, researchers have employed the minimum values as well as maximum values, including (0.1, 0.1) and (0.9, 0.9) respectively. Hence, E1 (0.1, 0.1) gives the maximum values, including 0.46420 and 0.69060 for V1 and V2, respectively, but it indicates greater uncertainty in decision-making. E9 (0.9, 0.9) gives the average value of durability, including 0.24270 and 0.41850 for V1 and V2, respectively. Further, E5 (0.5, 0.9) gives the minimum value of durability, including 0.21100 and 0.35550 for V1 and V2 respectively. All other fluctuations due to values of alpha and beta are presented in Table 31 for V1 and V2 respectively. Although E0 (0.5, 0.5) gives the concentrated values of durability, including 0.28520 and 0.47000 for V1 and V2, respectively. The outcomes through the values of alpha and beta (as 0.5) specified that a balanced environment of practitioners' judgments might give the best

Table 31: Sensitivity Analysis.

	Version 1	Version 2	Version 1	Version 2	Version 1	Version 2	Version 1	Version 2	Version 1	Version 2	Version 1	Version 2	Version 1	Version 2	Version 1	Version 2	Version 1	Version 2	Version 1	Version 2	Version 1	Version 2
Experiment Number	E1		E2		E3		E4		E5		E0		E6		E7		E8		E9		E10	
(Preferences of Participants) α	0.1		0.5		0.5		0.5		0.5		0.5		0.1		0.3		0.7		0.9		0.9	
(Risk Tolerance of Participants) β	0.1		0.1		0.3		0.7		0.9		0.5		0.5		0.5		0.5		0.5		0.9	
Durability	0.46420	0.69060	0.36870	0.57990	0.32630	0.51900	0.24650	0.40910	0.21100	0.35550	0.28520	0.47000	0.29100	0.45790	0.28780	0.45920	0.27890	0.46050	0.27510	0.46520	0.24270	0.41850

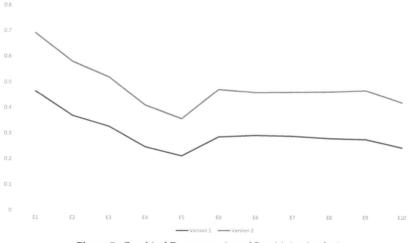

Figure 7: Graphical Representation of Sensitivity Analysis.

outcomes. After going through the outcomes of the sensitivity analysis, it has been determined that fluctuation in the values of overall durability is not negligible. The preferences of participants and the risk tolerance of participants affect the value of durability.

9.7 Statistical Investigation

Statistical validation is the procedure of establishing that a measure is supportive in the sense that it is related to other variables as expected in theory. Two experiments were conducted for statistical validation: a pre-tryout and a tryout. A minimal set of data is required for the pre-tryout. The tryout is carried out on a wider collection of data if the outcomes of the pre-tryout are favourable. The assessment's acceptance is determined by satisfactory test outcomes.

9.7.1 Design Module of an Experiment

Experiments are employed for testing and exploring a given theory. Through experiments, theoretical predictions are tested against reality [18]. Experimentation and data collection are the tools by which theories are validated. The goal of an experiment is to collect sufficient data to obtain a statistically decisive result [19]. The experiments are performed to validate the proposed framework for durability assessment and improvement. In the pre-tryout, one module of BBAU software design is employed as input.

With the support of priorities of durability characteristics, researchers measured the durability of a module, i.e., V1, and then, according to the suggestions, the given module was modified by the practitioners, i.e., V2. A comparison of the assessment values indicates that the durability of V2 after modification is greater than the old one. After analysing the outcomes of the pre-tryout, since no significant changes were noticed, a try-out was carried out with the larger set of data. Ten modules of BBAU software are employed as input. The same procedure is repeated for ten modules. Statistical interpretations are made based on the outcome.

9.7.2 Pre-Tryout

The pre-tryout has been carried out on a module of BBAU software. In Chapter 5, the durability of V1 and V2 is measured. The difference in durability between V1 and V2 is presented in Table 32.

Table 32: Improvement in Durability.

	Version 1 (Old Version)	Version 2 (Modified Version)	Durability Improvement (In Percentage)
Software Durability	0.28520	0.47000	39.32 %

Hence, it can be said that suggestions and frameworks imposed on V2 functioned well and durability improved by 39.32 percent, as evident in Table 32.

9.7.3 Review and Revision

A critical review of the outcome strengthens the acceptability of the proposed framework and the usability of the assessment. In a similar league, the outcomes obtained from the pre-tryout were analyzed. For the revision of the calculation, the classical method, as explained in Chapter 6, was employed. We obtained a 91.9% correlation between the fuzzy and classical methods. Therefore, the researchers adapted the same framework for testing on a large set of data.

9.7.4 Tryout

Statistical validation is an ongoing activity and hence there are degrees of validity: the more the evidence, the greater is the validity of the approach being used [18]. A tryout is carried out to collect more and more evidence for validation of the proposed framework. The tryout contains ten modules of the same design. These are the modules developed by the organization's team 1 and rated by team 2, again. After the assessment by the authors, the impacts of durability on ten modules are presented in Table 33.

Table 33: Reassessing the Durability for Ten Modules.

Software Module	Version 1 (Old Version)	Version 2 (Modified Version)	Durability Improvement (In Percentage)
Module 1	0.27480	0.31760	15.57 %
Module 2	0.28600	0.35990	25.83 %
Module 3	0.28900	0.34560	19.58 %
Module 4	0.30260	0.32670	7.96 %
Module 5	0.31780	0.36120	13.65 %
Module 6	0.34560	0.42230	22.19 %
Module 7	0.32780	0.36230	10.52 %
Module 8	0.23570	0.32670	38.60 %
Module 9	0.34250	0.41230	20.37 %
Module 10	0.38790	0.45230	16.60 %

9.7.5 Statistical Analysis

Statistics is a mathematical tool employed for organizing, gathering, analyzing, and interpreting numerical data. Statistical analysis is carried out on ten modules to display statistical significance or validation of the proposed framework. As the sample size is small, *the two-tailed t-test* is applied to find the level of significance and reject the null hypothesis.

Because the rejection or acceptance of a null hypothesis is based on either the *0.05 alpha (α) or the 0.01 alpha (α)* level of significance for one-tailed or two-tailed tests, the rejection of the null hypothesis is based on the *0.05 alpha (α) level of significance for a one-tailed test.* The complete procedure of the following statistical analysis is summarised as: The first step starts with the formulation of the null hypothesis and alternate hypothesis. The values of V1 and V2 are put under statistical analysis to conclude whether there is a significant difference between the pretreatment data and the post-treatment data. The obtained t value will determine whether to reject the null hypothesis and accept the alternative hypothesis.

9.7.5.1 Hypothesis Testing

The null hypothesis states that no significant association exists between two or more factors [3, 19], whereas the alternate hypothesis states that the relationship exists. The rejection of the null hypothesis strengthens the case for adopting the relationship or the alternative hypothesis. The following null and alternate hypotheses were made to validate the proposed framework:

Null Hypothesis (H_{01}): Durability-based suggestions using durability assessment cannot support assessing and improving the life span of the software.

Alternative Hypothesis (H_{11}): Durability-based suggestions using durability assessment can support in assessing and improving the life span.

9.7.5.2 Statistical Interpretation

By observing the values of durability in Table 33, it can be inferred, quite evidently, that the suggestions for all the modules have worked well. The values of durability for various modules of V2 are relatively greater than the values of durability for various modules of V1. By observation, it seems that the treatment worked well. The values displayed that the durability in all the ten modules was measured and, hence, the durability was improved. The initial claim that the durability assessment framework can assess and improve proved true. A graphical representation of the comparative study and improvement is presented in Fig. 8 for both V1 and V2. However, these steps in the assessment will not be able to prove the acceptability of the assessment. To establish the effectiveness of the assessment approach and validate its accuracy it must be verified whether the difference in the values in V2 is due to the given suggestions or is just a sampling error. All in all, the level of significance of the proposed framework must be computed. While examining the inferential data

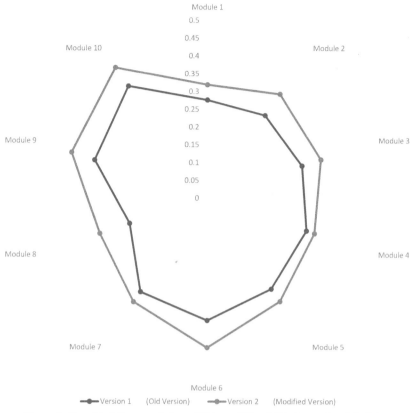

Figure 8: Graphical Representation of Values of Durability for various Modules.

analysis, it was found that the t-test for the situation given below is appropriate for the purpose: "When the same group of individuals takes a pre-test, then the group is exposed to a treatment". The group is again tested after treatment to determine whether the influence of the treatment has been statistically significant as determined by mean gain scores [19]. The t-test was carried out to determine the level of significance of the approach.

9.7.5.3 Level of Significance

To find out the significance of the difference between the means of values of V1 and V2, the means of both V1 and V2 values are measured as presented in Table 34. The Pearson coefficient of correlation comes out to be 0.887. The coefficient represents that the values of V1 before the researcher's suggestions and V2 after the researcher's suggestions are highly correlated. The degree of freedom is 9 for values of V1 and V2. For

Table 34: t-Test for Durability Improvement Data Analysis.

t-Test for Durability							
	Mean	Std. Deviation	Std. Error	No. of Samples	Pearson Coef.	Degree of Freedom	t- Values
Software Durability (Version 1)	0.311	0.043	0.002	10	0.887	9	2.26
Software Durability (Version 2)	0.369	0.045	0.003				

the application of the t-test in the scenario, the homogeneity of variances, i.e., the F value, must be tested. Homogeneity can be obtained by dividing the larger variance by the smaller. The large variance is 0.001842 for V1, and the smaller one is 0.00206 for V2. The larger to smaller ratio yields an F value of 0.89. Since the F value is less than 1.83 (the F critical value for 2 variances of the degree of freedom 9), it is concluded that the variances are homogeneous. This test provides the ground for the applicability of the t-test. The t value comes out to be 2.26. As the value exceeds the t critical value of 1.83 for a one-tailed test at the 0.05 level for 9 degrees of freedom, the null hypothesis H_{01} is strongly rejected and the alternate hypothesis H_{11} is accepted. Hence, it is validated that the durability assessment framework can be measured and, with the support of the suggestions, durability can be improved.

We used the Fuzzy AHP method for assessing the software's durability, encompassing both V1 and V2. Furthermore, to achieve the best potential outcomes, durability characteristics were measured according to their respective priorities.

Any novel technique must be validated before it can be accepted by the practitioners working in the said field or by the industry. It is the validation that establishes the approach's utility in practice by the experts or by the industry for wide scale use. The framework's utility for durability assessment is tested through a systematic validation procedure. Practitioners' review was done at first for the purpose of theoretical validation. Various specialists in the field measured the framework and determined it to be satisfactory. Statistical validation was performed as a second step. Pre-tryout and tryout were parts of statistical validation. A pre-tryout just requires a modest amount of information, but a tryout requires a bigger amount. The pre-testing was done by using a BBAU software design module.

The researchers advanced to the next level, the tryout, after a good pre-tryout. The test was conducted on 10 modules. The modules were examined, and values for V1 and V2 were determined. The framework's values for V1 and V2 were statistically analysed to prove that the framework has successfully measured the durability, and has improved it. The t-test was employed, and it was discovered that the t-values derived from computations on V1 and V2 values surpassed the t-critical values. As a result, one by one, the null hypothesis, which was formed at the start of the statistical analysis, was rejected, and alternative hypotheses were accepted. According to the researchers, the durability estimation framework can assess the durability of a design and give recommendations to improve it for an enhanced life-span.

9.8 Conclusion

Since the birth of software, the field of software engineering has been mostly overlooked. There could be a variety of reasons for this. It used to be a simple operation to accomplish by just applying some passwords or installing some software. With the passage of time, complicated antivirus software has supplanted easy-to-install software. Because of the computer's numerous connections, it is vulnerable to viruses, making it insecure for handling personal and sensitive data. Much work has been done in the field of software to offer optimal service at the lowest possible cost. Durability necessitates ongoing maintenance. Maintenance is becoming more expensive and time-consuming by the day. An accurate assessment of durability will not only reduce the maintenance time and costs involved but also extend the shelf life of the software in use.

Points to Remember

- Durability is influenced by five characteristics: dependability, usability, security, trustworthiness, and human trust.
- Identifying, prioritising, and evaluating the components is, in a nutshell, a crucial procedure.
- A software product is long-lasting if it performs well for the user over a long period. During software development, identifying and classifying durability characteristics aids in improving the service life.
- Design characteristics like coupling and reusability are affected by scalability. Affected design aspects of scalability may be measured and enhanced by using CCC and CMI metrics. Furthermore, CCC aids in calculating the ratio of all classes associated with the segregated characteristics.
- Dependability, trustworthiness, and human trust are crucial characteristics at the first level.

- Design properties such as coupling and cohesion are affected by business continuity. The affected design properties of business continuity can be measured and enhanced by using CCC and CMW metrics.

Review Questions

Objective Type Questions

1. .... is a crucial characteristic at level 1 of the hierarchy of software durability?
   a. Psychological Acceptability
   b. Dependability
   c. Auditability
   d. Time-efficiency

2. Which defuzzification method is used in the software durability assessment?
   a. Centroid method
   b. Alpha cut method
   c. Weighted Average method
   d. Center of largest area method

3. A .... is the estimation of something in terms of quantity, quality, or some combination of both?
   a. Rank
   b. Rating
   c. Questionnaire
   d. Tool

4. The technique employed to determine how independent variable values will affect a particular dependent variable under a given set of assumptions is defined as ....
   a. Sensitivity Analysis
   b. Empirical Validation
   c. Theoretical Validation
   d. Historical Data

5. ....is the highest weighted attribute of software durability.
   a. Reliability
   b. Dependability
   c. Human Trust
   d. Trustworthiness

Short Answer Type Questions

1. Enlist the second level attributes of software durability.
2. What ares traceability and feasibility?
3. Define sensitivity analysis.
4. Define hypothesis testing.

Descriptive Questions

1. Explain in detail the sensitivity analysis and the process of assessing it.
2. Which design characteristics are influenced by software durability characteristics?

References

1. Kumar, R., Zarour, M., Alenezi, M., Agrawal, A. and Khan, R.A. 2019. Measuring security durability of software through fuzzy-based decision-making process. International Journal of Computational Intelligence Systems, 12(2): 627–642.
2. New Data: Software as a Service Industry Revenue up 23% This Year as Shift to the Cloud Continues. 2017. Available at: https://www.geekwire.com/2017/new-data-software-service-industry-revenue-23-year-shift-cloud-continues/ Last Visit on Dec 25, 2021.
3. Agrawal, A., Zarour, M., Alenezi, M., Kumar, R. and Khan, R.A. 2019. Security durability assessment through fuzzy analytic hierarchy process. PeerJ Computer Science, 5: e215.
4. Millet, I. and Saaty, T.L. 2000. On the relativity of relative measures–accommodating both rank preservation and rank reversals in the AHP. European Journal of Operational Research, 121(1): 205–212.
5. Chowdhury, I. and Zulkernine, M. 2010. Can complexity, coupling, and cohesion metrics be used as early indicators of vulnerabilities? In Proceedings of the 2010 ACM Symposium on Applied Computing, pp. 1963–1969.
6. Abbadi, Z. 2011. Security metrics what can we measure? In Open Web Application Security Project (OWASP), Nova Chapter Meeting Presentation on Security Metrics, Volume 2.
7. Siddiqui, S.T. 2017. Significance of security metrics in secure software development. International Journal of Applied Information Systems, 12(6): 10–15.

8. Yadav, S., Sunil, S. and Uttpal, S. 2014. A review of object-oriented coupling and cohesion metrics. International Journal of Computer Science Trends and Technology, 2(5): 45–55.

9. Mohammed, O.S. and Taha, D.B. 2016. Conducting multi-class security metrics from enterprise architect class diagram. International Journal of Computer Science and Information Security, 14(4): 56.

10. Alshammari, B.M. 2011. Quality metrics for assessing security critical computer programs. PhD Thesis, Queensland University of Technology.

11. Krishna, G. and Joshi, R.K. 2010. Inheritance metrics: what do they measure? In Proceedings of the 4th Workshop on Mechanisms for Specialization, Generalization and inheritance, ACM, p. 1.

12. Kumar, M.D.S. and Prasad R.S. 2015. New metrics for system understandability of inheritance hierarchies. International Journal of Research Studies in Computer Science and Engineering, 2(3): 59–62.

13. Peterson, R.S., Wong, B. and Sirer, E.G. 2011. A content propagation metric for efficient content distribution. In: ACM SIGCOMM Computer Communication Review, 41(4): 326–337.

14. Taha, D.B. and Mohammed, O.S. 2017. Conducting security metrics for object-oriented class design. International Journal of Computer Science and Information Security, 15(8): 20–27.

15. Agrawal, A. and Khan, R.A. 2014. Assessing impact of cohesion on security: an object-oriented design perspective. Pensee Journal, 76(2): 45–54.

16. Rating Definition by Oxford Dictionaries. 2018. Available at: https://en.oxforddictionaries.com/definition/rating, Last Visit Oct 25 2018.

17. Briand, L., Emam, K.E. and Moraska, S. 1995. Theoretical and empirical validation of software product metrics, Technical Report Number- ISERN-95-03. International Software Engineering Research Network, Version 1.

18. Zelkowitz, M.V. and Wallace, D. 1977. Experimental validation in software engineering. Information and Software Technology, 39(11): 735–743.

19. Support or Reject Null Hypothesis in Easy Steps. 2009. Available at: http://www.statisticshowto.com/support-or-reject-null-hypothesis/ Last Visit Nov 18 2018.

Useful Links

https://www.tutorialspoint.com/software_testing_dictionary/durability_testing.htm

https://peerj.com/articles/cs-215/#supp-1

https://www.service-architecture.com/articles/database/durability.html

https://www.plm.automation.siemens.com/global/en/industries/automotive-transportation/strength-durability.html

https://www.amazon.jobs/en/jobs/1795397/software-development-engineer-s3-storage-durability-team

CHAPTER 10

Software Durability Testing

10.1 Objectives

In the present era of incessant attacks and cyber threats, a new trend is gaining a strong foothold. This is evident from the fact that the intruders are now shifting their tactics from hacking to data integrity and durability attacks. Vulnerabilities in source code are putting the software business at risk all the time. Although static source code analysis tools are improving, there is still a gap between what they can identify and what should be discovered. A prescriptive framework has been presented for critically examining source code in order to filter out the vulnerabilities and categorise their severity levels. The proposed framework in this chapter will aid in improving application software durability. As a result, identified vulnerabilities will be remedied, and a long-lasting code base will be created with suggested recommendations. In light of the above premise, the objectives that have been set forth for this chapter are:

- To ensure that the system's durability is achieved as per the assessment or not.
- To figure out what is durability testing, how is it performed, and what criteria should be met for testing software durability.
- To identify the types of durability testing and their significance for improving the quality of software.
- To identify the gaps in assessing and testing durability and the risks associated with it.
- To describe in detail how long code can last and to suggest a framework for analysing source code that can be used to make software that can last.

10.2 Durability Testing

Durability testing is a non-functional form of testing software in which a software application is evaluated under a heavy load for a lengthy period of time to estimate the behaviour of the software application in long-term use. The most important objective of durability testing is to make sure that the application can handle a lot of traffic without losing its responsiveness [1]. This type of testing is done at the conclusion of the performance run cycle. In fact, it can take more than a year to do a durability test. It is possible to apply external loads, such as Internet traffic or user actions. Durability testing, in contrast to load testing, typically lasts for a few hours.

"Durability testing integrates a full set of features of software for a complete end-to-end solution to ensure the longevity *of software."*

"Durability testing is a performance testing technique used to determine the characteristics of software under *various load conditions for a specific time period. This testing helps us figure out how stable transaction response times were over the course of the test."*

Durability testing is a crucial stage in estimating a software product's estimated lifespan. By spotting the problems earlier in the software development process, it improves repeatability and lowers risk exposure.

10.2.1 Purpose

Testing for long-term durability and durability of software applications and products is an important step in the development process [2-3]. It is extremely vital to have good test coverage to verify the durability of a software programme entirely and make sure that it's running well for a long time as per the specs. Software durability testing makes sure that the testing is being done properly and, as a result, the system is ready for use. Furthermore, the purposes of software durability testing are as follows:

- The main purpose of durability testing is to detect memory leaks.
- To determine how the system operates over time in order to ensure its longevity.
- To ensure that the system's reaction time is the same as, or better than, it was at the start of the test after a long period of time.
- To figure out how many users and/or transactions a system can handle while still meeting the performance targets.
- Durability testing helps the developers to figure out how many more resources (like processor capacity, disc capacity, memory consumption, or network bandwidth) they will need for future requisites.

- Durability testing is usually done by overusing the system or cutting back on certain system resources and then watching the results for a long time.
- After a "typical" amount of time, it is done to make sure there are no flaws or memory leaks.

10.2.2 Challenges

- The test takes a long time to complete. As a result, doing durability testing on a project with tight deadlines is tough.
- This isn't something that can be done by hand. It needs an automation tool and an expert who knows how to use it.
- Determining how much load is worth applying for how long might be difficult.
- If the test environment is not correctly separated from the real production environment, application or network failures during the durability test can wreak havoc on the entire system, resulting in permanent data loss or corruption.
- The customer notices any unhandled exceptions.

An Example

The banking application is an apt example of where durability testing is necessary and can be employed. The application is tested on the bank's closing days to see if it can withstand a continuous predicted load or a significant number of transactions over an extended period of time.

10.2.3 Benefits and Limitations

We can't get rid of software since it is an inseparable element of our existence. Anyone can see a computer with 12 tabs open, a mobile phone with half a dozen apps, one used every hour, an iPad, an Alexa device, or an automatically regulating air conditioner; even the engineers are wearing smartwatches these days! Software is something everyone uses daily [4–5]. And it all hinges on working software. When our software fails, how do we feel? Everyone feels frustrated and distracted if a piece of software takes three extra seconds to load. We have communication breakdowns when the communication software does not convey messages as it should. Hence, testing software for its durability comes under the quality assurance process and is a necessary element of any software development. The key benefits and limitations are as follows:

Benefits

- It ensures an application's long-term viability and exposes flaws that would otherwise go undetected by other performance tests. When it is used for a longer period, for example, developers may not notice the memory leak issue during volume testing or stress testing.

- It strengthens the application: It detects potential performance degradation issues that may arise over time and then fixes them, making the programme additionally robust.

- It explains the system's long-term behaviour when it is under stress. To put it another way, it keeps track of the system's long-term viability.

- The developer can utilise the data from the durability testing to validate or improve their infrastructure needs. The tool helps you figure out how the workload will change the system under load over time.

- It detects performance issues that may arise after a system has been operating at a high level for a long time.

- Typical faults found in smaller targeted performance tests ensure that the application remains available even when subjected to a large amount of traffic in a short period.

- The durability test is also used to see if there is any decrease in performance after an extended period of execution.

Limitations

- Determining how much stress to apply and for how long might be difficult.

- Durability testing could result in application and/or network failures if the test environment is not isolated, causing significant downtime.

- Over-stressing the system for a long time could cause data to be lost or corrupted that can't be fixed.

- Even after the stress is relieved, resource consumption remains high.

- Some application components aren't functioning correctly.

10.3 Basic Steps to Perform Durability Testing

After the developers have finished developing the software, they would want to ensure that it would last [3–6]. In this row, durability testing corroborates how long the software service can perform its role without causing damage. These tests are put together by imitating the conditions that would normally arise during the course of the software's lifetime.

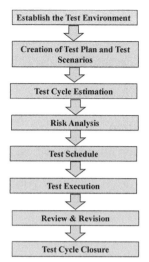

Figure 1: Steps of Durability Testing.

Durability testing can check for any issues that may arise with any software, as seen in Fig. 1. Depending on the software, the following eight fundamental processes can be used to do testing:

10.3.1 Establish the Test Environment

Establishing test environments offers a slew of new challenges, such as figuring out how to manage all of them. It's not always easy to recreate a tester's production environment exactly. Aside from that, the testing engineer must devote a significant amount of time and effort to manually creating those environments. The server that the testers use to execute the test cases they have generated is known as a test environment. The test environment consists of more than just setting up a server on which tests can be executed. Hardware and network settings are also required. This includes determining the durability test's hardware, software, database (and its size as the test progresses), and operating system. It also necessitates the formation of a team to conduct the durability testing, as well as the assignment of roles and tasks within the group. The test environment should be ready before the test is run, and it should be far enough away from the real system to be safe.

10.3.2 Creation of Test Plan and Test Scenarios

Test Scenarios are designed to guarantee that a website's or app's entire functionality works as planned. Gathering input from clients, stakeholders, and developers is the best way to generate accurate test scenarios. This ensures that all conceivable user situations are covered and that all business flows of the software, in the plan, are thoroughly tested. Test cases must be created, reviewed, and finished. This is also the time to plan how the tester will execute the tests. The application's breakpoint should be determined, as should the amount of load that will be provided to the application during a durability test.

10.3.3 Test Cycle Estimation

Test estimation and execution are just as critical as the development cycle for the success of any project. It's critical to stick to the estimate if the tester wants to earn the client's trust. It includes figuring out how long each test phase is and how many times it needs to be done.

10.3.4 Risk Analysis

In software engineering, risk analysis is the process of analysing the risks associated with a testing project. For the project's success, risks should be identified and related remedies determined prior to the start of the project. This is an important stage in the testing procedure. The test cases are prioritised based on the risk factor. The risks and challenges that a tester may encounter during a durability test are listed below:

- Is the durability test going to remain consistent with time?
- Are there any other minor issues that have not yet been resolved?
- Is there any external interference that has not yet been addressed?

10.3.5 Test Schedule

A test schedule includes all of the testing phases or tasks, target start and end dates, and assignments. Additionally, it needs to outline the testing's monitoring, approval, and evaluation processes. Determine the budget, objectives, and timeline for this. The software durability test schedule is always longer than other tests; thus, the timeline for this must be determined before testing begins.

10.3.6 Test Execution

Without a question, the most essential and "happening" step of the Software Testing Life Cycle, as well as the entire development lifecycle, is test execution. The process of executing code and comparing expected and actual results is known as test execution. This entails finally starting the durability test.

10.3.7 Review and Revision

No software is perfect, but testers can maximise their efforts to gather as much information about the product's quality as possible, focusing on the areas with the greatest potential for business risk. While none of these things are new, there are several components of the model that should be examined due to their importance and are sometimes overlooked, such as goals, testing teams, shift-left testing, shift-right testing, atmosphere and platform, and so on.

10.3.8 Test Cycle Closure

A Test Closure is a document that summarises all of the tests performed throughout the software development life cycle, as well as a full analysis of the flaws and mistakes detected. In other words, "Test Closure" is a message that is written before the testing process is fully completed. This letter includes a report on test cases completed, the number and type of faults discovered, defect density, and so on. Close the test cycle using the exit criteria that were established during the test preparation step. It could be determined by the number of flaws discovered, the length of the test, and so on.

10.4 Durability Testing Execution Procedure

Durability testing evaluates non-functional error-prone circumstances such as the application's efficiency for a longer time, the application's behaviour to act under particular conditions, the volume of data flowing through the application databases/interfaces for a longer period, and so on [6–7]. The life cycle of durability testing begins with the examination of non-functional areas, the test strategy required, the testing flow design, and the analysis of test findings. The following are the main objectives of durability testing throughout its execution:

- Durability testing, also known as longevity testing, is a type of non-functional testing that looks at how well a software system can handle a lot of stress for a long time.
- Memory leaks, slowdowns, problems connecting to databases, and other important problems are found during this testing.
- It strengthens the application and prepares it to withstand heavy weights indefinitely.
- Durability tests are mostly automated because doing them manually would not only be time consuming but also onerous.

- The test should start with the construction of an isolated test environment, then move on to the design of test plans, the estimation of the test cycle's time, risk analysis, test schedule preparation, durability test execution, and finally the test cycle's closure.

Durability testing was less important, and it's possible that just a small percentage of the world took advantage of the technology and satisfied the standards of modern hardware and software. The scenario has now shifted. When a startup starts or releases a website or a mobile app, the question is whether the application can handle X number of users for a longer period. Even the end users anticipate a quick answer. Every day, the designer must consider how to apply more fine-tuning so that a large number of consumers may be served quickly and for a longer period. How can the effectiveness of implementation be assessed now? What are the results' measurements? On what basis should these parts be included in software durability testing? To answer all of these issues, a method is constructed, which is divided into several stages as illustrated in Fig. 2.

According to Fig. 2, the results of durability testing are as follows:

- After a thorough look at the system, learn about the system's major durability situations and how the load is distributed.

- With the help of various project tracks, identify and prioritise the important objectives for durability testing.

- Use the results of previous releases as a guide for future releases and set up and use the data model.

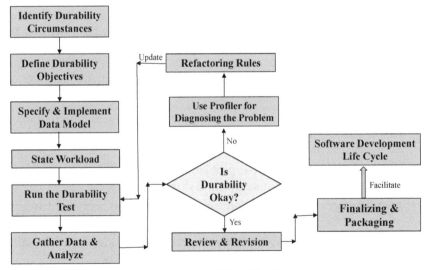

Figure 2: Flowchart of Durability Testing.

- For any extra work, make sure that the durability test environment and the durability test tool can handle it.

- Run durability tests for the specified scenarios that simulate the identified peak time.

- Set up durability monitoring to keep an eye on the test and uncover data throughout the execution phase and analyse it. If the durability is achieved, a review and revision phase is started, otherwise, it goes to the next phase.

- The next phase is using a profiler to diagnose the problem and make the refactoring rules for durability tests.

- Finalization and packaging are done in the last phase, and the software is delivered for further processing.

10.5 Types of Durability Testing

Has any company experienced a failure that may have been avoided if durability testing had been used? To answer that; the bulk of companies have [8–9]. Even the most dependable websites can crash during the peak load of a Christmas sale. Transaction processing may fail due to issues with longevity, data transfer speeds, network bandwidth, or throughput. Durability testing is critical because it reveals important details about the software's longevity, scalability, stability, and reliability. However, because durability testing involves a large range of specialised test types that must be performed in a precise manner, planning an effective durability test strategy is complex. Furthermore, software durability testing is a method for verifying a system's quality over a long period and under a variety of stress scenarios. Using this method, we can determine the reaction time stability throughout the test. Different types of software durability testing are depicted in Fig. 3.

10.5.1 Testing Load

It keeps track of the application's ability to execute under expected user loads. The goal is to find performance flaws before the software goes live. For durability, testing load tests for the quantity of load that can be passed to a system for a particular length of time.

10.5.2 Testing Stress

This entails putting a high-traffic or data-processing application through its paces. The goal is to find the starting point for a request. In durability, it tests for the stress passed on data processing software to estimate the time for how long it can handle the stress.

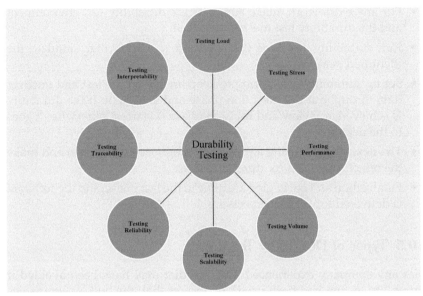

Figure 3: Categories of Durability Testing.

10.5.3 Testing Performance

Durability testing assesses the software's performance under load over time. It is done by putting different kinds of stress on the software under test over a long period of time to make sure that the performance criteria for production loads and the lengths of time till they last are met.

10.5.4 Testing Volume

There are a lot of under-volume tests. Data is kept in a database, and the software system's overall performance is monitored. The goal is to test the software application's performance in various volumes.

10.5.5 Testing Scalability

Scalability tests are used to determine how well a software application scales to handle a larger number of users for a longer period. It aids in the development of additional software capabilities. If any tester wishes to run any of these tests on their server, they'll need a variety of tools that are compatible with their test strategy.

10.5.6 Testing Reliability

The goal of a reliability test is to look at things like how well a piece of software works and how well it works over a long period.

10.5.7 Testing Traceability

The ability to trace tests forward and backward across the development lifecycle is known as traceability in software testing. This test case is meant to show how well a system can be traced over a long period.

10.5.8 Testing Interpretability

Interpretability is the degree to which a human can consistently predict the model's result. This testing determines the interpretability of the system over a longer period and with a higher load of memory.

10.6 Basics of Code Durability

10.6.1 Durable Code

The word "durable code" refers to a program's long-term longevity, usefulness, and maintainability [10]. It includes both good and terrible code. It gives project managers information on the coding methods and styles used by a team of developers. This level of quality, whether excellent or awful, is entirely subjective. Depending on the situation, various teams may adopt different meanings.

10.6.2 Code Reviews

As the world becomes more interconnected through the use of faster and larger digital networks, the software industry is constantly seeking to enhance the mechanism for building maintenance-free, durable software programmes [11]. A code review is a collaborative endeavour with no obvious leader or owner that does not result in a defined product for a client. Rather than discovering difficulties with durability, the code review process identifies defects. There have always been several schools of thought on the importance of long-lasting code, but no clear consensus on what constitutes durable code has emerged. Durable code should be as important to the software industry's culture as it is to the software development process.

The main goal of this cultural shift is to inculcate such a strong sense of durability in people that it becomes second nature to them. Source code with long serviceability may be produced by non-durable coding methods resulting from poor habits and behaviours during the development process. Humans are the creators of the software. As a result, the software is frequently prone to flaws. There are numerous methods for achieving a high code value that will last a long time, such as:

- *Regular Code Reviews:* A recent study suggests that software professionals consider code reviews to be the most effective technique to increase programming durability. Developers can interact and exchange expertise through these reviews, which improves their work. In addition, reviews ensure that the code meets the defined criteria.

- *Functional Testing:* This testing is critical because it pushes the developers to focus on software functionality for long-term durability from the start, reducing unnecessary code. The goal of software development is to create an application that meets the specific needs of its consumers.

- *Clear Requirements:* In agile software development, most software development projects start with a document for the collection of requirements, or storey cards. A project with clear, attainable criteria is significantly more likely to achieve high quality and durability than one with vague, poorly described needs.

10.6.3 Understanding Code Review

The idea of establishing such a system in any fast-paced agile company may seem like cruel punishment to anyone who recalls how code reviews used to be done with a squirm and a shudder [12]. Code reviews, like everything else in the world of computing and long-term software development, have evolved significantly, and there are now a variety of options to choose from. Only in software engineering fields where there is very little room for error, like avionics or businesses where people's safety is important, long formal code review processes are no longer needed, even though they have always worked well.

10.6.4 Common Code Review Approaches

A good peer review strategy for code review necessitates a balance of well-documented protocols and a welcoming, collaborative atmosphere [13]. Overly rigid peer evaluations might hinder productivity, while those that lack traditional protocols are frequently unproductive. Managers must find a happy medium where peer review may be fast and productive while also encouraging open dialogue and information sharing among peers. The following are some common ways to conduct code reviews:

(a) *The Email Thread*

When a piece of code is geared up for review, it is emailed to suitable colleagues, who can assess it as soon as their workflow permits. A code-inspection meeting with five people in a room isn't as adaptable and flexible as this method, but an email thread of recommendations and different opinions can quickly become tangled, leaving the original coder to work through it all on her own, which isn't ideal.

(b) Pair Programming

One of the hallmarks of Extreme Programming (XP) is that it places engineers side by side (at least figuratively), working on the same code and double-checking each other's work as they go. It looks like it will incorporate code review into the programming process, and it's an excellent way for experienced engineers to mentor junior colleagues. Since the authors and even the co-writers are sometimes too close to their work, other types of code review may provide greater objectivity. Pair programming may also use more resources in terms of time and personnel than other methods.

(c) Over-the-Shoulder

The over-the-shoulder technique is one of the simplest, easiest, and most intuitive ways to engage in peer code review and is more comfortable for most developers as compared to XP's pair programming. Once the code is complete, simply find a qualified colleague to sit at the desk (or go to theirs) and examine it while the tester explains why they created it in the way they did. Although this informal technique is "lightweight", it can be a little too light if tracking or documentation procedures are not implemented.

(d) Tool-Assisted

This is the most popular choice among coders, since software-based code review tools, some of which are browser-based or seamlessly integrated into a range of common IDE and SCM development frameworks, are undoubtedly the easiest and most efficient way to review code. Many of the problems with the previous methods can be fixed with the help of software tools. These tools keep track of colleagues' comments and proposed solutions to defects in a clear and coherent sequence, allow asynchronous and non-local reviews, send notifications to the original coder when new reviews arrive, and keep the efficiency of the whole process high by avoiding meetings and requiring no one to leave their desks to contribute.

(e) Tracking the Progress

Regardless of the form of peer review one selects, metrics are important in the world of code review, especially with so many development teams still undecided about its ultimate efficacy as a regular practise.

(f) The Future of Peer Code Review

Code review is simply one part of a software development team's quality assurance strategy, which also includes other types of testing and static analysis. It is, nonetheless, an essential component, since it often identifies "hidden" flaws that may not present a problem now but may inhibit the product's future evolvability, as well as destroys bugs just after they hatch and before they have time to grow into unmanageable beasts.

10.6.5 Importance of Code Durability

For every programme to be implemented successfully, code durability and quality are critical. It should be the most significant KPI for determining the software project's usefulness and efficacy [14]. However, sustaining code durability is not easy because it necessitates consistency in efforts and a focused attitude on the part of the software development team to satisfy the durability and quality objectives. This is critical for a software project, yet many developers frequently ignore durability when they are under pressure to perform tasks in a short amount of time.

Code writing should be viewed as a necessary investment with a quick payoff. To do this, the code should be readable, consistent, and documented, making it easier to review and resulting in less development time and longer-lasting code. Software that is well-designed and similarly less complex is more resilient and lasting, and it can be tested more readily. When a developer fails to pay attention to code durability, it might lead to more rework and maintenance in the code. This could raise the price of the software in the long run.

10.6.6 Measuring Code Durability

It's difficult to assess code durability. This is because defining the appropriate code durability is quite difficult [15]. For example, many people might claim that the code must function well most of the time, but consider this. Some people specify and apply numerous metrics to the code, and many of these metrics can be reported using tools. Well, sometimes the best way to determine code durability is to use a qualitative method, such as having someone read the code and providing feedback.

When the developers follow certain regular standards or have a style guide for producing code, it can make things a lot easier (from formatting to naming conventions). Inquiring about the code's durability or maintainability will assist them to understand the code's durability better and with enhanced clarity. Good code durability is critical for software since its absence can result in financial loss, a waste of time, or a significant amount of money spent on maintenance. If the code's durability isn't good enough, these funds or efforts could be better spent on improvements or adjustments.

10.6.7 Characteristics of Code Durability

(a) Efficiency

The efficiency of the code is closely tied to the software's longevity, performance, and speed, and can be used to assess its durability. It is a well-known reality that no one enjoys using software that takes an excessive amount of time to complete a task. It is vital to delete unnecessary or duplicate code to improve the efficiency of the code. In addition, try to write code that can be reused, saves resources, uses the right data types, functions, loops, and so on.

(b) Reliability

It refers to the software code's ability to perform consistent and error-free actions every time it is executed. This is a critical feature of good code durability. This is because the software would be meaningless if the code behaved differently every time it was run with the same input in the same environment, and if it broke down frequently without generating any errors. A code can be more trustworthy if it is properly checked and tested in all possible ways, as well as if the correct error and exception handling is used.

(c) Robustness

The code's robustness refers to its capacity to handle faults while the programme is running, even under exceptional circumstances. This is an important aspect of the software's code durability. External circumstances do not affect the behaviour of a robust code, making it straightforward to alter. The fewer combinations that potentially produce a bug in the code, the more robust the code is. It is predictable, making it simple to integrate and maintain. The best way to make your software more robust is to test it in all possible situations, both expected and unexpected, and to use correct error and exception handling, let the user easily debug the programme by giving clear and understandable error messages, and so on.

(d) Portability

This refers to the code's capacity to run on a wide range of devices and operating systems. Since it would be a waste of time and resources for the programmers to write the same code again if the machine or environment changed, this is crucial for code longevity. However, there are many ways to check if a piece of code is portable. It's crucial to test code frequently across different platforms rather than delaying it until the end of development. A minimum of two compilers should be used, and the compiler warning levels should be as high as possible.

(e) Maintainability

This refers to adding new features, modifying the existing ones, or addressing faults with minimal effort, while also ensuring that it does not damage other modules that are linked to it. This is an important aspect of code quality since software frequently requires new features or problem patches. In addition, the tester should ensure that the changes made do not introduce any flaws in the code's functionality.

10.6.8 Maintaining Code Durability

It is critical for an organisation to maintain a high level of code durability. Rather than working on durability after the code is finished, the developers should focus on it from the beginning of the project. There are times when a developer will discover that if she/he considers the durability of the code from the beginning of the project, the overhead of improving the durability is significantly reduced. Here is a list of a few items to keep in mind when maintaining quality.

(a) The System's Structure

The design and structure of coding are one of the most important components of it. Developers must be familiar with the universal design patterns, which are well-known among the general public and thus easily understood by the rest of the team. The code is durable and may be readily extended in the future, thanks to the usage of suitable principles. The developers must have a clear picture of how the entire project will look after it is completed to generate the draught and blueprints. Furthermore, mixing different things all over the code makes it even more jumbled and difficult to understand by others reading it, and sometimes even by the developer who wrote it in the first place. When transferring modules and components, there should be fewer dependencies. This makes the code more durable and requires less upkeep.

(b) Naming convention

By just paying attention to little details like naming conventions, file structure, variable names, and so on, a codebase can be made more legible, durable, and understandable. Developers are known to change from time to time, and if on-boarding takes a few weeks or months, it may have a negative impact on the organisation. A good idea is to use the same wording for both modules and classes in documents and everyday conversations to avoid confusion.

(c) Coverage of Tests

Even with 90% or nearly 100% test coverage, it is not always possible to cover all conceivable scenarios and faults. This has an impact on the product's quality and durability. Because software is constantly evolving, developers do not want to break anything else at the same time when altering something. Furthermore, the developers must comprehend the need to generate test coverage in the first place. Education, trust, and effective communication are the cornerstones of a successful product development process, which means greater collaboration with more experienced developers.

(d) Readability and optimization

Write code that is straightforward and easy to understand by the developers, as the time and resources spent on hard reading code will far outweigh the benefits received through optimization. If the tester needs to be optimized, it should be treated as a standalone module with DI, 100% test coverage, and no changes for at least a year.

(e) Prioritizing Architecture

Many people claim that they work quickly because they don't have time to consider architecture. However, as a result of their actions, 99 percent of them end up in serious trouble. It's pointless to write a code without considering the architecture. Before beginning, one should have a good understanding of what the code will do, what it will be used for, how modules and services interact with one another, what structure it will have, how it will be tested and debugged, and how it will be updated, and so on.

(f) Formatting of Code

Indentation and formatting should be used in code that can be read. This makes sure that the application's structure is consistent, visible, and long-lasting.

10.6.9 Improving Code Durability

As previously stated, comments, good naming, and adequate indentation can all help to increase durability. Commenting properly enhances code maintainability and aids in issue investigation. It cuts down on the time and effort needed to learn an existing code base. Without comments, a developer might easily become lost in the code and lose sight of its purpose. The importance of appropriate naming in maintaining the program's maintainability cannot be overstated. It enables the programmers to quickly comprehend what the code is doing as well as to correct errors or make changes. It is not a good idea to use meaningless names like "a", "b", and "c". Developers, on the other hand, can always choose meaningful names.

10.7 Building Durable Software through Source Code Analysis

Whatever mitigation measures have been established in recent years to address durability, the challenge of maintainability has remained the same. Software firms are now required to evaluate their operations to establish application durability requirements, strategies, and weaknesses. The need to develop a software durability policy to safeguard the software programme has become crucial [1–5]. According to the software industry, developers should write more resilient code in the first place. Long-term programming should be a goal for executives from the start. The company's lifecycle process will be updated to put software durability experts in the loop as soon as project needs are set.

Non-durable applications are a problem in the software industry. The only benefit is that the definition of durability has shifted from exclusive to inclusive. If durability teams are integrated into development teams, software companies will obtain earlier feedback on the durability of software or applications, cutting the costs of developing these solutions. Because the cost of boosting durability, including flaws, after deployment could be hundreds of times greater, there is a need to shift from reactive to proactive durability management, supported by appropriate approaches. Durability must be incorporated into the workflow.

Because of the increased demand for long-lasting software, software developers should consider development to be identical to long-term software development. Designing for security and employing long-term approaches and standards does not guarantee long-term software; rather, it facilitates the delivery of long-term software. Experts in the field of durability have established that tiny code defects are to be blamed for the lack of durability. Many studies have found that well-known programming flaws account for the majority of the reasons for poor durability. As a result, long-lasting software can be created by utilising long-lasting source code. We'll go through the principles of writing long-lasting programmes from source code in the ensuing sections.

10.8 The Gap in Practices

The software industry's adoption of software durability solutions has left a lot to be desired. The software industry spends billions of dollars on maintaining hardware and software durability. In today's race to produce cutting-edge business solutions, incorporating a quick development cycle by using third-party software or open source software adds a new degree of risk that must be handled right away to keep the application from failing. There's never been a better or more important time to invest in long-term durability than now. As a result, in any software company, the best durability standards should be a big part of the software development process.

The software industry is putting forth efforts to examine and measure durability. Despite spending a large amount of money on upkeep, quality continues to deteriorate at an alarming rate. Quality is frequently jeopardised due to non-durable source code. Assessing the long-term durability of software applications should be a priority method. The fundamental issue with the software industry is that long-term development has yet to be recognised as a revenue-generating activity. One of the main reasons why organisations don't train their developers in producing long-lasting code is, indeed, revenue constraints. Unfortunately, only durability failure convinces many software companies to spend money on durability solutions! However, sustaining software after a failure is prohibitively expensive and damaging to their brand.

10.9 The Framework

It is a well-known reality that source code will always include flaws, regardless of the amount of time, effort, or approaches employed to create a durable embedded software product. However, it is always possible to develop a technique that reduces the overall vulnerabilities in the source code and makes it significantly more difficult to exploit the vulnerabilities in the source code, which further gives birth to non-durability. Because non-durability in the source code causes a substantial percentage of maintainability problems, writing durable code is difficult and time-consuming. The software industry and the state-of-the-art still have an opportunity to improve to provide an effective as well as a standardised method that can be applied more equitably across software businesses.

To bridge the gap between the developers and the creation of durable source code, the entire process of scanning, detecting, and reducing durability gaps and faults during source code analysis must be integrated. An integrated and prescriptive framework is provided, taking into account the requirement and importance of a roadmap or framework for building durable source code with "necessary and desirable durability features". The proposed framework was created with the goal of being highly implementable and prescriptive.

As shown in the diagrams, the production of durable source code is divided into three phases, each containing prescriptive steps. A framework for writing long-lasting software source code has been presented, based on integral and basic components. Figure 4 depicts a high-level representation of the framework.

To obtain the gaps and defects in the data repository, the initial phase begins with "Execute and Monitor." Vulnerabilities and flaws need to be

Figure 4: General Overview of the Framework.

categorised and prioritised in the second phase, which is called "Classify and Control". This is a very important job that has been given to this phase. All source code data repositories will be consolidated into a single repository in the third phase of "Refine and Manage", and a suggestive measure in the form of prioritised durable source code writing guidelines will be generated for quick reference by software engineers. A short description of each of the steps in the procedures shown has been done to try to symbolically show the spirit of writing durable source code and make the framework prescriptive in nature.

10.9.1 Phase-I: Execute and Monitor

This phase begins with the use of analyzers to scan the source code. The Dataflow Analyzer detects fraudulent data flow. The Semantic Analyzer searches the source code for non-durable functions. The Flow control Analyzer monitors the order of processes to discover incorrect coding structures. The Configuration Analyzer parses and evaluates the application deployment at the end. Vulnerabilities and defects will be verified by the practitioners. The blacklist and whitelist codes that have been identified will be documented. Figure 5 depicts the prescriptive steps involved in executing and monitoring the source code.

10.9.2 Phase-II: Classify and Control

Access Control Vulnerabilities, Information Flow Vulnerabilities, and Application Programming Interface (API) Conformance are the three of several categories in which security vulnerabilities fall. These vulnerabilities and defects are classified in this phase. These classified vulnerabilities will now be prioritised as per their severity levels to save money and time during mitigation. Prioritized vulnerabilities will be assessed by using the High, Medium, or Low Indexes. The code will be repaired or blocked to minimise vulnerabilities with a high severity

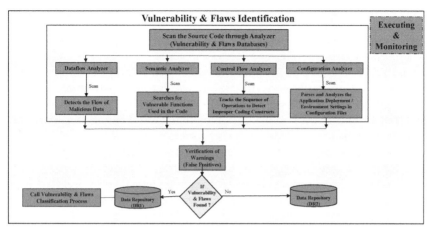

Figure 5: Phase-I Execute and Monitor.

level. The technique for calculating the probability of exploitation will be run for vulnerabilities with a medium severity level. If the likelihood is high, the vulnerability will be classified as having a high severity level and will be mitigated accordingly. If the likelihood of exploitation is low, the vulnerability falls under the category of low-severity vulnerabilities, which will be handled with recommended methods. Finally, an analysis summary report describing the actions related to the source code will be created. Figure 6 shows the steps that are supposed to be used to classify and control the source code analysis process.

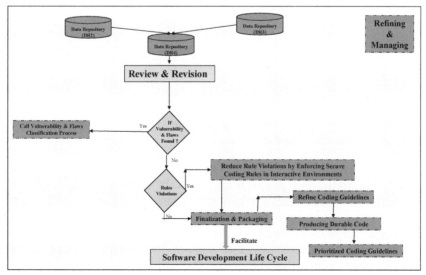

Figure 6: Phase-II Classify and Control.

10.9.3 Phase-III: Refine and Manage

After the successful completion of Phase II, all source code repositories will be combined into a single repository. The source code will be personally examined once again. Suggested measures will be used to mitigate the identified logical faults and vulnerabilities. Enforcing durability coding principles in interactive situations will also help to identify and reduce rule violations. Figure 7 shows the steps that should be taken to improve and manage the source code analysis process.

Source code analysis will be completed and will begin facilitating a long-term software development life cycle after it passes the exit criteria based on time, cost, and objectives. Figure 8 depicts an integrated and prescriptive approach for managing software durability source code.

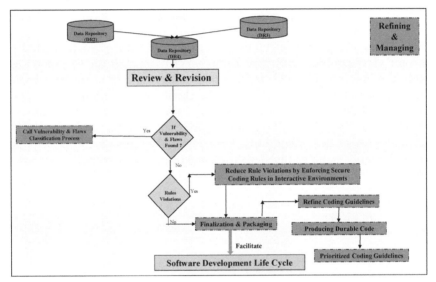

Figure 7: Phase-III Refine and Manage.

10.10 Significance of the Framework

Vulnerability Scanning of Source Code is one of the most significant ways of delivering long-lasting code. Most durability practitioners are currently adopting this practical approach. In essence, using durability strategies as a durability framework while generating source code would allow any durability issues to be identified and corrected long before the software programme is launched. The framework will also ensure that the code is audited for conformity. This will not only improve durability but also save time, money, and resources that would otherwise be spent on

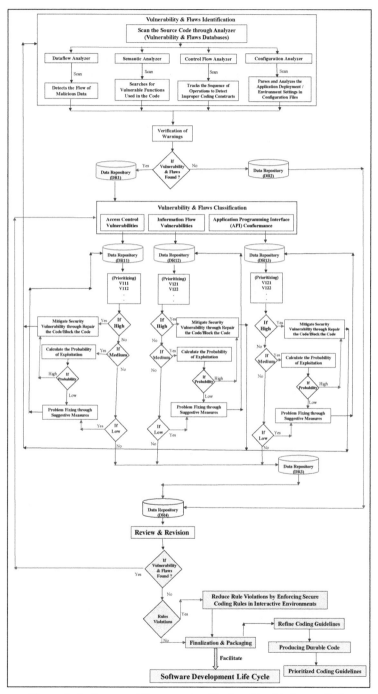

Figure 8: An Integrated Framework to Produce Durable Source Code.

redevelopment or repairing the software application once it is deployed. The proposed framework's goal is to be as practical as possible. The framework will guide the developer through the code to make the source code more durable as well as more robust and reliable. We are certain that executing all three phases of the suggested framework would ensure commercial and public faith in the long-term web application development mechanism while saving time, money, and effort around the world.

When the proposed conceptual framework is implemented, it will assist the durability experts and programmers in identifying source code faults and determining the optimal mitigation strategy. It can be used by software source code developers from all over the world, resulting in standardisation and durability improvements. To standardise the framework, further experimental trials and statistical analyses on a broad scale with typical representative samples may be required. The following observations were made after a close look at the parts of the theoretical foundation for writing durable code:

- The proposed framework includes writing durable code with a subjective rating like "very low", "low", "average", "high "very high", etc.

- The framework helps to evaluate the durable source code and provides the cost estimates for writing durable code, which facilitates the estimation and planning of new activities.

- The framework will be able to identify the faulty and vulnerable codes early enough to decrease the rework.

- Viable experiments should be designed to validate the proposed framework.

- Pre-tryout and tryout should be conducted on the proposed framework, and the results gained from the tryout should be analysed and interpreted.

- Informal review and revisions should be carried out throughout the entire phases of the durable development process.

10.11 Conclusion

This chapter gives a brief overview of durability testing, its impact, and the types of durability testing. More emphatically, the Chapter maps a series of crucial steps to be adhered to in durability testing. In the future, a tool can be used where we will walk through the steps of using it and improve our understanding of durability testing. A further description of durable code and how to write it with its attributes is detailed in this chapter. This chapter proposed a three-step framework to produce durable software applications. The proposed framework helps in identifying the types of durability vulnerabilities that arise due to a programmer's mistake. It also identifies the cause of these errors. A successful application of the proposed framework will identify and alleviate maintainability and durability issues in source code and provide a suggested solution for writing code that is more dependable. As a future intent, we envisage that different software projects will be installed on the framework to make sure that it works to deliver the intended targets in durability testing.

Points to Remember

- Vulnerabilities in source code are continuously exposing the software industry to serious risk.
- Durability testing is a non-functional type of software testing where a software application is tested with a high load extended over a significant amount of time to evaluate the behaviour of the software application under sustained use for a long period.
- It can be challenging to reproduce the production environment precisely. In addition, the testing engineer must spend a lot of time and effort manually developing those environments.
- Adoption of software durability solutions by the software industry has left much to be desired. The software industry is spending billions of dollars on maintaining durability and hardware.

Review Questions

Objective Type Questions

1. Durability testing integrates a full set of features of the software for a complete end-to-end solution to ensure .... of software
   a. Reliability
   b. Longevity
   c. Endurance
   d. Maintainability

2. A codebase can be made more readable, durable, and easier to understand by simply taking care of small things like .... conventions
   a. Coding
   b. Naming
   c. Maintaining
   d. Enhancing

3. The .... of the code is its ability to deal with the errors while the program is being executed
   a. Durability
   b. Robustness
   c. Readability
   d. Maintainability

4. .... refers to the addition of new features, modification in the existing ones, or fixing the bugs with minimum effort, and also taking care that it does not affect the other modules that are related to it.
   a. Maintainability
   b. Robustness
   c. Durability
   d. Reliability

5. .... testing is important because it encourages developers to focus on software functionality for durability from the outset, reducing extraneous code.
   a. White box
   b. Functional
   c. Grey box
   d. Alpha

Short Answer Type Questions

1. What are the two attributes of software durability?
2. How is the framework useful for software durability assessment?
3. How to improve the code durability?
4. What are the phases in the software durability framework?
5. What is the use of portability in improving software durability?

Descriptive Questions

1. What are the characteristics of software durability?
2. Enlist and explain the different types of durability testing.
3. Explain the framework of software durability in detail.

References

1. Agrawal, A., Alenezi, M., Kumar, R. and Khan, R.A. 2019. A source code perspective framework to produce secure web applications. Computer Fraud & Security, 2019(10): 11–18.
2. Grover, M., Cummings, J. and Janicki, T. 2016. Moving beyond coding: why secure coding should be implemented. Journal of Information Systems Applied Research (JISAR), 9(1): April 2016.
3. Hentzen, S. 2002. The Software Developer's Guide. Whitefish Bay: Hentzenwrke Publications. eBook Collection (EBSCOhost).
4. Assal, H., Chiasson, S. and Biddle, R. 2016. Cesar: Visual representation of source code vulnerabilities. In IEEE Symp. on Visualization for Cyber Security.
5. Backes, M., Rieck, K., Skoruppa, M., Stock, B. and Yamaguchi, F. 2017. Efficient and flexible discovery of PHP application vulnerabilities. In IEEE European Symp. on Security and Privacy.
6. Chess, B. and McGraw, G. 2004. Static Analysis for Security. IEEE Security & Privacy, 2(6): 76–79.
7. Oliveira, D., Rosenthal, M., Morin, N., Yeh, K.C., Cappos, J. and Zhuang, Y. 2014. It's the psychology stupid: how heuristics explain software vulnerabilities and how priming can illuminate developer's blind spots. In Annual Computer Security Applications Conf.
8. Assal, H. and Chiasson, S. 2018. Motivations and amotivations for software security. USENIX Symposium on Usable Privacy and Security (SOUPS). August 12–14, 2018, Baltimore, MD, USA.
9. Green, M. and Smith, M. 2016. Developers are Not the Enemy! The Need for Usable Security APIs. IEEE Security Privacy, 14(5).
10. Greenberg, A. 2015. Hackers Remotely Kill a Jeep on the Highway—With Me in It. https://www.wired.com/ 2015/07/hackers-remotely-kill-jeep-highway/. [Accessed May-2017].
11. Grieco, G., Grinblat, G.L., Uzal, L., Rawat, S., Feist, J. and Mounier, L. 2016. Toward large-scale vulnerability discovery using machine learning. In ACM Conf. on Data and Application Security and Privacy.
12. Smith, J., Johnson, B., Murphy-Hill, E., Chu, B. and Lipford, H.R. 2015. Questions developers ask while diagnosing potential security vulnerabilities with static analysis. In Joint Meeting on Foundations of Software Engineering. ACM.
13. Nunes, P., Medeiros, I., Fonseca, J.C., Neves, N., Correia, M. and Vieira, M. 2018. Benchmarking static analysis tools for web security. IEEE Transactions on Reliability, 67.3: 1159–1175.
14. Smith, Justin, Brittany Johnson, Emerson Murphy-Hill, Bill Chu and Heather Richter Lipford. 2018. How developers diagnose potential security vulnerabilities with a static analysis tool. IEEE Transactions on Software Engineering 45(9): 877–897.
15. Awan, Jawad Hussain, Shahzad Memon, Shariq Mehmood Pathan, Muhammad Usman, Rahat Ali Khan, Shazia Abbasi, Abdul Qudoos Noonari and Zahoor Hussain. 2017. A user friendly security framework for the protection of confidential information. Int. J. Comput. Sci. Netw. Secur. 17.04: 215–223.

Useful Links

https://www.wilsoncenter.org/sites/default/files/cybersecurity_in_mexico_an_overview.pdf

https://eandt.theiet.org/content/articles/2019/01/top-german-politicians-affected-in-major-data-breach/

https://www.techworld.com/security/uks-most-infamous-data-breaches-3604586/

https://www.businessinsider.com/british-airways-customer-data-stolen-2018-9?IR=T

https://www.wired.com/story/2017-biggest-hacks-so-far/

https://www.checkmarx.com/2017/12/31/recap-biggest-data-breaches-2017/

https://www.crn.com/slide-shows/security/300083246/the-10-biggest-data-breaches-of-2016.htm

https://digitalguardian.com/blog/biggest-and-most-impactful-data-breaches-2016

https://www.garlandtechnology.com/blog/cyber-security-year-in-review-major-data-breaches-of 2015

Chapter 11

Future Prospects of Durability into Software Engineering

11.1 Objectives

Indisputably, software durability is now one of the most desired attributes of high-quality software. Despite the huge investments in the development process, the practitioners are unable to meet the requisites for durable software; the majority of the available systems are still non-durable. This is because it is quite difficult to identify the contribution of durability early in the software development process, which has a negative or positive impact on other important factors. The practitioners are constantly looking for new strategies or methods for analysing and estimating the software's durability to satisfy the end users and provide them with service assurance throughout the operational time of the system. Against this backdrop, the core objectives for this chapter are as follows:

- To define the expectations of the practitioners working in the domain of software durability and assess if these expectations are being met.
- To identify the myths associated with software durability assessment and dispel them.
- To discuss the overall impact of the book on software quality and software durability.

11.2 Issues and Challenges

Technically, issues and challenges deal with various parts of an event or organisation, and while they share some characteristics, they also differ.

An issue is a problem with a deterministic or certain solution, but a challenge could be the difficulty in achieving the intended goal with an unknown or non-deterministic solution [1]. However, when dealing with issues that create roadblocks to reaching the goal, both terms are frequently interchanged. Our goal is to identify the concerns and obstacles that the software designers and developers face during the software durability analysis and estimation process. Any software organisation's major goal is to create high-durability software, but achieving this goal necessitates the adoption of durability attributes from the start of the development process [2]. The following are the most common concerns and challenges that software engineers face:

- Inadequate Project Infrastructure: The whole environment in which the software product can be built is referred to as the project infrastructure. Inadequate infrastructure developed by any software sector to build a software project has a direct impact on the software's durability and delivery time, which, in turn, has a direct impact on the proposed software project's estimated budget [3]. Because a well-established project infrastructure is the basis for making software that lasts a long time, poor project management will have a big effect on how long a software product lasts in general.

- Identification and Specification of the Requirements: Requirements collection and specification in advance is a hard undertaking [4]. During this stage of software development, it is not necessary to analyse and collect all of the requirements that are important to the stakeholders. In fact, most of the Stakeholders do not have a complete understanding of the requirements they want in their software system. While obtaining and analysing these needs ahead of time makes the process more difficult and error-prone, the most common issues seen at this stage are requirement ambiguity, inconsistency, and incompleteness. Because a software system's correct and effective operation comes from consistent and thorough requirements analysis and specification, any issues or problems have a direct effect on how long the software will last.

- Managing Durability Assurance: The terms "durability assurance" and "durability control" are frequently interchanged, but the truth is that they are not interchangeable [2–3]. As illustrated in Fig. 1, durability assurance encompasses a broader domain than durability control and is regarded as a super class, whereas durability control is considered a sub-class. Durability assurance gives you peace of mind that criteria will be met. Another definition says, "*All the planned and systematic operations conducted inside the software durability that can be shown to provide confidence that a product or service will fulfil requirements*

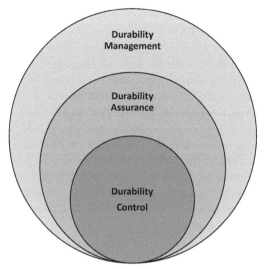

Figure 1: Durability Control and Durability Assurance.

for durability". It monitors and tracks the software processes and methodologies used to assure software durability. From requirement specification to software integration, it encompasses and supervises the entire software development process. Maintaining durability assurance becomes more difficult for software engineers because they have to produce a durable system within a limited budget. Furthermore, the ever-growing demand for software often forces engineers to produce end products that are inexpensive and ready to be used in a minimum time. Hence, the intense competition to meet the business targets in a backdrop of limited financial resources negatively affects the durability of the software.

- Maintaining Durability Control: Throughout the software development process, durability control provides the preservation of durability variations [4]. It assists software development companies in maintaining or improving their level of durability. The process includes a series of assessments, evaluations, and tests to guarantee that the software being developed meets the user's requirements. In case of any failure in the end software in terms of the practitioner's requirements and demands, the software process is connected to a feedback loop to optimise the process. Durability control activities might be automated, semi-automated, or human. The feedback loop is critical for overcoming the flaws that arise during the development process. Thus, durability control has a significant impact on the capacity of the software in meeting the stipulated standards. However, maintaining durability control is a difficult undertaking, especially for large and complex projects.

- Dynamism in the User's Requirements: The proverb *"wants are boundless, but resources are limited"* is also applicable here [5]. The user's needs aren't always obvious at the start of the process. The constant change in the needs is what makes the entire software development process ever-dynamic. With practice, the user acquires a better understanding of the software and its operating environment. Hence the user's established criteria can be modified, or new needs can be introduced to the software being developed development. It's difficult for software engineers to keep track of these details while focusing on producing long-lasting software. If requirement dynamics aren't considered when making the software, the longevity of the end product will be compromised.

- Software Security Infrastructure: Software designers and d*evelopers frequently overlook security as a feat*ure of software [6]. As a result, the number of possible security threats and data breach instances is rapidly increasing. It is estimated that 96% of all online apps have at least one significant vulnerability. Security is one of the most difficult problems for software engineers to solve because of its complexity and cost. Complexity reduces a software product's usability in the user environment and affects its user-friendly nature, reducing its business continuity in the software market. Implementing security from the start raises the software's expenses. However, persuading the users to invest more for strengthening the software's security is a difficult task that meets with little or no success! Hence, the target of providing suitable security architecture for software development so as to create long-lasting final software is more of a concept and less of a reality. Due to several vulnerabilities left untended in the final product, such a system is highly prone to attacks. Thus, without optimal usable-security, the software cannot be regarded as durable software.

- Estimation of Software Project Budgets: The cost of a project is one of the most important aspects that affect the overall process and the longevity of software products [7]. The foundation for long-lasting software is a precise estimate of project costs. Determining the amount of time and resources that a software project will use until it reaches its completion stage is a difficult undertaking, and efficiency in this area contributes to accurate cost estimation. Cost estimating is inherently tough, but the human inability to foresee correct outcomes makes it even more challenging. Furthermore, the one-of-a-kind nature of software projects makes it even more difficult for software professionals to deliver an accurate budget estimate of the project in question. As a result, precise cost calculations and budget estimation for a software project are intrinsically complicated problems for software specialists to solve. And, because a project manager can't afford high-durability resources and experienced software engineers on a low-durability budget, errors in cost estimates and budget estimation will have a negative impact on software durability.

- Integration with Other Systems and Applications: Producing a software product is more than just a worry for software developers in the present-day context. The emerging technologies and trends in commercial operations have created a slew of new challenges [8]. The durability of developed software products should allow them to integrate with other applications and systems without compromising the efficiency and effectiveness of the system. Integration of third-party tools and technologies, as well as proprietary programmes like ERP systems and inventory management databases, is now standard practice in business. Integration presents a higher problem in that it remains hidden throughout the development process, only presenting itself at the conclusion. All of these difficulties must be addressed during software development, which is a difficult task for software developers. Otherwise, the developed software would lose its commercial viability in the market and have a negative impact on the software industry.

Hence, each of the above-mentioned concerns that software engineers confront while developing long-lasting software solutions need decisive countermeasures. There may be more challenges that obstruct the creation of software durability solutions, but these are the most typical ones that most of the software development organisations face.

11.3 Durability Meets the Practitioners' Expectations

The best quote of the twenty-first century is "The practitioner is king". This is the unmistakable reality of today's practitioner-centric world [9]. Not only durability assurance testing vendors, but any firm, cannot thrive, let alone be lucrative if it does not address the needs of its practitioners [2–3]. Practitioner's expectations must be met in order to generate repeat business and establish a brand. It's no different in the field of software durability testing. Software durability assurance is currently being funded by companies all over the world [4–5]. Effective software testing not only meets the practitioner's expectations but also ensures long-term viability and lowers expenses. As a result, software testing must satisfy both of these requisites.

Effective testing scenarios ensure not only practitioners satisfaction, but also increased durability and cost savings [6–7]. As a result, the practitioner's happiness has become critical. In layman's terms, businesses should not only provide services and measures to meet the needs of practitioners but also go above and beyond their expectations. This also shows that a referral from a potential practitioner is the only kind of referral that can be trusted.

In this context, a Practitioner service durability assurance is a method that can assist a company in identifying and analyzing the practitioner's expectations and problems with the software. Practitioner expectations and corporate goals are centrally communicated through the durability assurance process [8–9]. When the practitioners outsource their needs to a user, they're putting their faith in the user not only with the sensitive information at stake, but also with the durability and care with which they'll look after them. Let's take a short look at the top five primary testing expectations practitioners have of their external durability assurance testing vendor:

11.3.1 Get Practitioner's Software to Market Faster

Given the digital timelines of the day in which the world moves at a highly competitive pace, *this should have been done sooner"*, is an oft-quoted fact [7]. In today's dynamic marketplace, the practitioner is continually diminishing, with a particular focus on time-to-market. That is why they decided to outsource their requirements in the first place. The ideal approach, according to one practitioner, is to outsource their testing needs to the best durability assurance. The company allows the vendor to work autonomously and without relying on others. They expect the user to be the nimble programmer who will be invaluable. Their fundamental expectation of the user is to prioritise speedy collaborative effort, flexible strategic planning, and early delivery above all else.

11.3.2 Bring in Domain Knowledge

Practitioners choose to outsource their target areas, particularly software testing, because it is very convenient [2]. They anticipate that independent software durability assurance testing providers will have the required domain knowledge in software testing. If the organization's domain is healthcare, for example, testers must have healthcare domain expertise in order to not only satisfy the requirements but also improve the output. Developers will need skilled coders and in-house niche experts to comprehend the needs from both the practitioners and end-perspectives. This market research is unavoidable for them because they have significant investments at stake as well as an incredibly crucial end product in the form of software that is perfectly designed for their end-users.

11.3.3 Core Expertise

A critical distinction for software testing businesses is core subject matter expertise combined with hands-on experience [1–2]. If the developers don't have the right resources at hand, doing it in-house is a waste of time and money, which could be better spent on something else. This enables businesses, particularly small and medium-sized ones, to outsource a significant portion of their software testing requirements. It not only enables them to allocate assets for the most appropriate tasks, but also ensures that their revenue and project budgets are not squandered. Developers are expected to use the best and subject-matter-related resources to save on training costs while also avoiding the mass confusion that might occur without prior knowledge. They expect the developers to have core expertise, so it's to the practitioner's best advantage to learn the basics of the project and get to work straight away. Outsourcing is expected to shorten the pipeline and cut down on the time it takes to get a product on the market. It will also give a business a crucial competitive edge.

11.3.4 Cut Costs

According to Business Matters, the primary reason why the practitioners choose to outsource their durability assurance requirements is to reduce project costs [1–3]. Developers should already have an expert team with trained specialists, and since a person is specialising in testing, they should have state-of-the-art testing tools built into the software. This saves a lot of money on infrastructure. However, it should also be ascertained that the software in use is of the highest quality and that all licenses are valid and in place. Just because the developers or testers get an advantage by saving the practitioner's money, it doesn't imply that they have to cut expenditures on their end as well.

11.3.5 Take it a Notch Higher

Go above and beyond the expectations of the practitioner [2]. Instead of slapping the code together, attempt to adhere to the highest standards of durability assurance. As a capable testing partner, one is expected to conduct market research in order to determine the practitioner's fundamental voice. To avoid bottlenecks during the product launch process, try including focus groups, issuing acceptance tests, and recruiting beta testers ahead of time. Developers should work not only for the practitioners but also aim at producing excellent software for them.

Developers must have a well-thought-out and out-of-the-crowd testing plan. That is what will set them apart from the crowd. Finalizing software specs and counselling the organisation on its long-term software strategy will help them stand out from the crowd. They not only give important advice, but they also lay the groundwork for a long-term relationship with practitioners by pointing out the pros and cons.

11.4 Needs and Importance

Durable software must include extra, often redundant, code to perform the necessary checks for exceptional conditions [3–4]. This reduces the program's execution speed and increases the amount of storage required by the program. For the following reasons, durability should always take precedence over efficiency:

11.4.1 Software is Now Cheap and Fast

There is little need to maximize the usage of equipment [3]. In a strange way, faster functions lead to higher expectations from the user, so you can't completely ignore efficiency.

11.4.2 Non-durable Software is Liable to be discarded by Users

Because of a single non-durable software product, an organization's ill-repute for non-durable software is likely to damage its future sales [3–5].

11.4.3 Software Failure Costs may be Enormous

The cost of software failure is many times larger than the cost of control software in some applications, such as software that regulates a reactor or assists an airliner in flying [4].

11.4.4 Non-durable Software is Difficult to Improve

Because most of the execution time is spent on small programmed areas, it is usually feasible to adjust inefficient software [5]. Since modifications must be done all over, software that does not survive is more difficult to improve.

11.4.5 Inefficiency is Predictable

Users can alter their work to accommodate for the fact that programmes take a long time to run [6]. Durable software, on the other hand, frequently surprises the user. Non-durable software might have hidden faults that can compromise the software and user data without warning and with unforeseeable repercussions.

11.4.6 Non-durable Software may Cause Information Loss

Information is expensive to obtain and preserve of a few, and it is sometimes worth more than the software that processes it [5]. Making copies of essential data to protect it from data corruption caused by software that doesn't last takes a lot of effort and money.

The long-term viability of software is influenced by the software development process. A repeatable defect-prevention technique is more likely to provide long-lasting software [4]. The link between product and process durability, on the other hand, is not clear. Users routinely express their disappointment with the software's inability to last. It's possible that this is due to faulty software development. On the other side, incomplete specifications are a common cause of apparent non-durability [4]. Although the software performs as expected, the specifications do not specify how it should respond in uncommon situations. In such cases, software developers must use their expertise to create long-lasting software that performs meaningful and important actions [5]. The longevity of software is a measure of how well the users perceive it to be in terms of providing the services which they require. Durability is typically described as the likelihood of something working without breaking for a specified period of time in a specified environment and for a specified purpose.

Software durability is a new issue that jeopardises the software industry's long-term survival and erodes practitioners' confidence [5]. Moreover, there is a slew of other considerations that underscore the importance of software durability products. And if the final result isn't long-lasting, it'll cause major organisational problems. Several organisations around the world have faced historical disasters as a result of software durability issues, which were outlined at the beginning of the chapter. Since the users' needs are typically concerned with the software's functional requirements, durability ensures the software's non-functional requirements, which are mostly unseen until the product is placed in the user environment [5]. As a result, the software engineers will have a harder time evaluating the non-functional needs early in the development process, requiring more resources. We'll discuss the relevance of software durability and the demand for it.

- A high-durability product ensures an end product's real-time performance efficiency, which means faster response times, higher throughput, more efficient resource use, and higher user satisfaction. Response time, and resource utilisation all play a role in ensuring that the programme performs all of the needed duties successfully and efficiently.

- A high-durability software product provides the long-term viability of an end product that performs well in the user environment. Mainly, a product's usability ensures that the user is protected from errors, that the product is simple to operate, and that it is simple to learn with a user-friendly interface. This surely improves a software product's business continuity.

- Durability is one of the most important features of high-durability software and a product that lacks it cannot be classified as such. Durable software products guarantee a software product's fault tolerance and recoverability. Fault tolerance keeps the software running even if one or more of its components fail, and recoverability maintains the software's ability to return to a consistent state after a failure and recover lost data. This demonstrates the critical relevance of long-lasting products in today's world.

- Durability ensures that a software product's security is optimal, protecting it from both internal and external threats and attacks. A software product's ideal security mechanism protects businesses against attacks while also improving the user experience. As the number of attacks and threats against organisations that store sensitive and important data grows every day, so does the demand for long-lasting software.

- Durability products enable the longevity of modularity and modifiability, making it simple to modify the software product as needed to meet the future requirements of the defined user environment without affecting the performance of other components. It enhances the long-term usability of a software product.

- Durability of the software products guarantees software portability, allowing them to work on a variety of systems regardless of any software or hardware changes. So, the software solutions are better able to run on a variety of platforms and meet even the most demanding user needs without needing more resources.

11.5 Evolving Trends in the Development Process and Integration with Durability Concept

The current market conditions are exceedingly difficult for businesses as a result of the calamity ushered in by the COVID-19 pandemic [6–7]. Businesses are confronted with significant challenges, and technology is supporting them in maintaining their market share and generating money. Some excellent software development and technological advancements are supporting businesses in meeting the growth targets in the given scenario. As a result, the global software sector is predicted to develop at a compound annual growth rate (CAGR) of 4% to $968.25 billion by 2021. It will even reach $1493.07 billion in 2025, with an 11 percent CAGR [8]. Furthermore, software development trends change all the time, but in 2022, we can expect some of the most popular ones to reign supreme [9]. Businesses will have to adapt to these changes if they want to stay in business. There is a discussion on the top software development trends that will rule the software world.

11.5.1 Automated Code Reviews

Human reviewers are finding it increasingly difficult to keep up with the current volume of code [2]. Automated code review tools can help solve this problem by finding defects and potential issues in a fraction of the time it takes to evaluate the code manually. They also make it easier to maintain coding standards across an organisation. Although automated reviews aren't perfect, they are far more dependable than manual reviews. If newly hired software engineers want their programme to be the best available one, they must follow this trend. A developer can save up to 50% on time spent on code reviews by using the automated code review technologies. Automated code reviews have several other benefits. Other than these, the following aspects also need to be reckoned in:

- Errors and potential problems should be identified as soon as feasible.
- Ensure that coding standards are followed throughout a company.
- Reviews are faster and more accurate than manual reviews.

11.5.2 Coding Standards

Software engineers may be able to alleviate this dissatisfaction by focusing on the code standards. It ensures that all of a company's code is written in a consistent manner [3]. Coding standards also aid in the readability and maintainability of code. It's essential since these factors can have a significant impact on the overall durability. Companies should pay attention to coding standards if they want their products to last. However, the developers have different opinions about the impact of code style on readability, maintainability, and overall durability. Some of the advantages of focusing on coding standards include:

- The code is written logically way.
- It aids in the improvement of code maintainability and readability.
- Increases a product's overall durability.

11.5.3 Cybersecurity with DevSecOps

The most important cybersecurity trend is expected to be DevSecOps [2–3]. To increase the entire security of software products, it combines development, security, and operations. DevSecOps allows for the early detection of potential security threats. It also makes the process of patching vulnerabilities faster, i.e., after they've been discovered. The Advantages of DevSecOps can be traced as:

- Since the software is created with security in mind, it is more secure.
- Potential vulnerabilities are detected and fixed earlier.
- It simplifies the process of repairing these flaws once they've been detected.

11.5.4 Software Durability Standards

Durability has always been a major factor in software development. It is expected to grow even more important in the next years. The surge in outsourcing and the growing popularity of development solutions and services are just a few of the factors that have led to this. To be successful, software applications must meet durability criteria. When outsourcing, it's especially crucial because the contractor's reputation is on the line. Focusing on software durability standards has many advantages, including:

- Software products have a higher chance of being successful.
- Outsourcing will prioritise durability over timeliness and cost.
- Software products have a higher chance of being successful.
- Outsourcing will prioritise durability over timeliness and cost.

11.5.5 Cost Management Solution

Durability concepts apply financial principles and procedures for the company's operations [4–5]. It aids in the management of expenses, cash flow, and risk for businesses. It is critical for software development outsourcing since it allows organisations to control the costs and predictability in a better way. The following are some of the advantages of employing durability concepts:

- Astute management of expenditure, cash flow, and other possible issues help in minimizing the risks entailed in any venture.
- Costs can be kept under control, and predictability can be improved.
- When software is created with financial goals in mind, it is more efficient.

11.5.6 Low-code or No-code Solutions

In the past, software development required teams of dedicated coders and professionals to bring solutions to life [6–7]. Even the most courageous entrepreneur with a wonderful app idea would require the assistance of a team of software developers to finish the project. The entry barrier has remained high in many circumstances because software development may be a costly and time-consuming process. However, the software industry's tendency toward low-code development changes this equation by making it simple to construct programmes using graphical user interfaces rather than complex programming languages. Low-code development platforms usually contain drag-and-drop interfaces that allow the programmers to visualise programmes without delving too deep into the intricacies, rather than having to hand-code every component of an application. For business applications, low-code development is gaining popularity since it allows the developers to create new software without investing additional time or money. There are several advantages to using low-code or no-code solutions. The features that need underlining in this context are:

- Employing a visual interface, such as low-code or no-code solutions, may build the software products faster.
- Build in a language with a huge user base to save money.
- Software products that are developed with easy-to-learn code, such as low-code or no-code solutions, are easier to design.

11.5.7 Durability Assurance Solutions

The usage of durability assurance is required in the software development process [3–4]. It's used to ensure that the things fit the particular criteria before they're released to the broader public. By combining a durability assurance solution with the development solutions, software development organisations can improve the durability of their products by conducting automated tests on them before they're released to the public. Developers will also employ analytics tools to acquire data on how customers interact with their products. They'll utilise this data to make important decisions about their software's long-term sustainability, such as making changes based on user feedback or adding additional testing before releasing a product. Some of the benefits of using durability assurance systems are as follows:

- When software products are tested with durability assurance solutions before being deployed, they have a higher level of durability.
- Collecting statistics on how the consumers engage with software items helps the developers to make key decisions about the software's long-term viability.

- Software development outsourcing increases the longevity of the products by using durability assurance solutions, development solutions, and analytics.

11.5.8 Cross-Platform Development Tools

Previously, developing apps meant starting with a single platform, such as iOS or Android [5–6]. By following the creation of the first app for one platform, the software developers could create a second version for a different platform, which would involve committing resources to code porting between operating systems. The utilisation of contemporary cross-platform development tools is one of the development trends that makes life easier for developers and users. Using development environments such as Google's Flutter or Microsoft's Xamarin, software developers can design apps that operate on virtually every major desktop and mobile platform. These new software technologies can fully exploit the native APIs and user interfaces, allowing the developers to construct native-like programmes without sacrificing performance, unlike earlier cross-platform development tools.

11.5.9 Continuous Delivery and Deployment

Software development cycles were once notoriously long and arduous [7–8]. Because new features or functionalities were commonly bundled together in one release, users had to wait until a new version was generated, tested, and made available for download. Whether the product had significant advancements or little bug patches, this development technique left a lot to be desired. As progress stagnated, it became easier for the competitors to come up with their ideas and offer better options for the end users. In recent years, continuous delivery and continuous deployment have become two of the most popular software development methodologies. Both methodologies aim to produce software in shorter cycles of feature development, bug fixing, and experimenting to deliver it as quickly as feasible. With continuous delivery, apps are delivered into production for human download, whereas software is updated via automated deployment with continuous deployment. However, both methods have their advantages: rather than waiting for new features to be released, software development teams can work continuously to add fixes and new features as soon as they're available.

11.6 Significant Contributions of the Book

A series of disasters and chaos caused by insecure software indicate that software durability can be a life or death situation at any time. In the efforts to address this formidable challenge, software companies are currently working on extending their software services [8]. Evidently, software durability measurement and enhancement are one of the most talked-about topics in businesses. Recognizing and troubleshooting some of the key durability issues during software development can also help to decrease maintenance time and expenses incurred [9]. Long-term viability is one of the supporting properties of durability because long-term usage does not demand frequent maintenance [2]. As a result, the maintenance costs and time are minimised. The software durability assessment could have a big impact on how long the software lasts.

The quality and shortcomings of software can be shown through research into software durability standards and their effects on timeliness. Given the reported lack of knowledge of the idea of software durability, the accurate evaluation of software durability remains a key issue. There is no evident answer to the question *"What views are related to software durability?"* Finding a proper method of analysing software durability and the bulk of the components that go into it is quite challenging [1–3]. As a result, software engineers, developers, and practitioners must undertake a software durability assessment. Durability is a way of supplying dependable, dynamic security to support and facilitate all business activities, such as cloud, mobility, and durability enhancement. The following are the main advantages of a software durability evaluation:

- The life expectancy of software has been extended.
- The software development life cycle's maintenance costs are decreased.
- Software maintenance and repair expenditures were lowered.
- User happiness has improved, as has the product's market worth.
- Prioritized software durability qualities and recommendations could aid in the development of long-lasting software.
- The topic of software durability is still in its infancy, and only quantitative software durability assessment can help forecast how long software will be serviceable.

Throughout the development life cycle, a constant quantitative assessment of software durability is extremely desirable. Nothing important, exact, or unambiguous exists in this area, according to the literature review, that may be utilised to quantify software durability at an early stage of development. As a result, of the lack of a framework or model for calculating software durability, it is worthwhile to establish a methodology for calculating software durability. The primary goal of this study is to get a comprehensive grasp of the software durability idea and the necessity to create long-lasting software.

11.7 Impact of the Book

The current study makes significant inroads in the identification of software durability features and includes numerous macro-level direct or indirect discoveries. Estimation practise at an early stage is advantageous for a long-term software development. The software durability evaluation provides principles for developing long-lasting software [1–3]. An analysis of software durability and recommendations based on the importance of software durability attributes revealed several things, including the requirement for software durability in the present day to meet the ever-evolving needs of the users. Using evidence from the literature and context, the authors attempted to estimate software durability [2].

The second phase of this empirical study peruses several software durability estimation to demonstrate the concept by carrying out each step outlined in the framework. The ultimate goal of using MCDM methodologies is to recommend a more decisive, accurate, and quantitative assessment of the longevity of the programme being developed. In this context, the proposed model in the Book clearly follows the given execution sequence. Quantitative evaluation helps to figure out which parts of the software need greater attention to make them last longer.

It is necessary to correlate software durability features with other common software attributes, such as human trust, reliability, and trustworthiness, in order to provide a substantial and improved measurement of software durability. According to a review of the literature, no known work looks at software durability and quality throughout the design phase. Statistical analysis was used to validate the suggested model for the quantitative assessment of software durability. This methodology appears to be effective in determining the life expectancy of software and reducing the cost and effort spent on maintaining software defects that crop up from time to time. Stats back up the claim that an expert's opinion is important when figuring out how long the software in the suggested model will last.

We discovered that software durability estimation, done in the very initial stages of software development, is extremely desirable [4–5]. The recommendations posited in this Book can be emphatically enumerated as:

- The developed approach can be used to test the alternative theories that haven't made a place in the literature due to a lack of theoretical and empirical support.
- The established "Framework" provides a step-by-step method for assessing durability characteristics in the early stages of the development phase.
- The proposed approach can be used to keep a track of how long the software lasts during the design phase.

- The durability properties are used to determine how long a piece of software or an application will last.
- The development criteria presented here will the organisations in ensuring software's long-term viability.

Three basic important criteria are used in the models described to assess software durability: dependability, human trust, and trustworthiness. These characteristics are quite important and are linked to other software and durability characteristics. Although the software durability evaluation model has been proven, its applicability can still be investigated for a larger set of data [1]. Test cases in the form of a developer's handbook may be created to test software durability based on the model's results in the initial phases of the process. The proposed framework can be implemented in a variety of ways [2].

Some suggestions for the development team to reconsider the design to attain the set of durability indices could be made. The properties of software, such as human trust, dependability, trustworthiness, and usability, all contribute to its long-term viability. Developers are working hard to preserve human trust, dependability, trustworthiness, usability, and other qualities for a longer length of time to meet software needs [3]. The reason for this is that developing long-lasting software requires a significant investment in terms of time, money, and effort [4]. The long-term viability of software justifies all of the effort put into its development.

As a result, the maintenance costs and time are minimised. In addition to human trust, dependability, trustworthiness, usability, and so on, a new pillar, software durability, can be added to the software. According to a US Federal Report, software that functions for a longer amount of time is in demand [5]. Hence, the tenability of more investigations and conclusive results to achieve optimal levels of software durability remains undeniable. However, there is no literature on how to develop longer-term software during the development process. In fact, such is the lacunae in this context that we could trace only a few research endeavours that had been done in the design phase of the development cycle (connected to improvement through assessment) to improve software durability. Hence, this book places itself as a repository of well-thought-out studies into software durability assessment throughout the design process.

11.8 Successful Strategies for Software Developers

Software design is not a one-time built-in process; instead, it is based on the reuse of current market criteria. This study's main focus is on analysing the software's service-life in terms of quality [7]. The goal of this study is to improve software's service life by making it more secure and durable. The phases that make up the process are chronicled below. Furthermore, when executed iteratively, progressively, and in parallel with other activities, tasks, and primary objectives, it would also be effective in achieving durability. The phases are:

- To make durability a necessary component of software quality.
- Determination of deterioration threat models about durability.
- Create a plan for long-term viability that encompasses trustworthiness, human trust, usability, security, and dependability.
- Identify and research their possible sources. Calculate the risks associated with these well-known assets' long-term viability.
- Sort them as per the severity of their negative effects.
- Find and investigate the long-term requirements of an arrangement's usability as a quality indicator.
- Identify new attributes that will allow the software to have a secure service life for a set period.
- Determine the impact of durability subfactors on the overall software.
- Examine the software's durability hazards.
- Make it a goal to reduce software design complexity by ensuring longevity, which improves maintainability.
- Improve the service-oriented design of software to improve software quality.
- Calculate durability parameters by using existing or newly built models.
- Standard architectural design tools could be improved to make them more durable.

At present, the software industry is battling with the complex task of bridging the gap between software durability crisis and the escalating demand for software [8]. To eke out effective and economically sustainable solutions, software engineers need to build products quickly and that too at competitive costs. Competition in any business is in the foreground for enhanced services and better-quality products at cheaper rates for the user. However, intense competition to woo the end users with budget-friendly software solutions in minimum time has led to the crisis of low-durability software in the software industry. Responding to this debacle, some vital recommendations that will help the software practitioners to maintain the durability of software and garner better business can be listed:

- Software designers and developers should follow these formal and well-known guidelines while developing software products throughout the software process. Adopting informal and traditional guidelines results in low-durability software products.

- Before starting any project, there should be a thorough study of the feasibility of the project and the envisaged results. This strategy not only helps to avert any major upheavals that might crop up at the later stages of the project, but also enables the programmers to segregate and economise on the resources and engineer a product that aligns with the intended results. Since the proper cost estimation plays a vital role in building durable products, software professionals should use tools and methods like the COCOMO model to make very accurate budget estimates.

- An efficient and comprehensive communication mechanism should be established to communicate thoroughly with all types of stakeholders concerning the software project. That results in accurate identification of the user's requirements.

- Durability should be taken into account when designing the architecture of software, so that the end product has all the qualities that software with high durability should have.

- There should be proper and adequate establishment of project infrastructure before beginning a project. Inadequate project infrastructure will lead to defective resulting products.

- No matter what the functional requirements are, the main focus should be on non-functional requirements like reliability, security, usability, and maintainability.

- Developed products should possess the durability of integration with third-party tools and other applications.

11.9 Recommendations for Security Practitioners

It's vital to remember that COVID-19 is only supposed to be temporary for a few weeks or months [6–9]. However, for IT and cybersecurity professionals, this might exacerbate an already difficult situation. Throughout the crisis, they must consider the aftermath as they invest, build, and deploy new capabilities. The Book examines the pandemic's effects both during and after this period.

- *Some organizations will need to move to new operating models:* To overcome the limitations that exist in providing lasting methods for employees who work from home or are remotely connected, cybersecurity and IT rights would require a thorough investigation and fast attention [6]. Staff help and remote control would become crucial. Before allowing the updated software to connect to the network again, cybersecurity specialists must keep a strict vigil on how employees utilise software and access the network when they go from home to the workplace.

- *Companies will need to reset their security of software to ensure there are no outliers:* To check for any digital gaps in the fence, it will be necessary to restart both physical and digital systems [6]. Device and data access rights granted during the epidemic would need to be audited to see if they should be revoked or amended to facilitate distant work. IT infrastructure would need to be inspected for holes, bad routes, or fraudulent identities. The reason for this is that cybercriminals may have discovered ways to gain access to services that were previously thought to be secure.

- *New cyber risks that appeared during the pandemic must be understood:* Security and durability experts, for example, would need to look into the digital capabilities of vital business functions to guarantee that they can withstand cyber-attacks during a lockout [6–7]. They will look into critical supply networks, particularly digital ones, to stay going during a health crisis.

- *Corporate IT security architectures should be reassessed:* This comprises access tools, support requirements for large-scale remote access, and risk-based and context-based security authentication techniques [7].

- *Advanced technology must be deployed:* Threat detection and response skills must include advanced capabilities afforded by next-generation technologies such as artificial intelligence, big data, and machine learning [7–8]. These are necessary to identify and respond to negative behaviour at machine speed without the need for human interaction. Additionally, businesses should consider how to protect themselves against cyber-attacks in the event of a pandemic.

The lessons acquired by everyone throughout the crisis would also need to be communicated to the officials in charge of software durability [6, 9]. This will aid them in developing appropriate countermeasures in the event of a pandemic-like disaster in the future. Security and durability solutions must be re-calibrated, particularly in terms of provisioning, scalability, remote administration capabilities, and cloud-based availability. They should also collaborate with trusted partners ahead of time to plan for dynamic scalability and the delivery of services and solutions. Planning necessitates both imaginative and meticulous efforts. Leaders face a rising responsibility to adopt creative techniques and consider new operating technology. Automation, in particular, will improve operational efficiency and reduce reliance on human intervention.

11.10 Conclusion

It is self-evident that completely durable software cannot be created; thus, the goal of evaluating software durability as the parameters of perfect and durable software cannot be accepted. As a result, the goal is to reduce the maintenance burden for long-term serviceable software. From the preceding debate, it is clear that developing long-lasting software will be a new problem for the software business. It's just as crucial as establishing other quality qualities like dependability, usability, and supportability. It has also been noticed that obtaining durability early in the development process improves software quality. This Book explains how to make software last as long as possible and gives a general plan for doing so. In this way, assessing durability offers a fresh perspective on building long-lasting software. In the absence of any standard index values or details for durability assessment, it is difficult to validate the results. Experts working in the field of software development review the framework and approach. In this league, our Book provides a thorough examination of the concept of software durability, its estimation, and its application in real-world scenarios. During the software development process, the latest challenges in computer and software-related research are extending the life span of services. The study's goal is to evaluate software longevity throughout the early stages of development. The system accomplishes this by combining software and durability attributes, prioritising the attributes based on their impact on software durability, and making recommendations to developers. The paradigm developed here could aid in determining software's long-term viability. With the help of this study, researchers may be able to help come up with new activities and ideas for long-term software development.

Service practitioners who up their game and protect their firms' services, technology, and data from novel or amplified threats by extra-advanced cyber criminals will be critical contributors to the economic recovery. Because various elements are required, computer security with longevity is a difficult task. In this digital era, the current pandemic crisis and the argument in this book clearly demonstrate the need for effective impact analysis. All practitioners in a software or software development procedure desire an organised orientation to aid efficient durability. This book analyses the impact using MCDM processes and provides a table of prioritised impact analysis. As they adjust to the new normal post-crisis, businesses will be pushed to optimise the available resources, reduce expenditures, and speed up their digital revolutions. To do more with less, durability leaders would have to embrace these initiatives by using emerging technology and service models. It's critical to conduct things in the most cost-effective manner possible. Additional computational modelling is a useful tool for estimating important transmission characteristics. The proposed prioritisation model also includes automated instruments, decision analysis, Fuzzy-AHP for calculation, and dynamic analysis, all of which are vital in pandemic management. The Fuzzy-AHP tool is used to prioritise the results that are accessible.

Points to Remember

- It is hard to figure out how durability affects the other important factors, and whether that effect is good or bad, in the early stages of the software development process. Durability control activities might be automated, semi-automated, or human. The feedback loop is critical for overcoming flaws that arise during the development process.

- As a capable testing partner, one is expected to conduct market research to determine the practitioner's fundamental voice. Try including focus groups, giving acceptance tests, and finding beta testers ahead of time to avoid bottlenecks during the product's launch process.

- The software development process has an impact on the software's long-term viability. A repeatable procedure geared toward defect avoidance is more likely to produce long-lasting software. However, the link between product and process durability is not straightforward.

- Durability concepts apply financial principles and procedures to a company's operations. It aids in the management of expenses, cash flow, and risk for businesses.

- It is obvious that there is no way to create software that will survive indefinitely. This means that determining the specifications of excellent and long-lasting software cannot be the purpose of software durability testing.

Review Questions

Objective Type Questions

1. Durability attributes ensure .... requirements.
    a. Functional
    b. Non-functional
    c. Both
    d. None of the above

2. Durability attribute efficiency is defined for
   a. Code
   b. Design
   c. Both for code and design
   d. None

3. Which of the following is not the direct or indirect durability attribute?
   a. Reliability
   b. Security
   c. Maintainability
   d. None

4. The life-test sample plans that are terminated when a pre-assigned number of failures occur in the sample is
   a. Failure-terminated
   b. Time-terminated
   c. Operation-terminated
   d. Sequential

5. Which one of the following is not a challenge in durability engineering?
   a. Inadequacy in project infrastructure
   b. Managing durability assurance
   c. Accuracy in budget estimation
   d. Coding and testing

Short Answer Type Questions

1. Draw the diagram of durability control and durability assurance.
2. Write a short note on non-durable software may cause information loss.
3. Describe some of the advantages of "employing durability assurance solutions".
4. Explain the issue of "inadequate project infrastructure" regarding software durability.
5. Write any five primary objectives for maintaining durability in software.

Descriptive Questions

1. Explain the needs and importance of durable software in detail.
2. What are the development trends for durability concepts and modernized expectations of the practitioners?
3. What are recommendations for practitioners to maintain software durability?

References

1. Kapoor, A. 2022. Top Software Development Trends Expected to Dominate in 2022, Available at: https://enlear.academy/top-software-development-trends-expected-to-dominate-in-2022-48617c351198.
2. Testrig Technologies. Software Testing: Top 5 Expectations Of Customers From QA And Software Testing Companies, Available at: https://www.testrigtechnologies.com/software-testingtop-5-expectations-of-customers-from-software-testing-companies/.
3. Ciklum. 7 Evolving Trends in Software Development, Available at: https://www.ciklum.com/blog/7-evolving-trends-in-software-development.
4. Digital Marketing Software Market. Digital Marketing Software Market by Component, Software (CRM Software, Email Marketing Software, and Social Media Advertising), Service, Deployment Type, Organization Size, Industry Vertical, and Region-Forecast to 2022, Available at: https://www.marketsandmarkets.com/Market-Reports/digital-marketing-software-market-52158190.html.
5. IBM. Custom software development, Available at: https://www.ibm.com/topics/custom-software-development.
6. Baz, M., Alhakami, H., Agrawal, A., Baz, A., and Khan, R.A. 2021. "Impact of covid-19 pandemic: a cybersecurity perspective," Intelligent Automation & Soft Computing, vol. 27, no.3, pp. 641–652.
7. Kumar, R., Khan, S.A., and Khan, R.A. 2015. Revisiting software security: durability perspective. International Journal of Hybrid Information Technology, 8(2), 311–322.
8. Kumar, R., Zarour, M., Alenezi, M., Agrawal, A., and Khan, R.A. 2019. Measuring security durability of software through fuzzy-based decision-making process. International Journal of Computational Intelligence Systems, 12(2), 627.
9. Agrawal, A., Zarour, M., Alenezi, M., Kumar, R., and Khan, R.A. 2019. Security durability assessment through fuzzy analytic hierarchy process. PeerJ Computer Science, 5, e215.

Useful Links

https://vdoc.pub/documents/the-future-of-intelligence-challenges-in-the-21st-century-6bqumb91iem0

https://www.scribd.com/doc/75871605/MCA-Assignment-Semester-2-3-Full-Sikkim-Manipal-University-SMU

https://enterprise.verizon.com/resources/executivebriefs/2020-dbir-executive-brief.pdf

https://www.computerworld.com/article/3412197/top-software-failures-in-recent-history.html

Index